*War & the Politics*
*of Identity*
*in Ethiopia*

# EASTERN AFRICA SERIES

# War & the Politics
# of Identity
# in Ethiopia
## Making Enemies & Allies
## in the Horn of Africa

KJETIL TRONVOLL
Professor of Human Rights, Peace & Conflict Studies
Norwegian Centre for Human Rights,
University of Oslo

James Currey

# Contents

# Preface & Acknowledgements

Researching political development in Eritrea and Ethiopia inevitably – and regrettably – leads to the study of conflict. After war in the Horn of Africa, it is more likely that new conflicts emerge rather than peace. Apparently, the historical, political, and cultural contexts of the region foster political elites which are more inclined to favour violent strategies rather than peaceful mechanisms to advance their political agendas or to solve disputes. In view of the lack of democratic bodies and procedures, and institutions of checks and balances, the people are inevitably exposed to the whims of unaccountable political leadership.

The two leaders of Eritrea and Ethiopia, Issaias Afwerki and Meles Zenawi, have broken more or less all the promises they gave when assuming power in 1991 after their resistance armies, the EPLF and TPLF/EPRDF respectively, managed jointly to topple Mengistu Haile-mariam's Derg regime. Promises of peace, development and democracy were made, and, perhaps naively, believed in by many of their citizens and the international community. Their biggest failure has been the flawed policies of 'peace-building', which have led to the continuation of conflicts and wars in the Horn of Africa. In this regard the Eritrean leadership has the dubious record of having been in armed conflict with all its neighbouring countries during the past decade. Furthermore, during this period Eritrea has developed into a one-man dictatorship in which President Issaias Afwerki is holding his people hostage to his own omnipresent ambitions and ego. Concomitantly, in Ethiopia the government has proved that its rhetorical support for democracy and international law is just that – rhetoric and meagre compliance.

In view of the tightrope balance between Eritrea and Ethiopia – in which the non-implemented decision on boundary demarcation looms as a fore-warning of future conflict, animated by ongoing proxy wars – and the precarious geo-political situation in the Horn as such, it seems likely that political conditions will deteriorate in the near future, before possibly improving again.

This study represents the new transnational influence on academia, since it has benefited from studies, fieldwork and networks located in three continents: Europe, Africa and North America. It is thus impossible to mention all the individuals who have contributed in one way or another to the end result presented here.

This book is a revised and shortened version of my PhD thesis, defended at the London School of Economics in 2003. I wish to thank my supervisor Professor Henrietta Moore who provided crucial academic input to the formulation of the research focus and the shaping of the theoretical framework of my thesis. I really enjoyed and gained immensely from the stimulating and challenging discussions she offered during my time at the LSE.

The manuscript has benefited from comments from many colleagues and friends. In this respect, I am particularly grateful to Jon Pedersen, Jan Ketil Simonsen, Tekeste Negash, Fredrik Barth, Leif Manger, Alessandro Triulzi, Chuck Schaefer and Stig Jarle Hansen, who all gave me valuable and constructive advice. Needless to say, though, the end result is my responsibility alone.

The undertaking of this study has relied on the support and the facilities of several institutions, to which I owe my gratitude. First and foremost, Addis Ababa University and Mekelle University have been instrumental in granting me research permits in Ethiopia and in facilitating various practicalities in order to carry out my fieldwork, in addition to creating a social and scholarly 'home' for me in Ethiopia. Furthermore, the LSE, the Norwegian Centre for Human Rights, the Institute for African Studies at Columbia University, and the Center for African Studies at the University of Florida have provided stimulating and challenging academic milieus during my shorter or longer stays with them. In particular, I want to thank director Leo Villalón and the staff of the Africa Centre at UF who hosted me for a year while I carried out the final revisions of this manuscript. I very much enjoyed my stay in 'Gator' country. I am also grateful for financial support from the Norwegian Research Council (grant # 165669/ V10), which made it possible for me to concentrate on writing this book.

The fieldwork on which the book is based could not have been carried out without the help of my research partner and friend, the late Mekonnen Berhane from Tigray, Ethiopia. Sadly, Mekonnen passed away before he could see the end result of our fieldwork. Mekonnen's knowledge, intellectual capacity and personal capabilities made it possible for me to carry out research during a tense and troublesome period in the war zone of Tigray. His academic background, deep knowledge of Tigrayan and Ethiopian history and society, personal wit and easy-going attitude made him the perfect research partner. More than a research partner, though, Mekonnen Berhane was a close personal friend who is truly missed and will never be forgotten.

My sincere appreciation is also offered to the many friends, contacts and informants I made in Ethiopia during the course of my research in the country. Since much of the information presented in this book may be perceived as sensitive by the current government, I shall not reveal the names of these crucial contacts here. I believe those concerned will know my gratitude to them.

Finally, one person in particular deserves my greatest appreciation and thanks, my wife Hege. She has been extremely supportive and understanding with regard to my many fieldtrips and endless hours in the office writing this study and others. I am also grateful that my two daughters, Cecilie and Victoria, seem to be catching an interest in Africa.

# Selected Glossary

| | |
|---|---|
| *addena* | 'our country', homeland |
| *adi* | village, 'home area', 'homeland' |
| *adi abo* | 'fatherland' |
| *akni abat* | 'founding father', first settler |
| *arbegnas* | patriots/resistance during Italian occupation |
| *arriena gerreb* | 'we have united around our rivers', slogan from the first *Weyane* |
| *askari* | regular Eritrean indigenous troops serving in the Italian colonial army |
| *awag* | Imperial decree |
| *awraja* | administrative province (under *kilil*) |
| *awrajanet* | 'regionalism', parochial in-fighting between districts/kin-entities |
| *baito* | local, elected administrative council |
| *balayina batach* | superior-inferior |
| *banda* | irregular Eritrean indigenous troops supported by and affiliated to the Italian colonial administration |
| *blatta* | title of scholar |
| *bun* | coffee |
| *bunnabet* | coffee house |
| *chiguraf-gwoses* | communal land-tenure arrangement (see also *diesa* and *shehena*) |
| *dekki kebessa* | Eritrean 'highlanders' |
| *dewta* | term for a rank-and-file protest against TPLF leadership in 1989 |
| *diesa* | communal land-tenure system (see also *chiguraf-gwoses* and *shehena*) |
| *Ethiopiawinet* | 'Ethiopianness', Ethiopian unity |
| *ferenji* | foreigner |
| *gemgum/gimgimma* | an evaluation process of critique/self-critique |

xi

| | |
|---|---|
| *gesgassa* | shorter military campaigns (razzias) during Imperial reign |
| *gontsi* | conflict |
| *gult/gwilt* | fief rights |
| *gultenya* | bearer/owner of *gult* |
| *habbo* | 'guts', resilience, courage |
| *habbonya* | bearer/owner of *habbo* |
| *habesha* | Ethiopian Christian Orthodox highland people and culture |
| *hayet* | 'cubs', popular term for TPLF fighters |
| *henay mifdai* | to obtain revenge/retaliation |
| *hidmo* | traditional stone/mud house |
| *hiliwuna* | survival |
| *hinfishfish* | chaos/pandemonium, term for TPLF dissent-process in 1977–8 |
| *hizb* | people |
| *injerra* | flat, soft 'bread', staple food |
| *kalai weyane* | second *weyane* (TPLF revolution) |
| *kebelle* | administrative unit (neighbourhood) (*tabia* in Tigrinya) |
| *kebessa* | Eritrean highlands |
| *kilil* | regional state |
| *kinea* | metaphorical use of language ('wax and gold') |
| *kushut* | lowest administrative level in Tigray, village, local community |
| *la'lewot ta'htewot* | superior-inferior (same as Amharic *balayina batach*) |
| *ma'anta* | intestine or 'guts' (see *habbo*) |
| *medeb* | assignment/agenda: political decision of TPLF communicated to the people to follow up/implement |
| *Medir Bahir* | 'The land on the Sea', the Eritrean part of Abyssinia |
| *men'nenetena* | identity |
| *min'nesele* | secession |
| *nagarit* | war-drums (calling peasants to the war during the Imperial reign) |
| *neftenya* | 'bearer of gun', Amhara settlers outside the core Abyssinian highlands |
| *negus* | king |
| *negus negast* | king-of-kings/emperor |
| *netsela* | sash |
| *Qu'alsi* | 'The Struggle' the civil war between the TPLF and the Derg |
| *ras* | regional prince, feudal title |
| *risti/rist* | land rights |
| *ristenya* | bearer/owner of *risti* |
| *salsai weyane* | third *weyane*: the new (2001) Tigrayan opposition to the TPLF |

because of their emotional impact in combination with their ambiguity and multivocality. They enable people to experience and express their affiliation to a group or state without compromising their own individuality (Cohen 1994b: 17–19). Indeed, the members of a group may not recognise the idiosyncratic understandings to which their fellow members put their shared symbols, so that they are unaware of the alternative interpretations of meanings. Hence we may find a variety of ethnic or nationalistic expressions within one group, reflecting *individual* life histories and experiences. Since boundaries have referents to personal consciousness, social interaction, and cultural symbolism, the implication is that the concept of boundary is essentially contestable. People have different experiences, life histories, and preferences, thus their understanding and interpretation of boundaries of identity differ. Boundaries are 'zones of reflection', as Cohen phrases it, on who one is – on who others are. 'There is no axiomatic rule which stipulates that the boundaries of selfhood are less significant in this regard than are those of collectivity. The subordination of self to society is achieved by power' (Cohen 1994a: 74). In times of war and conflict, in which a regime's identity politics is maximally geared to create dichotomisation in order to mobilise the citizenry against the enemy, it is thus important to keep the focus on individual agency, since people living in war will both comply with and encourage the politics of war, and resist and reject it, too.

The above understanding of the concept of boundaries, I believe, manages to capture and explain the complex and contradictory processes of identity formation taking place during war. It can be used to study the formation of ethnicity and contrasting collectives (as addressed in Chapter 4), just as it can simultaneously explain shifting alliances and allegiances (as described in Chapter 5). Moreover, this notion of boundaries can be used to explain individual positioning in relating to collective identities (as Chapter 6 explores). Boundaries can also be used to make sense of competing national discourses, the exclusion of groups and the creation of enemy images (as Chapters 7 and 8 discuss). But how do we go about identifying and analysing the relevant boundaries and their facets of concern for our study?

## 'MAPPING' BOUNDARIES OF IDENTITY

Our conventional understanding, based on a number of studies, proves that boundaries of identity can be politically constructed, infused with cultural content and made politically relevant by imposing distinctions between groups with the intention of creating dichotomisation and enmity for political purposes (such as military mobilisation against an enemy). This book shows how such a process was created by those in power in order to separate the Tigrinya-speaking people straddling the Eritrean-Ethiopian border. However, the novel approach employed here demonstrates that cultural boundaries can just as well be used to connect and create cross- and trans-boundary identities, as to distinguish and separate identities. Anthropology's preoccupation with difference, distinctions and the categorisation of collective groups, has led us to view boundaries only as socio-cultural phenomena of separateness. By implication, we have overlooked the fact that collective boundaries also *connect* groups (cf. Barth 2000; Cohen 2000). If we open up to such an understanding of boundaries, we shall more easily explain the constant making and remaking of enemies and allies and shifting identities during wartime.

As our point of departure, let us agree that boundaries both distinguish and connect peoples as individuals and collectives. People relate to and negotiate a number of identity boundaries simultaneously, as ethnic, national, local or political identities are continuously formed, challenged and recreated in response to ongoing social, cultural and political processes. However, an identity boundary is perceived and conceptualised differently – both from within (as self-identification) and from without (as identity ascribed to others) – according to scale and the social field to which the boundary relates. Anthony Cohen explains that 'as one goes "down" the scale so the "objective" referents of the boundary become less and less clear, until they may be quite invisible to those outside' (1985: 13). A national identity is much more discernible when one's focus is oriented towards the social field of the political regime and the state, as cohesion theory (or diversionary theory, as it is also called (Levy 1998)), advocates. However, as Cohen explains, 'as you go "down" this scale, they ["objective" referents of the boundary] become more important to their members for they relate to increasingly intimate areas of their lives or refer to more substantial areas of their identities' (1985: 13). The fact that individuals emphasise and understand boundary markers or referents differently from how these are perceived from the 'top' is significant in this study. Boundaries of identity relate to any scale, or social field, in which the actors in the study are operating. A peasant may be equally present within a social field and relate to a discourse of identity as the regime does. 'Identity' is produced and perceived by all social actors within all social fields, something many authorities on the theory of nationalism tend to overlook within their top-down and state-biased perspective. Nationalism implicates all segments of the population and it is thus neither 'top-down' nor 'bottom-up' (Herzfeld 1997: 10).

Herzfeld's critique of conventional theories of nationalism as lacking an understanding of scale is appropriate, and relates also to how we ought to treat the state as an entity in our analysis. The state is important, since we are exploring socio-political processes created by state actors. In order to integrate statehood into our analysis, we need to see the state as a multifaceted actor, not merely as a symbol or idea. As such, it is the feature of the policies of the regime which is of interest, since it is important to understand and describe the power represented and exercised by the state as a specifiable third force in the processes of boundary construction between groups (Barth 1994: 20). Different regimes employ different strategies to perpetuate their power and to implement their political agenda and as actors they will therefore pursue dissimilar policies towards ethnic categories and movements in the populations they seek to control: 'identity management, ethnic community formation, public laws and policies, regime interests and measures, and global processes thus fuse and form a complex field of politics and cultural processes' (Barth 1994: 20). In an African context the state has in particular been instrumental in designing and enforcing a state nationalism in the aftermath of colonialism: a state nationalism which was presented as authentically African, Clapham explains, but 'which simultaneously redefined pre-colonial identities and political structures as the source of a divisive and illegitimate "tribalism"' (1996a: 35).

To set out the interconnected forces that interweave with the state in complex fashion, Barth (1994) proposes that we model the processes separately on three levels or social fields – micro, median and macro – distinguishing them only for the sake of analytical clarity and to explore their interconnections. At the micro level, my analysis will thus focus on the war and processes that influence experience and the formation of identities: on persons and interpersonal interaction related to relevant political, social and cultural discourses (in Chapter 5). The perception of the 'enemy' is influenced by policies and parameters designed by actors located at different analytical levels. At the second analytical level I move up the scale in order to focus on the processes that create and establish collectives and mobilise groups for various purposes and by various means (in Chapter 4). Here I shall in particular present how political actors (the TPLF/EPRDF, in particular) influence the perception of enemy images. Many actors within this social field are in a position to impose decisions which directly influence the construction of identity boundaries and dichotomies. Finally, at the macro level I relate to the agencies of the state and devote attention to the legal framework of bureaucracy that allocates opportunities and impediments according to the regime's policies and decisions, but also by means of the manipulative and deliberate use of force and violence (in Chapters 6 and 7). Many actors – individuals, parties and organisations – operate at this level trying to influence and manipulate the regime's various identity policies, and thus constitute important contributors to the formation of perceptions of 'enemies,' 'allies,' 'identities' and ideas of nationalism as such. This will illustrate how the politics of identity works both ways: it creates distinctions and enmity, but also connections and alliances.

In order to explain these identity shifts, a particular focus is given to how the Ethiopian government redesigned its politics of identity to fit and manipulate the new political landscape created by the war. During the war it became clear that identities (however inexplicit), boundaries (however elusive and nebulous), and authenticity (however contested and contestable), were matters in which the government and the people invested huge value (cf. Cohen 2000: 5). The war impacted on Ethiopian society in different ways, as it was translated from politico-military strategic theory to actual practice (cf. Nordstrom 1995a: 95). However, the war proper was not the only war that took place; concurrently there were conflicts between ethnic groups and political parties, social classes, generations and genders, all taking place within, and ineradicably shaping, the war and the regime's identity politics (Nordstrom 1995a: 105). Identity politics thus comprises the strategies used (by regimes and other actors) to manipulate the ambiguity and contradictions of identity for political ends. This is precisely what this book aims at exploring.

## ETHNOGRAPHIC REPRESENTATION AND AUTHENTICITY DURING WAR

Anthropologists and other social scientists working in conflict and war zones have to consider a massive stream of information and a cacophony of voices eager to explain and communicate war, violence and sufferings, sometimes in a context of disordered chaos. So also in Tigray and Ethiopia during the Eritrean-Ethiopian war. Nordstrom claims that 'the louder the story, especially when it comes to violence and war, the less representative of the lived experience it is likely to be. In the midst of wars of propaganda and justification, the most silenced stories at war's epicentres are generally the most authentic' (1995: 139). In my experience, however, this is not necessarily true. I agree that the most silenced and muted stories may *appear* as more authentic because they represent such a stark contrast to the continuous cacophony of other voices and noises also witnessed by the anthropologist. In this flux of disturbances the silent voice of a humble informant may also appear to be a safe haven for a somewhat confused and paralysed anthropologist who is forced to digest an immense number of observations under a strong threat to his or her own personal safety. Under such circumstances, where anthropologists also want to associate with the silenced victims of war, we are also exposed to 'ethnographic seduction', as Robben (1995: 83-4) terms it – we *want* to believe the stories we are told by victims. However, I doubt if such voices are more representative of the context of war than, for instance, the pleas of local NGO workers, or the accusations of aggression by politicians, or the orders for mass evacuation of villages given by military commanders because of enemy shelling and bombing.

Representativeness in contexts of war and violence has to be localised and positioned within the setting in which the violence takes place. In this sense, Nordstrom is overlooking her own main assertion that violence is not something fixed, easily demarcated and singularly perceived. The expression of violence differs according to context, time-span, personal life histories, and so on. Violence is a fluid phenomenon, which affects individuals to a varying degree according to a variety of factors. 'Its manifestation', write Robben and Nordstrom, 'is as flexible and transformative as the people and cultures who materialize it, employ it, suffer it, and defy it' (1995: 6). Thus the voices of violence also take on different expressions, some loud and clear, others muted and blurred, some sound

and coherent, others unintelligent and contradictory, but all simultaneously part of the 'cacophony of voices' which the anthropologist has
to relate to accordingly.

Simons claims that 'with a few notable exceptions, anthropologists have
barely studied modern wars, and when modern war is treated as a subject,
it is the why behind the fighting and the aftermath of it – not the how or
the process – that receives most attention' (1999:74). Moreover, as noted
by Dennis Rodgers (2001), few anthropological studies of war and violence
have been based on actual fieldwork in the context of war/violence (with
the notable exception of, for instance, Carolyn Nordstrom's work), but
rather rely on interviews and other non-participatory methodologies which
are frequently retrospective (as, for instance, Daniel 1996; Feldman 1991).
This book stands out in this regard, as it uses fieldwork-based data
gathered during the Eritrean-Ethiopian war.

The chaos of war, and the impact warfare has on socio-cultural
processes, makes it difficult, if not impossible, to know how to identify and
circumscribe relevant units of study, least of all the classical anthropological notion of a bounded society. Instead, the anthropological focus
is defined as a field of relations and social processes which are of
significance to the actors involved in the study. This makes it possible to
explore non-sited relations and the way in which they influence and are
influenced by the different sites and fields where they 'touch ground'
(Appadurai 1991; Barth 1992: 25; Hastrup and Olwig 1997: 8; Marcus
1995a: 105; Nordstrom 1997).

This study adopts a twin technique: it follows the *'contexts of conflict'* to
examine the understanding of the metaphor of *'who is the enemy?'*. With
such an approach, I was able to 'touch ground' in several localities in
Ethiopia where the Eritrean-Ethiopian war had made a noticeable impact,
and pose the guiding question of how people related to, discussed and
conceptualised the 'enemy' – whatever appearance it took. This allowed
for tracing historical trajectories, contextual influences and various
discursive fields, accommodating changing impressions and landscapes
across sites and time-span. More importantly, though, it facilitated a
variety of perceptions and localised understandings of boundaries of
identity: my own and others.

The Eritrean-Ethiopian war (1998-2000) was a comparatively un-
problematic war to relate to as a field anthropologist, since the front lines
were sharply demarcated, which generally limited the active war-zone to
a stretch of territory on the border itself. The fighting took the form of
trench combat and aerial bombardment and shelling of enemy positions
along the border. Doing fieldwork close to the front line was thus relatively
safe. Nevertheless, the psychological pressure of war and the tense
atmosphere created by omnipresent military and political security
surveillance imposed certain limitations on my presence in the field. This
said, however, it was only on one occasion during the two-year-long war
that I was directly hindered from working in the war zone of Tigray. In

the run-up to the main military offensive called 'Operation Sunset' in February 1999, all foreigners remaining in Tigray were asked to leave for Addis Ababa since the whole region was declared a military security zone for a brief period of time.

One final comment on carrying out ethnography during war, or in politically suppressive and human-rights-abusing states, may seem appropriate. Eritrean and Ethiopian communities have experienced war, political authoritarianism, drought and famine for the better part of the last four decades. 'Wrong' political sympathies held by ordinary men and women, or accusations of such, have in many cases entailed brutal torture, a sudden death or mysterious 'disappearances'. War and terror are not only memories, but lived experience for the majority of the Ethiopian people. Recent human rights reports from internationally recognised organisations tell stories of new human rights violations and political persecution of opposition sympathisers, both before, during and after the Eritrean-Ethiopian war. As a field anthropologist in such a tense and conflict-ridden political environment, one needs to be extremely cautious not to expose informants or others with a politically negative attitude to the regime's policies to the authorities. Doing political anthropology in Ethiopia today entails discretion, care, and most of all awareness of the extremely complex political field within which one is manoeuvring.

To take sides actively in the field with one or another part of the political 'game' – as certain anthropologists' are advocating (cf. Scheper-Hughes 1995) – might be the decontextualised morally correct thing to do; however, it might also jeopardise the lives of one's informants and contacts. This is the crucial dilemma of doing anthropological study in politically charged contexts. The answer to this issue must necessarily be found by careful balancing of one's moral and ethical obligations to speak out against injustice, on the one hand, and to protect the anonymity of one's informants, on the other. Being 'out there' in the field, conducting the research and facing the obstacles, demands considered and subtle solutions. Under such circumstances, the most important asset a field anthropologist may have is experience of the area and the situation of the research, thus having knowledge about how to read the political map and the game played, in order to avoid being cornered or risking unwanted exposure of one's informants.

# Chapter outline

The theoretical framework provided in this Introduction will form a backdrop to the following narrative chapters. *Chapter 2* describes the main features of the ethnography of Tigray and highland Ethiopia (*Habesha*). Emphasis will be placed on explaining people's attachment to land and the conception of hierarchy and alliances among the Ethiopian Christian

Orthodox highland population. This debate will introduce *Chapter 3*, in which the historical trajectories of wars and enemy images in Tigray and Ethiopia are outlined. The discussion will concentrate on presenting the development in Tigray starting from the mid-nineteenth century, and the subsequent Italian invasion of Ethiopia and the battle of Adwa, through the first *Weyane* uprising against the oppressive central government in 1941 and concluding with the EPRDF takeover of government in Addis Ababa in 1991. *Chapter 4* is the first empirical chapter addressing the Eritrean-Ethiopian war. It concentrates on presenting discourses on Tigrayan identity and how self-ascribed Tigrayanness is constituted, and viewing it in relationship with and contrast to the Eritrean and Amhara 'others'. This will feed into the discussion presented in *Chapter 5*, where the effect of the war at the grassroots in Tigray is analysed. Various opposing views on the war are presented, and it will become obvious that the war also has a disintegrating and fragmenting capacity. Thereafter, *Chapter 6* moves up the scale and focuses on national discourses of identity. The war set in motion processes which re-established 'Ethiopia' within the national political rhetoric in a language reminiscent of the former centralising governments in the country (the Derg and the Imperial regime). However, competing and clashing discourses of nationalism will also be highlighted, exemplified with material from southern Ethiopia and from the opposition political parties. *Chapter 7* will conclude the empirical presentation of the effect of the war, by focusing on two groups of people – Ethiopians of Eritrean descent and Oromos – who became politically stigmatised by the war and were thus contrasted as 'others' in the official nationalist rhetoric. The *Conclusion* chapter will unpack Ethiopian nationalism and make clear the processes of identity formation during the war, thereby summing up and concluding the theoretical argument of the book.

# Notes

1 This account is an interpretation established on the basis of a number of interviews conducted on both sides of the border.

2 'Agreement between Eritrea and Ethiopia', Algiers, 12 December 2000.

3 See 'Decision of Eritrea-Ethiopia Boundary Commission', Statement by the Council of Ministers of the Federal Democratic Republic of Ethiopia, Addis Ababa, 13 April 2003; and 'Statement on the Determination of the Border', Government of Eritrea, Asmara, 13 April 2003.

4 The EPLF was officially re-named the People's Front for Democracy and Justice (PFDJ) in 1994, in order to signify the transition from a military liberation movement to a civilian government. However, both Eritrean party/government officials and the civilian population still refer to the Front as the 'EPLF', a term which will also be used in this study.

5 The TPLF was instrumental in the establishment of the EPRDF in 1989, and the TPLF ideological basis is reflected in the programme of the EPRDF. Moreover, the key EPRDF decision-makers are also the leadership of the TPLF. For instance, the TPLF chairman Meles Zenawi also holds the chairmanship of the EPRDF. Thus, in many circumstances,

it is difficult to distinguish between the EPRDF and its core component, the TPLF. In this book, I shall use the term 'TPLF' to describe a Tigrayan discursive field and empirical basis, and the 'EPRDF' in relation to a national Ethiopian discursive field and empirical basis. For an elaboration of the history of the establishment of the two movements, see below, Young (1997), and Vaughan and Tronvoll (2003).

6  'Derg' is Amharic for 'committee/council', and was the popular term given to the military regime which toppled Emperor Haile-Selassie in 1974.

7  Eritrea achieved *de facto* independence on 24 May 1991 when the EPLF army entered Asmara. *De jure* independence was proclaimed on 24 May 1993 following a national referendum.

# Two

## Land, Hierarchy & Alliances in Highland Ethiopia

To cultivate [the land] is to rule [the land]. (Abyssinian proverb)

In the densely settled highlands, land was the base on which all else rested – subsistence, religion, status and political authority. (Clapham 2001: 20)

The people of the present-day Tigray regional state[1] in northern Ethiopia and parts of the Eritrean highlands – pride themselves on being direct descendants of some of Africa's oldest civilisations; the kingdoms of Da'amat (ca.700-400 BC) and Axum (ca.100-800 AD) (Marcus 1994). These civilisations were founded on Africa's most efficient and innovative agricultural production system, where the ox and plough were paired to produce optimal yield (McCann 1995). The subsistence sedentary agricultural society of the Abyssinian[2] highlands developed well-organised local communities, where principles of kinship and descent guided the habitation pattern and access to land. Today, we find the descendants of the Axumites among the Tigrinya- and Amharic-speaking communities in the Ethiopian and Eritrean highlands. They are still predominantly sedentary agriculturists (83 per cent), growing *teff* (an indigenous grain), wheat and barley as main crops, together with beans, lentils, onions, potatoes and maize as supplementary crops. The ox and traditional plough (*maharas* or *mesrie*) are still their main means of production; the plough has remained more or less unchanged since its invention more than two thousand years ago. The Tigrinya-speakers straddle the river Mereb which divides Eritrea and Ethiopia. There are about one and a half million Tigrinya-speakers in Eritrea, whereas about 3.3 million live in Tigray. Their ethnic 'cousins', the Amhara population, on the other hand, constitute the second largest ethnic group in Ethiopia and amount to approximately 16 million (Central Statistical Authority 1998a).

With more than 2,000 years of continuous occupancy within the oldest state-polity south of the Sahara, it is a surprise and a paradox that the anthropological literature on the Abyssinian highlands and its people is so meagre. Reputable ethnographic studies of the Tigrinya-speaking[3] people of Ethiopia and Eritrea (available in English) can be counted on one hand. A wider field of anthropological studies has been conducted on the Amhara people, where we find a handful of core texts covering aspects of Amhara cultural traditions, livelihoods and cosmology. The literature on the Amhara has significant comparative value for the study of the Tigrinya-speakers, due to the social, cultural and historical relatedness between these two groups. In explaining the social and cultural characteristics of the people of Tigray, I draw on this literature, as is conventional within Ethiopian studies (cf. Levine 1974; Lipsky 1962; Longrigg 1945; Shack 1974). The groups differ in terms of language, but they have similar frameworks of social organisation, use the same system of production (ox-plough-using sedentary agriculture), are members of the same religion (Orthodox Christianity), subscribe to the same understanding of the historical trajectories of the Abyssinian/Ethiopian state, and have in historic and contemporary times constituted the main partners and adversaries in social and political interaction.

The relationship between people and land, and its significance for the sense of belonging, spatial and territorialised identity, is the main focus of the ethnographic presentation in this section. Moreover, I touch on the customary understanding of socio-political hierarchy among the peoples of the Abyssinian highlands, in order to explain the never-ending 'Abyssinian' struggle to define oneself, individually or collectively, as the superior part in any alliance or relationship involving social status and political legitimacy/hegemony.

# Ethnographic representation and interpretation of Ethiopia

On the problem of the representation and interpretation of the ethnographic context in Ethiopia, Wendy James has commented that:

> until very recent times, professional ethnographic writing about Ethiopia was dominated by essentially nineteenth-century styles of civilization-description and evolutionary explanation, at several removes from people and events 'in the field'. The ethnography of imperial Ethiopia remained enmeshed within a defining framework of ideas, expressed particularly openly in Western fiction, which derived from an old oriental-romantic tradition of African princes far removed from the humdrum world of colonial administration which had become the norm in other parts of Africa. (1990: 96)

The scholarly representation of Ethiopia has thus been flawed by the illusion of orientalism (Said 1978), as traditional ethnographic writings undertaken were strongly influenced by foreign visitors, travellers,

and the crucial common denominator to all of them is an inbuilt notion of and drive towards alliance-building.

First, the *awrajanet* (regionalism) phenomenon has deep-rooted historical trajectories which become relevant in contemporary conflicts and political identity discourse. *Awrajanet* is both a notion of local territorialised identity ('my homeland is my region') *and* a process of infighting between representatives from different regions in order to put oneself in a dominant position vis-à-vis the other regions. So, if representative A from region X wants to dominate representative B from region Y, he will enter into an alliance with representative C from region Z and maybe even representative D from region Y itself, in order to conquer B. The sub-partners of the alliance (C and D) will gain authority as a reward when A has installed himself in a dominant position, as in a patron-client relationship. (This intricate play between authority figures will be exemplified with historical and contemporary cases throughout the book.)

Secondly, the systems of land tenure (*risti* and *gult*) in the Ethiopian highlands were not so much systems which guided relationships between claimant and land, as rules regulating the relationships between the claimant and other persons. *Risti* rights were not directed towards a specific plot of land with fixed boundaries and a permanent location. *Risti* rights related instead to a principle of usufruct rights in a larger tract of land held corporately by the descendants of the first settlers in the area. On this basis, explains Donald Donham, 'each land tract was subject to overlapping and contradictory rights, and successful men were often able to increase their "hereditary" *rist* lands through a variety of political stratagems' (1986: 16). This presupposes alliance-building and negotiation with local individuals and kin-groups in authority in order to activate the latent *risti* rights of the claimant. Moreover, the historical *gult* (fief) rights held similar characteristics of inter-personal relationships. A *gult* grant was a grant of power to dominate the people on the land, more than control of the land itself. The granting of *gult* from the emperor thus involved a fragmentation of authority, since the *gult* lord again appointed all his functionaries and followers. Thus, Donham concludes, 'the only way the emperor could influence the appointment of his followers' followers was to revoke the appointment of his follower. Each link in the hierarchy was a personal one, and each person was bound only to those immediately above and below' (1986: 9).

The legacy of this system of compartmentalised authority still resides in Ethiopia. For example, when as a researcher I was given a general research permit issued by Addis Ababa University in the capital, I needed a new letter of permit from the regional state authority, who again would send me to the *woreda* (district) for a new letter introducing me to the *tabia* (area) chairman, who again would follow me around to the various *kushet* (village) chairmen for personal introductions. A permit granted from the central authorities in Addis Ababa is only valid to the second highest level of authority, which has to convert that order to the third level, and so on.

It is a matter of practical survival that such a system of fragmented authority, carried on throughout the centuries, has inspired alliance-building across and between hierarchical levels in order for the different persons in authority actually to govern and implement their decisions.

This leads us to the third and last concept, that of hierarchy. Although the elaborate feudal hierarchy was abolished with the fall of the Emperor in 1974, a strict socio-political hierarchy is still operating in Ethiopia. The Derg military junta soon developed their own administrative apparatus, reaching out to every village and every household under their domain. This new structure – popularly termed the *kebelle*-system[10] – was deliberately put in place to extract surplus from the peasantry, in a similar vein to the feudal system. Christopher Clapham notes that it became so efficient that it managed to 'exact grain from peasants at a time of famine, which in turn those peasants could only acquire by selling livestock and buying the grain on the open market' (2002: 17/19). With the fall of the Derg regime in 1991, the new EPRDF government managed in a short time to replace the old party cadres in the *kebelle* system with their own EPRDF cadres or affiliates, co-opting the structure and hierarchical control over the Ethiopian domain (see, for instance, Tronvoll and Aad-land 1995: 29–31).

During the Imperial system many scholars have commented that every person in the highlands had an inborn ambition to climb the hierarchy as part of their socialisation. The workings of the bilateral system of descent encouraged this social mobility, since 'almost everyone saw himself or herself as descended from local notables' (Donham and James 1986: 7). In order to work, live and climb under such a system of authority, it was essential to make alliances with other individuals trapped in the same system. Many Ethiopians have commented that a similar understanding of the workings of the hierarchy is also experienced today.

The Tigrayans and Amhara thus have a socio-cultural inclination towards making and re-making alliances in order to move up the socio-political hierarchy or gain some personal benefit. However, the Tigrayans and Amhara are not only culturally inclined to make alliances as individuals, but also as collectives. This is what this book explores and analyses in the following chapters: the process of defining new enemies, rejecting old allies and creating new ones within the context of war.

# Notes

1 The Tigray regional state shares borders in the north with Eritrea, in the east with the Afar regional state, in the south with the Amhara regional state, and in the west with the Sudan. The territorial area of Tigray is estimated at 80,000 sq. km.

2 I use the historical term 'Abyssinia' to describe the Semitic highland communities in present-day Eritrea and Ethiopia.

3 'Tigrinya' is a term describing the language of the people (the suffix '–*inya*' denotes

language). No common term describes the 'ethnic' group of all Tigrinya speakers. In Eritrea, the government has chosen '*Tigrinya*' to denote the people in addition to the language. The Eritrean Tigrinya-speakers themselves, however, use a different set of terms as group identifiers. *Dekki kebessa*, meaning 'people of the highland', is a term describing all Eritrean Tigrinya-speakers. If they were asked individually, however, they would use the term for their geographical location (*awraja*) – which corresponds with the larger descent group – as a group name, either *Hamasien*, *Seraye* or *Akkele-Guzai*. The Tigrinya-speakers of Ethiopia are in the English language generally termed Tigrayans. The Ethiopian government recently described them as *Tigrawi* (*Tigraway*), male and *Tigrawit*, female); however, few Tigrinya-speakers use these terms themselves. As terms of self-identification, the Tigrayans generally use their geographical location, as they do in Eritrea, being *Agame*, *Adwa*, *Shire*, *Enderta*, etc. In the Amharic language, *Tigre* is the term used to describe this group. Furthermore, due to the lack of consistency in transcribing Tigrinya and Amharic terms in English, a variety of different terms are used to describe the Tigrinya-speakers in different scholarly works, as *Tigrina*, *Tegrenna*, *Tigrigna*, *Tigrai*, *Tigray*, *Tigre*, and *Tigrayans*. To confuse things even more, Tigray (or Tigre) is also the name of the northernmost region in Ethiopia. Tigre is also the name of an ethnic group in Eritrea (found in the western lowlands) and the same term is also used for their language (which differs from the Tigrinya language). For the sake of clarity, in this book I will use the term 'Tigrinya-speakers' to denote both the Eritrean and Ethiopian peoples who speak that language. To describe the Eritreans I use the term *kebessa* (or Eritrean Tigrinya-speakers). To describe the Ethiopians, I use the term *Tigrayans*.

4  *Habesha* is a term used to describe the highland Orthodox Christian peoples and culture.

5  Central Statistical Authority (1998b) presents the following breakdown along ethnic lines in Tigray region: Tigrinya-speakers 94.75 %; Amhara 2.59 %; (Eritreans 0.92 %); Saho 0.73 %; Agew/Kamyr 0.42 %; Afar 0.24 %; Oromo 0.12 %; and Kunama 0.06 %. Of these groups, the Saho, Agew and Kunama may be labelled minority groups in Tigray, since they do not have any other separate ethnic regional state (unlike the Oromo, Amhara and Afar).

6  The districts (*awraja*) of Tigray proper in historical times were: Adwa, Tigre (also called Aksum), Tambien, Shire, Agame and Endarta (Erlich 1996).

7  One faction advocating Tigrayan secession and independence, the other regional autonomy in a federated Ethiopia.

8  I use the Amharic terminology here since it is recognised throughout the Abyssinian highlands. In Tigrinya, the terms *la'lowey ta'thowey* hold the corresponding meaning of 'superior inferior'. Another set of Tigrinya terms applicable to describe this relation is *gezaie tegezaie*, meaning 'ruler ruled'.

9  The Danish researcher Søren W. Nielsen (2002: 479) recently recorded 27 main levels – from the king at the top to the slave at the bottom – in Tigrinya Eritreans understanding of customary hierarchy, divided into the three main categories of aristocracy, ecclesiastics and commoners.

10  *Kebelle* is the lowest administrative unit in the towns (corresponding to Peasant Associations (PA) in rural areas during the Derg).

# Three

## Historical Trajectories
## of Enemy Images

I remember my father telling me about the Italian invasion [in 1935], and how they were helped by the askaris [indigenous Eritrean troops]. We thought that we had become friends during the 17 years of struggle [the TPLF revolution], but once again the Eritreans attacked us. We should learn now and never trust them again. (Tigrayan farmer, Wuqro 1999)

'The land is our father, the enemy our brother,' (Tig. '*Meretna Abona Eya Eti Tselaei dima Hawna*') was the expression used by an elderly Tigrayan peasant to explain to me the convoluted reasons for the Eritrean-Ethiopian war (1998-2000). This expression captures the essence of what constitutes social order in Tigray and the ancient highlands of Abyssinia – individuals' relationships to land and kin, and the conflicts surrounding these relationships. Land is a symbol of fertility and provides a person with a place of belonging and of resources, facilities which it is also the responsibility of a father to provide. The Tigrayans will defend their land as they will defend their own father. The enemy is cast as a 'brother' chiefly because most conflicts over land are between relatives wrangling over family land. Moreover, since Tigrayans share cultural, linguistic and religious attributes with the highland people of Eritrea, the kinship terminology is apt to describe their relations to the Eritrean adversary. To the elderly peasant, the expression 'the land is our father, the enemy our brother' summarises the two crucial aspects of the war; that they are fighting for their inalienable land rights against their own kin. As such, the expression, like the Eritrean-Ethiopian war in itself, signifies historical trajectories of conflicts and enemy images in Tigray.

War and violence are not a novel experience in the lives of the Ethiopian population. The region has been a theatre of war more or less continuously throughout the last few centuries (Ayele 1984; Erlich 1986; Markakis 1990; Tareke 1983: 18). As a consequence of the complexities and layers of war, the region has seen continuous shifts in allegiances and alliances that have created a multitude of overlapping and sometimes contradictory enemy images. To analyse wars and conflicts throughout history and pose the question 'Who is the enemy?', is thus a daunting task; here I shall therefore cover only more recent history and highlight a few key changes in the trajectories of enemy images. The chapter will illustrate how enemy images in Tigray and Ethiopia have been created, upheld and rejected by a number of wars and conflicts since the mid-nineteenth century.

Conflicts and narratives of violence in Tigray – both contemporary and historical – are related to the possession of land and to socio-political hierarchy. These two issues form a common thread in most Tigrayans' life histories, linking one generation to the next through common experiences of violence and through conceptions of shifting and enduring enemy images. Justification for new wars is often sought in history and finds a fertile ground in the societal embodiment of violence. Contemporary conflicts and wars draw heavily on heroic myths, national and ethno-national symbols, and enemy images from past conflicts in order to inspire the local Tigrayan population to sacrifice their lives in yet another war to defend their 'homeland' (*adi*).[1] The genealogies of violence span generations to forge landed belongingness, perceptions of relationships between rulers and ruled, and expressions of local and national politics. Violence influences the forging and break-up of identities in multiple ways, in as much as 'even the most horrific acts of aggression do not stand as isolated exemplars of a "thing" called violence but cast ripples that reconfigure lives in the most dramatic of ways, affecting constructs of identity in the present, the hopes and potentialities of the future, and even the renditions of the past' (Robben and Nordstrom 1995: 5).

# The wars of history (1855–90)

God fenced the paradise, Ethiopia, with fire! – Tigrayan expression.

In the mid-nineteenth century, Ethiopia emerged from one of its darkest and most troubled periods, called the Era of the Princes (*zamana masafint*, 1769-1855). During this period, no central power or government existed, and coalitions and alliances between regional lords were constantly formed and dissolved (Abir 1968; Bekele 1990: 26; Tegenu 1996). The constant warring made Ethiopia one of the most militarised societies in the world at that time. By the middle of the nineteenth century, it is estimated that there were at least 200,000 men under arms in the Abyssinian heartland, 'accompanied by an even greater multitude of camp-followers, so that there were a total of perhaps 'half a million idlers' who preyed on the population at large' (Pankhurst 1990: 148).

The Tigrayan regional governor and nobility were at the heart of the machinations in central Ethiopia, at the same time as regional ruling families from the various districts clashed in petty warfare in attempts to control the Tigrayan region (*awrajanet*) (Rubenson 1976: 36). From the point of view of the Tigrayan peasants, however, the enemy was at all times whatever adversary was defined by their local lord. Conflicts were created, sustained and solved by the nobility, drawing on the resources of the peasantry under their control to wage them.

The self-armed peasantry constituted the main source of military manpower in Tigray during historical times (and partly also today). 'When the *nagarit* war-drums sounded every season, the farmers followed their local masters on campaign,' describes Erlich (1996: 5). The weather usually allowed for two annual military campaigns (*zamacha*), in October/November and March/April, following the long and short rainy seasons and after the main agricultural tasks had been carried out. The *zamacha* could be called for both longer military occupation campaigns, as during the wars of subjugation in southern parts of Ethiopia under *Ras* and later Emperor Menelik, and also for shorter campaigns (*gesgassa*) against competing and hostile neighbouring princes (Marcus 1995c: 65–6; Tafla 1984).

Emperor Tewodros II (1855–68) managed to unite the Abyssinian heartland after the turbulent years of the Era of Princes (Beyene et al, 1990). His original policies were progressive, as he strove to create national unity and peace by transforming traditional provincial politics and parochial enemy images into national themes. Tewodros' methods of achieving these goals, however, alienated him from his subjects and supporters. To maintain power, war and violence again became the chief political tools of control. But authoritarian policies only helped further the alienation of the peasantry and, in Tigray, Tewodros even intensified the effects of severe drought and famine by destroying homesteads and crops in rebellious areas (Marcus 1994: 70).

The fall of Emperor Tewodros marked the final collapse of the central Ethiopian highlands – the territories lying around Lake Tana – as the political core of the Abyssinian polity. Thenceforth Tigray in the north and Shoa in the south, hitherto practically independent, became the real centres of power. After a series of battles, a Tigrayan regional nobleman proclaimed himself Emperor Yohannes IV at Aksum, the holy city of northern Tigray in January 1872. For the first time in the second millennium, Ethiopia was ruled by a Tigrinya-speaking emperor (see Gabre-Selassie 1975). Regardless of his ethnic background, throughout his 17 years on the throne he did his best to avoid becoming a parochial Tigrayan monarch. He made, for instance, Amharic, and not Tigrinya, the official language at his court (Erlich 1996: 2). Despite Yohannes' Ethiopian-centred policies, the TPLF and politically conscious Tigrayans of today interpret his reign as important for Tigrayan consciousness and political influence.

Following the death of Yohannes in the battle against the Madhist in 1889, the throne was fought over by several forces, both internal and external to Ethiopia. It was *Negus* Menelik of Shoa who managed to manoeuvre his way to the throne – by creating alliances both internally and with foreign powers – and assume the title of *negus negast* (king of kings) (Marcus 1995c). In this internal struggle over political hegemony between the Tigrayans and Shoa-Amharans during the years prior to the Italian colonisation of Eritrea, the contenders used all means possible to win the struggle, even collaboration with Italy, a foreign aggressor threatening Ethiopia's integrity (Erlich 1996).

## Foreign enemy images (1890–1941)

Since Tigray representd the northern Ethiopian frontier, it was also the access point for foreign influence and armies. During the late nineteenth century, Belgian, French, Turkish, Egyptian, Sudanese and Italian representatives and armies had been 'stirring the Tigrayan pot' for their own interests (Rubenson 1976). During three decades and the reign of three Emperors, northern Ethiopia and Tigray had been repeatedly attacked by foreign forces – a season of war which created, and cemented, the image of 'foreigners' as enemies (Prouty and Rosenfeld 1994: 312). Time and time again, the Ethiopian emperors mobilised the peasant army, not to fight against their own countrymen as had been usual, but against neighbouring forces and European colonial armies, battles which have left an imprint in the history of Tigray and Ethiopia, and which still are used as reference points for contemporary conflicts and enemy images (as discussed in Chapter 6). The conflicts with the Italians introduced for the first time *European* colonial aspirations in the Horn of Africa, where Italy colonised Eritrea in 1890 (Mesghenna 1988; Negash 1987).

Italy was helped to consolidate its power in the Eritrean highlands by the local highland (*kebessa*) elite who tried to use it as a tool to win the local power struggle over the Tigrayan nobility in controlling the Tigrinya-speaking highlands straddling the river Mereb (while at the same time the Tigrayan nobility and Emperor Yohannes were fighting off Shoa-Amhara attempts to come to power, also with the help of the Italians). However, when the highland elite understood that Italy had come as a permanent force, they changed sides again and asked their Tigrayan brothers for assistance in fighting the Italians (Mesghenna 1988; Negash 1987; Rubenson 1976). The Italians were not satisfied with the small sliver of land they named Eritrea, and continued their march southwards on the Abyssinian plateau, greatly helped by the machinations of continuously shifting alliances of the everlasting power-struggle within the Ethiopian ruling class.

### THE BATTLE OF ADWA (1896)

The most important event serving as a point of reference for Ethiopian identity in modern history took place soon after Emperor Menelik II ascended the throne. The Italians used their foothold in Eritrea to prepare their expansionist plan of an East Africa colony, stretching from the Red Sea in the north to the Indian Ocean in the south, composed of Eritrea, Ethiopia and Somalia. Although Menelik signed an agreement at Wuchale in 1889 that granted them Eritrea and marked an international border between the Italian colony and Ethiopia (Prouty 1986: 61), he was soon to discover the treacherous tactics of Italian colonialism. Italy translated and interpreted Article XVII of the treaty differently from Ethiopia. In the understanding of Menelik, Italy *could* be consulted prior to any contact with other foreign missions or governments. The Italians, however, translated the article in a way which *bound* Menelik to make all his foreign contacts through the agency of Italy, thereby reducing Ethiopia to the status of an Italian protectorate (Zewde 1991: 74). When Menelik discovered the Italian plot, he abrogated the treaty in 1893, a move that ruined Italy's hopes of subjugating Ethiopia without resorting to arms, and the war of colonialism began.

Although the regional princes were often at loggerheads with each other and with the emperor, the overt internal divisions were temporarily suspended when foreign forces threatened the empire. In late 1895, an Italian army contingent went into battle with Tigrayan forces at Amba Alage, but was defeated. This only inspired the Italians to return with an even greater force, in order to crush any Ethiopian defence and resistance. On the morning of 1 March 1896 a well-equipped Italian army of 17,700 men (10,596 of whom were Italians/Europeans and the remainder Eritrean regulars, called *askari*) moved in a surprise attack on Menelik's army, which raised approximately 100,000 troops in defence (Marcus 1995c: 172). The battle itself was fierce and intense, and after four to five hours of fighting the Italians were already retreating in disarray.

After the fighting ceased, Emperor Menelik dealt with the captured Italians differently from the Eritrean *askari*. The Italian prisoners of war were treated cordially, received medical attention and were later released without further conditions. The *askari*, on the other hand, were looked upon as treasonous since they were considered to be Ethiopians, although they were subjects of the Italian crown. They were therefore maimed (the right hand and left foot were cut off) as punishment not only because they were fighting the Ethiopians (as the Italians also had done), but because of the perception that they had betrayed their national identity as Ethiopians – and for that they had to suffer (Prouty 1986: 158).

The Ethiopian victory at Adwa echoed throughout Europe: an indigenous, black army had won a decisive battle against a European coloniser. It was the bloodiest of all colonial battles, leaving between 10,000 and 13,000 dead on each side. The European press flashed headlines like 'The Italians have suffered a great disaster ... greater than has ever occurred in modern times to white men in Africa' (Prouty 1986: 159). Haggai Erlich concludes that the survival of Ethiopia's independence was due not so much to the political awareness and diplomatic skills of its leaders that enabled it to withstand the pressure and emerge victorious;

rather, it was the 'ability of its natural leaders to mobilise and organise militarily as well as politically all levels of Ethiopian society' (1996: 4). The centuries of war and violence in the Abyssinian heart-lands had created a highly militarised society – a society in which warring traditions were more prevalent than the practice of peace.

In Italy, the defeat led to demonstrations against the government's colonial Africa policy. In Ethiopia, the victory secured the country's independent status throughout the colonial scramble for Africa. Moreover, it became the battle of legends and myths of Ethiopian heroism and nationalism. So much so that the victorious battle of Badme (not very far from Adwa) which came to an end on 1 March 1999 – where Ethiopian forces drove the Eritrean army off Ethiopian soil at a cost maybe ten times higher than Menelik's losses – was instantly termed the 'Second Adwa' (see Chapter 6). More importantly, though, the Adwa victory has thenceforth been used to forge an all-embracing sense of Ethiopian identity, contrasted with 'foreigners' of all kinds who interfere and meddle in Ethiopian affairs.

## CONSOLIDATING THE EMPIRE: SUBDUING ENEMY IMAGES WITHIN (1896–1935)

After the battle of Adwa, Menelik and the imperial army concentrated most of their attention on subjugating the people in the southern and western regions of the country (see, for instance, Donham and James 1986), laying the foundation for the most prominent internal enemy image in Ethiopia today: the perception of several ethno-political elites in southern Ethiopia that their people are subjugated and colonised by the Abyssinian highlanders (Holcomb and Ibssa 1990). This interpretation of history is reproduced and sustained also under current EPRDF rule (see Chapter 7).

Throughout the twentieth century Tigray was strategically important in serving as a buffer territory between Ethiopia's political core at Shoa (Amhara) and the Italian colony of Eritrea. The complex set of internal rivalries in Tigray was not only interwoven with the continuous power struggle in Ethiopia, but was also a pivotal issue in Ethiopian-Italian relations. Thus, even though many tend to consider the northern parts of Ethiopia as fairly stable during this period – in contrast to the southern parts of the country – this glosses over the intense political and military history of the period between the battle of Adwa and Italy's invasion in 1936, during which some 20 major battles were fought on Tigrayan soil (Erlich 1986: 172).

A common thread running through the wars and battles fought in northern Ethiopia during this period is the by now familiar pragmatic and flexible approach applied by the Ethiopian nobility to relinquish allegiances and establish alliances in order to promote themselves within the socio-political hierarchy. This internal power-play between the competing princes even continued when Ethiopia was under foreign attack. The historian Haggai Erlich goes so far as to say that 'collaboration with foreign forces against the country's rulers was part and parcel of Ethiopia's traditional politics' (1986: 130). Yohannes cooperated with the British to gain the throne from Tewodros, later to be undermined by Menelik who cooperated with the Egyptians and the Italians in the race for power. Tigray was at the centre of these machinations and Erlich claims that 'throughout the period from the death of Yohannes [1889] till the Fascist invasion [1935] practically all the leading figures of the province, at one stage or another, openly or secretly cooperated with Asmara against the authority of Addis Ababa' (1986: 131). The inspiration for collaboration between the foreign forces in Asmara and the Tigrayan nobility against the central authority of Addis Ababa did not, according to Erlich, stem from a separatist instinct or a modern sense of Tigrayan nationalism:

> Rather, it was always a means of obtaining promotion at home within the framework of the traditional Ethiopian power game. ... Indeed, the ultimate goal of the Tigrayan chiefs cooperating with the foreigners was to eliminate local rivals in order to be recognised as Tigre's *negus* by Ethiopia's emperors. (1986: 131)

## A RETURNING ENEMY:
### FASCIST ITALY'S OCCUPATION (1935–41)

Emperor Menelik suffered a massive stroke in 1909 which rendered him speechless and paralysed, and a struggle for the succession was immediately launched. After a brief interval with Lij Iyasou, political power was vested in Empress Zawditu's regent, *Ras* Tafari. Following her death in 1929, Tafari (then king, *negus*) was proclaimed *negus negast* (king of kings) by the crown council, at which point he took back his baptismal name Haile Selassie (Marcus 1994: 128-30). Emperor Haile Selassie was soon confronted with Italy's renewed aspirations to dominate the Horn of Africa, and, in Mussolini's words, 'We have old and new accounts to settle; and we will settle them' (Marcus 1995b: 160). The Italian army returned in force to avenge the humiliating defeat at Adwa, some forty years earlier. Eritrea was once again used as a bridgehead for the Italians to invade Ethiopia. And, once again, Eritrean native troops were mobilised and used as fighting forces to conquer their 'ethnic' brothers on behalf of the colonial power. Over 50,000 Eritrean troops participated in the war against Ethiopia (Negash 1987: 49). In October 1935, more than 100,000 Italian troops, in addition to the Eritrean *askari*, crossed the Mereb River and entered Tigray, and soon thereafter the town and symbol of Italy's defeat, Adwa, was taken, prompting proud statements in Rome that Italy had finally rectified the humiliating defeat at Adwa (Marcus 1995b: 167). Emperor Haile Selassie mobilised a peasant army of 250,000 men to confront the enemy, while in Tigray parts of his own nobility betrayed him in order to secure local political hegemony.

Fierce battles were fought during a period of six months, but the Imperial army was slowly pushed back towards Addis Ababa by a superior

Italian war machine. Harold Marcus sums up the war in one sentence: 'Modernity defeated Ethiopia – it was that simple' (1995b: 175). In May 1936, Emperor Haile Selassie, together with the royal family and a small group of followers, escaped to Djibouti and into the care of the British navy which transported them to Britain and exile in London and Bath during the Italian period which lasted until 1941. Ethiopia was conquered for the first time in its history, but the Emperor, mythically representing the 41st generation in the Solomonic dynasty, had escaped to become a symbol for the resistance to the Italian regime. Throughout the emperor's absence, *arbegna* (Ethiopian patriots/ resistance fighters against Italian occupation) conducted guerrilla warfare against the occupying army.

The fact that Italy used about 50,000 Eritrean colonial troops to help put down the Ethiopian resistance was viewed as treachery by Ethiopia, as it had been in the Adwa battle forty years earlier. Once again Italy had attacked Ethiopia with the help of Eritreans. Moreover, in recognition of past and future contributions by the Eritreans troops, Italy passed a decree in 1937 distinguishing the Eritreans from other subjects of the newly founded empire (Negash 1997: 17). The Eritreans were to be addressed and treated as 'Eritreans', and not as 'natives', as was the case with the 'Ethiopians', who had not undergone a colonial 'civilising' process. This contributed to cementing a distinction between Tigrinya-speakers north of the river Mereb and their ethnic brothers south of the river. The different classification and treatment of 'Eritreans', in combination with the influences of racist colonial ideology and rapid economic development due to Italian investments, soon made the Eritreans perceive themselves as more 'modernised' and 'developed' than their Ethiopian counterparts (Negash 1987; 1997). This distinction, formalised by the Italian colonial administration, would later develop into a classification of 'superiority/ inferiority' and thus could easily be converted into an active enemy image in times of conflict, as history later proved (see also Negash and Tronvoll 2000).

# Restoring Ethiopian sovereignty

The Italian occupation of Ethiopia (1935-41) came to an end as a consequence of the Allied forces' expulsion of the Fascist and Nazi forces from Africa. When the Fascist Italian army was defeated in Ethiopia, Emperor Haile Selassie resumed power in an independent Ethiopia. At the top of his agenda was the transformation of its archaic politico-adminis-trative structures in order to build a modern, centralised state. The Ethiopian polity had, for all practical reasons, been left unchanged during the last few centuries. Although a growing urban intelligentsia was fostered by Emperor Haile Selassie (Zewde 2002), they were not capable of becoming the bearers of modern nationalist concepts. Thus, Haggai Erlich claims that during the Italian occupation of Ethiopia a modern nationalist movement was virtually non-existent: 'Resistance to the Fascist conquerors, strong as it was, was conducted along medieval organisational patterns, with priests, monks and provincial warlords playing a dominant role' (Erlich 1981: 192).

In order to set in motion the centralising and modernising processes needed, Haile Selassie re-designed the Ethiopian state around his own absolute power (Erlich 1981: 193). This centralisation process did manage to transform parts of the archaic Ethiopian polity into the guise of a modern state, with a centralised government bureaucracy, state army, monetary institutions, educational institutions, etc. (Clapham 1969; Marcus 1995 (1983); Zewde 1991). However, this centralisation, based on the emperor's absolute power, created a growing resistance from the political peripheries of the country and a new enemy-image was produced: the state and its central government.

In Tigray, there were mixed feelings about the reinstatement of the Imperial regime in 1941. Italy had abolished the feudal plundering of the peasants, and Haile Selassie's re-imposition of the old tax system, though modified, was contrary to peasant expectations and certainly proved to be unpopular (Tareke 1984: 82). The growing resentment against the reinstalled imperial regime found fertile ground in the highly militarised and violent Tigray. Repeated battles in the region had taught the peasants how to operate modern weapons, and how to fight in larger units (Tareke 1996: 118). Moreover, the Italian invasion of 1935 created conditions that gave legitimacy and opportunities for rebellion. In addition to the *arbegna* (patriots), who continued their fight against Italy throughout the occupation, there were renegade elements, *shifta* (bandits), operating throughout the region. The distinction between *arbegna* and *shifta* was often blurred, since more often than not the peasants suffered equally from the activities of both (Tareke 1984: 87). Many of the *arbegna* were *shifta* prior to the Italian occupation, and thus continued as *shifta* after their departure (Fernyhough 1986). It has been estimated that by mid-1943 there were close to 5,000 armed *shifta* in north-eastern Tigray alone (Tareke 1996: 100).

Although *shiftanet* (banditry) has always been a feature of Ethiopian feudal society (Crummey 1986), its rampancy in the post-Italian period must be attributed to the inability of the new Imperial government to fill the power vacuum created by the departure of the Italians, according to Gebru Tareke. Within such a context, the traditional Tigrayan in-fighting (*awrajanet*) was rife. Consequently, banditry was an important sociopolitical activity for at least two reasons: first, by preying on the peasants it intensified their hardships and increased the potential for revolt, and second, when suppressed feelings erupted in 1943, many *shifta* joined the rebellious peasants as their military leaders (Tareke 1984: 87). The prevalence of banditry thus contributed to fragmenting the perceptions of 'enemies' and categories of 'relevant others' with which the people could

44

contrast their own identity. The internal struggle within and between the Tigrayan nobility, the emperor and the British (who controlled Eritrea after Italy's defeat), created an unstable political context in Tigray which paved the way for the peasant uprising called *weyane*.[2]

# The state as the enemy:
# the first *weyane* rebellion (1941–3)

The *weyane* rebellion erupted with full force in May 1943, after initial clashes in 1942. During the summer and autumn of 1943 several big battles were fought, involving 20,000 peasants against a force of 10,000 government troops (Tareke 1996: 109). This time the enemy was not foreign forces, but Ethiopians fought against each other. Peasants all over Tigray were forced to feed the Imperial army, and tens of thousands of cattle were confiscated, together with the lion's share of the harvest. The situation was extremely unstable, and a local poem expressed the prevailing mood among the peasantry:

> Do not pasture your cattle far from home,
> Bury your money deep in the ground.
> Do not store your grains, but keep the flour safe,
> People of Enderta [Mekelle district] and Tigrai are locked in a struggle,
> And our ruler is not yet known.
> (Quoted from Tareke 1996: 107)

This first Tigrayan uprising has been interpreted by the TPLF as an act of ethno-nationalism, signifying the struggle to liberate Tigray from Amhara rulers.[3] However, the two foremost scholars on the subject, Gebru Tareke and Haggai Erlich, agree on the point that the first *weyane* cannot be said to represent Tigrayan nationalism. 'It had its various social, political, even cultural backgrounds, and its ideological manifestations were couched in slogans advocating Tigrayanism, but in the final analysis Tigrayanism was more of a rallying slogan than a program to fulfil,' concludes Erlich (1986: 191). The leaders of the first *weyane* faced the problem of elevating the local, peasant-oriented rebellion to a broader, more ideological platform which could develop regional and ethno-nationalistic sentiments. They also lacked the political organisation to sustain a struggle through popular mobilisation. The primary enemy the *weyane* were fighting was the Amhara ruling class. They did not fight to replace the quasi-feudal order with an alternative political model, or to establish an independent Tigray. The motivations for the *weyane* differed in accordance with the social background of the participants, as explained by Gebru Tareke: 'The goals of the partners were obviously not the same: the dissident notables wanted a "fair share" in the territorial allocation of

was implemented by organising the peasants into armed resistance against the central authorities; as explained by the TPLF in their official history of the struggle: 'The decisive element for the beginning of an armed struggle is not a gun. Although it is true that a gun is needed to carry out an armed struggle and reach the needed objective, the most decisive element is the readiness of the people' (TPLF 2000: 71).

A twofold process created this readiness of the people. First, the actual repression and authoritarian policies exhibited by the central government created a reaction from the grassroots – a call for change. This call was thenceforth utilised by the TPLF, who carefully converted the Tigrayan history of exploitation by the Amhara-led feudal system of the imperial government, and the contemporary repression of Tigrayan cultural and linguistic expressions by the central military government of the Derg, into active support for the revolution. In order to anchor the Tigrayan revolution within Ethiopian history, the TPLF presented the Amhara under Emperor Menelik as the relevant other with which a Tigrayan identity could be contrasted. Since Menelik, and his Amhara court, had been striking deals with the Egyptians and the Italian foreign aggressor while the Tigrayan Emperor Yohannes was fighting them, Menelik was put forward as a suitable enemy image against which to promote Tigrayan identity awareness. Such an interpretation of history underpinned the first TPLF manifesto of 1976, which describes the loss of primacy to the Amhara in 1889 as ushering in 'the misfortunes of Tigray' (Abbay 1998: 193).

For an effective revolution to take place, people have to perceive themselves as oppressed and have to recognise an alternative political organisation as offering an effective revolutionary force and a desirable political future (cf. Kertzer 1988: 163). Aregawi Berhe, one of the founders of the TPLF and its first military leader, explained:

> Tigray was the cradle of civilisation in Ethiopia. Nevertheless we were deprived of all benefits during the Amharised regimes in Ethiopia. There was a feeling of collective anger, a collective anger that led to collective consciousness, which again led to collective action. This is the core of Tigrayanness. (Personal communication)

By appealing to a sense of regional, linguistic and cultural difference, and by blaming the Amhara for the lack of Tigrayan development, the TPLF managed to present itself to the Tigrayan peasantry as an organisation which could change these historical injustices and provide for a better and desirable future. By doing so it inspired the creation of a fundamentally new kind of consciousness, a Tigrayan 'ethnic' identity:

> Before, Tigrayan peasants' sense of difference had related primarily to their identification with Tigrayan elites who had competed with other lords in Ethiopia for the office of 'king of kings'. This hardly opposed Tigrayans to the cultural core – just the opposite. By the late 1980s, however, many Tigrayans had apparently begun to see themselves in a different light – as

another 'kind' of people, a people called forth by narratives of group injustice and suffering. (Donham 2002: 4)

It is important to observe that this transformation took place in a context of extreme violence, in which several wars were fought simultaneously against various politico-military enemies *and* the state. The TPLF also had internal difficulties during its formative years of 1977–78, a crisis known as *hinfishfish* (chaos/pandemonium). This factional struggle was partly based in differences of ideology and identity: one faction advocated Tigrayan secession and independence, the other regional autonomy under a federated Ethiopia. It was a clash of notions of what constituted a Tigrayan identity: could it be based on its own historical and cultural merits, or should it be affiliated to a wider Ethiopian identity discourse? I shall return to this intrinsic dilemma in the TPLF ideology, a dilemma that has surfaced at irregular intervals in the TPLF's history and caused severe internal problems. The core motivating factor for the *hinfishfish* may be located within another identity discourse, that of parochial sentiments, or the Tigrayan *awrajanet* phenomenon. The dissenting group within the TPLF argued that the Front's leadership was dominated by individuals from the districts of Shire, Adwa and Axum (all districts in north-western Tigray) – the 'SAA group' as it was labelled – and that they were biased in favour of their own people and districts. This ignited a purge of dissident voices within the Front, and the four ringleaders of the dissenting group were executed for their criticism of the leadership. This brutal way of handling internal criticism and diverging views had a stultifying effect on internal democracy and dissent within the Front. More importantly, it eradicated an internal discourse of parochialism and consolidated a *Tigrayan* platform of identity within the Front (on the *hinfishfish*, see Milkias 2001: 6-8; Tareke 1996: 217-8; Young 1997: 134-5). It was during these turbulent years that a Tigrayan identity discourse was shaped by the TPLF and seemingly embraced by the peasantry. As Donham argues: 'The experience of war, trauma, and death seems always to hold the potential for transforming people in the most fundamental ways' (2002: 4).

Other factors also played important parts in motivating the Tigrayan peasantry to take up arms against the central authorities. Gebru Tareke (1983: 20-1) argues that land scarcity and escape from recruitment into the Derg army were important mobilising factors. I have identified similar reasons in my analysis of the Eritrean peasants' recruitment to the EPLF during the same historical period (Tronvoll 1998). Tareke further claims that the Kalashnikov gun represented a symbolic value of power which also attracted many peasants to the TPLF, in a situation in which they had felt powerless for too long.

It is impossible to give a representative account of the innumerable atrocities and narratives of violence during the 17-year-long struggle in Tigray, which helped to create, recreate and cement locally perceived enemy images. It should be noted, however, that this was not a struggle against the Derg regime alone, but also against a host of other resistance movements. In Tigray in the mid-1970s, the Ethiopian Democratic Union (EDU), the Ethiopian People's Revolutionary Party (EPRP), and the Tigray Liberation Front (TLF), were the most prominent armed political organisations the TPLF had either to establish alliances with or defeat militarily (Young 1997). Also, the Eritrean Liberation Front (ELF) and the Eritrean Peoples' Liberation Front (EPLF) operated in areas bordering Tigray, and established alliances with or against the various Tigrayan movements. Thus, the TPLF's war of resistance had a number of enemies becoming their significant others: the Derg army representing the Amharised, authoritarian state; the EDU representing the feudal system and *ancien régime*; the EPRP representing the ideological Marxist adversary;[4] and the TLF representing both foreign influence (through ELF) and an even narrower nationalist agenda than the TPLF. In the three-year period 1975–78, the TPLF, according to its own sources, engaged in over 85 military campaigns 'in order to maintain its survival' (TPLF 2000: 76, page 67 in original). The alliance-building strategies were crucial for the TPLF in order to survive as an organisation in the field in the struggle against shifting enemies.

## THE MAKING, UNMAKING AND REMAKING
## OF THE TPLF-EPLF ALLIANCE

When the TPLF was established in 1975 in the aftermath of the fall of Emperor Haile Selassie (1916–74), the Eritrean liberation fronts (ELF and EPLF) had been operating for many years and had gained valuable political and military experience. Common linguistic and kinship ties joined people in the Eritrean highlands (*kebessa*) and Tigray together. It was therefore natural that the Tigrayans sought advice and assistance from the Eritrean movements across the border.

Before they entered the field and established the TPLF, representatives of the Tigrayan group (at that time called the Tigray National Organisa-tion, TNO) had been in contact with the Eritrean fronts, and the EPLF in particular. The first group of TPLF fighters, led by the current foreign minister Seyum Mesfin, was sent to the EPLF for military training and supplies in 1975 (cf. Berhe 2004; Young 1996). Soon, however, the growing cooperation between the two fronts was strained by the EPLF's relationship with the Ethiopian People's Revolutionary Party (EPRP). The EPLF trained EPRP troops in the Sahel at the same time as TPLF and EPRP turned against each other in Tigray. This led the TPLF to look for another alliance as a substitute, and its relations with the ELF improved. The latter was operating in the Badme area (the core conflict area of the 1998-2000 Eritrean-Ethiopian war) and had undertaken several military operations against Derg positions inside Tigray (Young 1996: 106; 1997: 112–13). The TPLF saw these attacks as furthering its own interests, and therefore established closer cooperation with the ELF. But this relation-ship soon came to an end, as the ELF began to assist a competing

Tigrayan movement, the Tigrayan Liberation Front (TLF), with which the TPLF found itself at loggerheads, eventually leading to strained relations with the ELF. Yet another change of alliances was needed. Sebhat Nega, a founding member of the Front and its former Chairman, explained the difficult choices of the TPLF:

> We were trying to balance the relations between the ELF and the EPLF, in particular when the situation with the ELF was aggravated. And when we were quarrelling with EPRP, EPLF was not happy. Anyway, we were in a dilemma. But we could not give in on our principles. We could not give up that the national struggle is the primary struggle, or the primary contradiction. And as time passed the ELF and the EPRP came closer. They became on good terms and formed an alliance. Then we clashed with EPRP and drove it out from Tigray. Finally, we were also in contradiction with ELF. In 1981 we and the EPLF jointly evicted the ELF from Eritrea. (Personal communication)

The confusing period 1975–76, which showed shifting, overlapping and contradicting alliances among and between the competing Eritrean and Tigrayan/Ethiopian fronts, illustrates the pragmatic and opportunistic promises of support which were made between the different movements.

Later during the struggle the initial TPLF-EPLF alliance was repudiated, as the two fronts turned against each other politically. The differences in ideology, politics and military strategy led to a total breach of relations between the two fronts in 1985 (Negash and Tronvoll 2000: 19-20; Young 1996); for three years, until 1988, the two movements had no cooperation or military coordination. This incident became an important point of reference during the 1998-2000 Eritrean-Ethiopian war. Many Tigrayans referred to the breach as an example of the historical continuation of Eritrean betrayal. The two fronts resumed cooperation in 1988, but not on such close terms as before the breach in 1985. The cooperation was basically of a military nature with the common objective of toppling the Derg regime. Although both fronts had everything to gain from close cooperation, both during the struggle against the Derg and afterwards, other issues of political ideology and development policy and a fight for hegemony made the alliance between them an unstable and shifting one. As such, it did not differ during these years from the alliances made between the competing nobility within the old Abyssinian polity, in the struggle to secure political positions and control a territorial base.

## TIGRAYAN PEASANTS' ALLEGIANCES

Peasant support was attractive for all warring factions in Tigray, and various fronts tried to present their interpretation of history and their 'enemy' as the relevant *other* for the Tigrayan peasants to mobilise against. At the same time the peasantry was also seen as a reservoir of potential support for the adversaries; thus the civilian population was also exposed to direct military campaigns. The most direct effect of this was the Derg army's strategy of counter-population warfare, or, as it was described: 'draining the sea to catch the fish'. The oppressive policies of the Derg government, which had alienated most segments of the Tigrayan population, in combination with growing support for the TPLF, meant that the government forces could not locate any secure bases in Tigray from which to start a pacification strategy (de Waal 1991: 141). As a result, they engaged in counter-population warfare with terrible consequences for the civilian population. For outsiders it is difficult to comprehend the massive scale of these violations. They were not isolated incidents, but a deliberate strategy to crush all opposition and resistance, a strategy which only cemented the impression of the central government as an enemy in the eyes of the Tigrayan population.

The civilians had to adjust and cope with the political machinations, the war, and the shifting politico-military realms; as a war-experienced resident of the southern Tigrayan town of Maichew explained: 'People had to be clever or tactical. It was a soldier's government and you had to give soldiers food, *tej* [mead], whatever they wanted. Parents gave their children to marry Derg soldiers to get security' (Young 1997: 119). But the exposure to violence was not only projected by the Derg. The TPLF, and the other resistance movements as well, exerted pressure on the peasants in order to get their support and to prohibit them from supporting other movements. This faced the peasants with a dilemma, as no matter what strategy they chose, they could be targeted by one or other political force.

Much of the support given to the TPLF from the peasantry was based on the two-fold objective of the revolution, to liberate the Tigrayan people both politically from the oppressive central government and socially from traditional prejudices and discriminatory cultural practices. Female emancipation was high on the agenda, as was equality for Muslims and low-/out-cast groups such as smiths and tanners. More importantly for TPLF popular support was the Front's position on the issue of land and land tenure. From the very start of its revolution, the TPLF addressed the grievances of the 'masses' and concluded that priority should be given to solving the issue of landlessness and alleviating the socio-economic status of the peasants. The means to solve these issues was land reform, giving equal access to land for all people in Tigray, both men and women, rich and poor. By carrying out the reforms in the areas they controlled, the TPLF increased its political legitimacy among the Tigrayan peasants, at the expense of the other resistance movements operating in the area (Chiari 1996; Hammond 1999; Young 1997).

## A CULTURAL REVOLUTION

Since the TPLF based its struggle on liberating Tigrayan society and culture (*bahli*), it made use of common Tigrayan symbols and cultural expressions to mobilise the peasantry for their cause. It is a strong tradition in Tigrayan society to express sentiments of joy and anger, and viewpoints and opinions on politics and war, through the medium of poetry and parables (Berhane 1994). Song and story-telling tradition was exploited in order to construct a culture of resistance against the enemy, both during the 17 years of struggle (1975-91) and during the new Eritrean-Ethiopian war (1998-2000). Jenny Hammond has noted down the following recollection by an old TPLF fighter on the strategy used from the first days of the struggle (1975) to win the confidence of the peasants.

> When we reached somewhere, we sang songs. There were only a hundred or so of us then with very old-fashioned guns, but everybody was happy. We really understood the meaning of culture and what part it plays in the revolution. To teach people new ideas, it's very hard. They have to use their own culture, their own language. They don't know anything about what struggle means by itself. In our culture, if someone has a gun and stands against the government, he is called a bandit. They don't know the difference between banditry and revolution. ... If you tried to tell them something directly about the revolution, they wouldn't believe it, because a peasant, no matter what you want him to approve, has already learned the opposite from his experience. So, when we taught them about the tactics of guerrilla fighting, we told them it's like the dog and the flea. The flea jumps on the dog's back. The dog starts scratching. Then the flea jumps to another place. Soon, everywhere there are fleas. They suck his blood and the dog becomes skinny and in the end, it will die. In the end, it's only because they see the revolution is very powerful that they join and feel that it's 'their' revolution. (Hammond 1999: 187)

The cultural department (*kifli bahli*) was one of the first departments the TPLF established, and the fighters assigned to it were active in producing new songs and educational parables, as well as collecting old ones from the peasants. Traditional Tigrayan parables, poems and songs were gathered from all over the region and revitalised in the service of the struggle. This created continuity with the political past of Tigrayan repression and enduring enemy images (the Amhara), and with Tigrayan customs and cultures to establish legitimacy for the new invention – the TPLF. In particular, songs and slogans from the first *weyane* were revitalised, linking and identifying the new struggle with the familiar and popular revolt of resistance against Amhara domination (Abbay 1998: 195).

The first song written by the TPLF – 'The Bell is Ringing' (*Dewel tede wilu*) – was recorded in the early days of the revolution (Hammond 1999).

> The bell is ringing
> For the Revolution
> The big bell is ringing.
> Rise up, all you people!
> Stand up for your rights!
> Take up your arms and fight
> Against the oppressors.

This cassette became very popular as it was the first widely distributed, popularised expression of Tigrayan resistance. The old fighter, interviewed by Jenny Hammond and quoted above, explained that: 'The national sentiment is very strong. It's our music, already in our blood, under our skin. Though the political meaning is there, it's the music itself ... it hurts. It breaks down your heart' (Hammond 1999: 188). The explicit intention of the TPLF was not, of course, to 'break down' the hearts of the Tigrayan people, but to strengthen the spirit of resistance by combining sentimental metaphors of Tigrayanness with a political ideology of Tigrayan unique-ness and claims of autonomy and self-administration. The success of the TPLF's 'cultural revolution' was also observed by the Derg security, which reported in 1987 that 'most of the TPLF army is made up of peasant forces who do not know why they are fighting. Due to their low level of political consciousness, they were only intoxicated by folk music' (quoted from Abbay 1998: 122).

The TPLF revolutionary songs concentrated chiefly on three themes: the strong and invincible force of the revolution and its vanguard, the TPLF; the longing for a just peace and Tigrayan autonomy; and criticism of the historical domination of Tigray by the Amhara elites and the feudal system as a strategy for creating enemy-images. The TPLF's use of Tigrayan culture, symbols and history to legitimise its political aspirations gave it grassroots support in the fight against both the Derg and other competing political movements in Tigray in the 1970s and 1980s. It was only the TPLF that mobilised the peasantry on the basis of Tigrayan nationalism and identity. Ghidey Zeratsion, the deputy chairman of the TPLF in its formative years, emphasised the importance of Tigrayan nationalism as a mobilising factor against the Amhara, politically represented by the EPRP and the Derg, for all sectors of Tigrayan society, including the traditional Tigrayan leadership.

> Nationalism was the main issue that gained support for the TPLF. The Tigrayan nationalism is high and bitter against Amhara rule. The Tigrayan feudals, rulers and the rich showed great resentment and hatred against Amhara rule. They had contested areas like authority, region and trade with the ruling Amhara class. The common man and the elite were conscious of and agitated by his national oppression. So it was not difficult for the TPLF to appeal to these feelings. (Personal communication)

The other resistance movements operating in Tigray (the EPRP, EDU and TLF) had thousands of members and supporters throughout the region. But as the organisations were defeated one by one by the combined pressure and hostilities from the Derg army and the TPLF, the civilian supporters of these organisations were forced to adjust to the new political reality and accept the growing hegemony of the TPLF – or be quiescent. By 1991, when the TPLF-led coalition the EPRDF entered Addis Ababa and the Derg regime collapsed, the TPLF had seemingly unanimous backing from its Tigrayan constituency. Or, as a former EPRP supporter in Wuqro expressed it when I asked him to explain his shift of support from EPRP to the TPLF.

> When the TPLF fighters managed to crush the EPRP base at Assimba, we knew that we could no longer rely on the protection of the EPRP against the TPLF or the Derg. For me it was an easy choice. I had to accept the TPLF as my organisation, since it also took over control of the area.

He concluded by citing an ancient Tigrinya proverb, metaphorically expressing the shifting allegiances of the peasantry:

> Any sun that rises to the east – is our sun
> Any king that sits on our throne – is our king

## From Tigray to Ethiopia – from TPLF to EPRDF (1989–91)

By 1989 the TPLF had achieved its primary objective – to liberate the whole of Tigray from Amhara state-domination. The second *weyane* had accomplished what the first *weyane* started. After the military liberation of Tigray, the victorious TPLF faced the dilemma of whether to cease its offensive military campaign against the Derg and adopt a defensive strategy to protect Tigray only, or to continue the struggle beyond Tigray in order to topple, once and for all, the oppressive central government in Addis Ababa. The leadership of the Front were unanimous in their decision to continue the struggle to overthrow the regime in order to settle the issue of suppressed ethnic groups in the whole of Ethiopia and not only Tigray. This decision had two consequences, one ideological and one practical. First, the Front had to readjust its ideological platform so that the revolution of Tigrayanness and political autonomy could also include an Ethiopian solution to the problem of other suppressed 'nationalities'. And, secondly, it had to establish alliances with other ethnic fronts outside Tigray in order to carry on the military struggle on 'foreign' ethnic soil.

The rank and file and the Tigrayan masses challenged this change of strategy, however, and at the beginning of 1989 thousands of fighters left the Front to return to their villages, stating 'We have liberated Tigray and that was our objective. We do not want to proceed any further. Let the Amhara, Oromo and the others fight for their own causes.' The protesting fighters received support from their home villages, who wanted their sons and daughters back. The protest and the standstill, called *dewta*, created severe problems for the TPLF in the final momentum of the war against the Derg. They were also a challenge for the leadership to restore both ideological and their military legitimacy in order to continue the struggle. Ideologically, the TPLF blamed the protesters for being 'narrow nationalists', focusing on their parochial concerns in such a way as to blur the revolutionary objectives. For almost a year the TPLF carried out an intense re-ideologisation campaign, to 'detribalise' a peasantry that had been 'tribalised' for 15 years (Abbay 1998: 201), or, in terms of the argument of this book, to re-focus on the issue of 'who is the enemy' and to define the answer in a broader manner than just identifying a Tigrayan adversary. The *dewta* standstill thus has its parallel to the *hinfishfish* protest of 1978, since both had an undertone of parochial concerns.

To pursue the struggle against the Derg beyond Tigray, the TPLF needed political and military allies from among other oppressed peoples within Ethiopia (Vaughan and Tronvoll 2003). In January 1989 the Ethiopian Peoples' Revolutionary Democratic Front (EPRDF) was established by the TPLF, together with the Ethiopian Peoples' Democratic Movement (EPDM), later renamed the Amhara National Democratic Movement (ANDM). The TPLF was the dominating party within the coalition and used the EPDM/ANDM as a vanguard to mobilise support among the Amhara peasants against Derg repression. In order to broaden the coalition against the Derg, the Oromo People's Democratic Organisation (OPDO) was established by the TPLF in 1990 after talks with the Oromo Liberation Front (OLF) in the late 1980s failed to include them in the coalition. The first members of the OPDO were Oromo prisoners of war captured from the Derg army by the TPLF. The OPDO aimed at recruiting support among the Oromo people in competition with the first Oromo movement OLF. After the fall of the Derg, yet another EPRDF partner was created in order to represent the multi-ethnic southern region of Ethiopia, named the Southern Ethiopian Peoples' Democratic Front (SEPDF). This happened after the establishment of the Southern Ethiopian Peoples' Democratic Coalition (SEPDC), an umbrella organisation for many small opposition parties in the southern region. The common denominator of all EPRDF coalition partners and affiliates is that they were initiated by the TPLF as part of a strategic policy of consolidating ethnic representation and control over the various regions of Ethiopia, through the establishment of ethnic-party alliances. As such, the TPLF brought the Abyssinian tradition of alliance-building into a modern multi-party context and a wider Ethiopian sphere, when it took control over Addis Ababa on 28 May 1991 after the escape of Mengistu Hailemariam to Zimbabwe.

# Post-revolutionary Ethiopia: deconstructing the 'nation' into ethnic-component parts (1991–8)

With the downfall of the Derg in May 1991, the main enemy of the TPLF/EPRDF vanished. The 17 years of constructing the Amhara ruling class as the principal enemy of the Tigrayan, and later Ethiopian, peoples ceased immediately. The EPRDF itself was now the new ruling class. In order to build up its legitimacy as the government, the EPRDF replaced the 'Amhara ruling class' with the 'unitary Ethiopian state' as the new main enemy of the people. Alessandro Triulzi (2002) observes that '[over] the past decade Ethiopia's past has been fought over and constantly redefined by a number of revisions and reformulations which have attempted to modify the prevailing historical narrative of the country's past and to adapt it to changing political situations'. Just as the Derg regime reconstituted the Ethiopian state and the content of 'Ethiopianness' in the 1980s in accordance with its political ideology (see, for instance, Clapham 1988; Donham 1999; Markakis 1990; Tiruneh 1993), the EPRDF had to do the same in the 1990s.

When the EPRDF entered Addis Ababa in 1991 the main challenge confronting it was to form a government and reform the state in order to establish political legitimacy among the wide range of Ethiopian peoples. One must bear in mind that the EPRDF represented only segments of the three main ethnic groups in the country (Tigrayan, Amhara and Oromo); in addition, the absolute majority of the population knew little or nothing about its ideology or policies. Just as political legitimacy for the new government following the 1974 revolution lay in solving the land question, no government following the Derg could hope to win legitimacy and support without addressing the issue of ethnicity in governance. This was grounded in the fact that all the main opposition movements operating at the time of the fall of the Derg were organised on an ethnic basis, and in the central government's subjugation of the various non-Amhara ethnic groups in the country. The new power-holders thus saw the need to redress the ethnic question and emphasised ethnic equality and autonomy within a new Ethiopian federal state as a means of abolishing the many ethnic enemy images that flourished in the country.[5] Only by granting every ethnic group in Ethiopia the right to autonomy and secession if so desired could the groups overcome their fear of belonging to the Ethiopian federation (as enshrined in Article 39 in the new Ethiopian Constitution). It was within such a context that the EPRDF spokesperson and speaker of the House of Representatives Dawit Yohannes expressed the dominant discourse on Ethiopian identities in an interview given on the occasion of the first federal and regional elections under EPRDF rule in 1995:

> The EPRDF is challenging the political environment of Ethiopia. We do not have loyalty to history, it has been proved to fail. Nor do we perceive containing Ethiopia as an absolute entity as our main goal, hence we also accepted Eritrean independence. We must find a solution that is beneficial for the Ethiopian people today, therefore history will not provide the answer. History has been used as a veil, covering up differences within Ethiopia. People have believed that we have had unity in this country, but it has never existed. What they call unity was a geographical entity dominated by one ethnic group. An Amhara peasant had never met an Eritrean, likewise an Afar nomad had never heard of a Nuer, let alone seen one. And this they call unity! At the stage Ethiopia is now you cannot force people to form a unity. (Personal communication)

In order to anchor this political argumentation within a politico-historical context, the EPRDF undertook an official revision of Ethiopian history, identifying its depth and point of departure with Emperor Menelik's rule at the turn of the twentieth century. This was grounded in the fact that the borders of contemporary Ethiopia were delimited and internationally recognised during his rule. By abolishing the deep historical trajectories of the Abyssinian state, and launching the '100 years of Ethiopian history' paradigm, the EPRDF signalled that it did not believe in the primordiality of the Ethiopian state, and that consequently the state could be re-configured into a different structure without too many problems.

The ethnic policies of the new Ethiopia were highly controversial at the time of their introduction and Ethiopians from all walks of life had their own opinions about them. However, more contentious than the ethnic federal policy itself was the EPRDF's discourse on Ethiopian identity and history, in particular for the urban middle-class and intellectuals. An Ethiopian academic and high-profile scholar vented his frustrations at the EPRDF attitude.

> One thing is their political ideology and practical politics. We can either like or dislike that. But another issue is the re-writing of Ethiopian history, claiming that the Ethiopian historical roots are only 100 years old! That's an outrageous lie! And when Meles is telling us that Ethiopia is only a territory and that, as a nation, Ethiopia has never existed, and the Ethiopian flag is only a piece of cloth without any symbolic value, he is as arrogant as he gets. They must understand that some passing Tigrayan peasants cannot annul the 2,000 years of Ethiopian history and tradition, just because they happen to oust the Derg/WPE from Arat Kilo! [meaning party/government offices]. (Personal communication)

The TPLF/EPRDF reconfigured the Ethiopian state by recasting 'spatial relationships in terms that enabled previously peripheral zones to capture direct control over sources of power that had previously been monopolised by the state, and to reconstitute these in ways that challenged the idea of statehood and threatened to displace it' (Clapham 2002: 23). The TPLF/EPRDF projected an image of representing the diverse groups of people captured within a state polity against their own will and for whom 'national unity' was no more than a pretext for repression (Clapham 2002: 26).

In order to understand the changes in identity discourse that took place during the Eritrean-Ethiopian war (1998-2000), it is vital to have this basic understanding of the EPRDF's hegemonic identity discourse prior to the war. As we shall see below, the discourses on identity in Ethiopia changed radically with the outbreak of the war. Suddenly, Ethiopianness rose like a phoenix from the revolutionary ashes, positioning itself at the centre of the political discourse on identity.

# Historical trajectories – current realities

Clearly, experiences of war and violence have been an intrinsic part of everyday life for generations of Tigrayans and Ethiopians during the last two centuries. By tracing the historical trajectories of enemy images, the analysis has unveiled the constant shifting of alliances and allegiances, which has influenced the enduring creation, rejection and recreation of the images of the enemy. In the Ethiopian historical landscape, no ethnic-political-military alliance has been perceived as given; and what may seemingly appear as a stable and consolidated alliance may elusively be broken due to external or internal factors. History has shown that the dynamics of alliances depends not only upon an external threat, but also upon the everlasting power-play between the alliance partners in order to position oneself above the other in the traditional Ethiopian socio-political hierarchy.

Moreover, this chapter has identified the strategy used by the TPLF in modern times to connect its struggle to a distant past. When the TPLF was established in 1975, its founders deliberately described themselves as the second *weyane*. The second *weyane* implied the continuation of the struggle from the first *weyane*, and an enduring enemy image. It signified that the Tigrayan liberation struggle had continued through the genera-tions, and that the futile peasant rebellion of 1943 was in no way a waste of life. The overarching narrative of the *weyanes* – first and second – tells of a continuation of the struggle in which the seemingly senseless deaths of thousands of Tigrayan peasants in 1943 were transformed into an appropriate sacrifice of revolutionary martyrs in order to conquer the enemy, the Amhara ruling class. This is supposed to be understood as a sacred event, and one which points to another sacred event, that of February 1975 and the establishment of the TPLF and the start of the second *weyane*. As such, the new revolution created its own relevant past and anchored the new struggle within a historical depth. Historical know-ledge was manipulated and interwoven into contemporary politics, thus giving historical legitimacy to the revolution.

In the post-revolution period, in which the TPLF/EPRDF dissolved the unitary Ethiopian state and re-configured it into an ethnic federal state, a different kind of enemy image was, at least officially, acknowledged. In the words of Meles Zenawi:

> The question we asked ourselves at the outset [was]: 'What should we base our internal policy on?' There were two fundamental ideas on which we based it. Our first question was, 'Now that the Derg is gone what is the people's primary pre-occupation? *What are the main enemies of the people?*' It was on the answers to these questions that we based the formulation of our domestic and foreign policies. *We identified poverty, ignorance and backwardness as the principal enemies of the Ethiopian people.*[6]

After assuming power in Addis Ababa, the TPLF/EPRDF concentrated on facilitating a rapid reconstruction and development plan for Tigray and Ethiopia as a whole, providing basic healthcare, education and agricultural aid to the peasantry. For seven years the Tigrayan people, at least, experienced peace and relative stability – without the presence of a threatening enemy – before the new Eritrean-Ethiopian war erupted in May 1998.

Parallel with the outbreak and escalation of hostilities, old alliances were broken and new ones established, turning friends into enemies and enemies into friends. Suddenly, historical trajectories of enemy images were turned into current realities. History was once again reinterpreted and inserted into the new political context to create legitimacy for the new alliances and enemy images. The discourses surrounding this politico-cultural production of allies and enemies will be the focus of the chapters to come.

# Notes

1 Note that *adi* is not a fixed geographical entity like 'Ethiopia'. *Adi*, as 'homeland', must be understood within the context in which it is used, designating the village, district, region, or country as the relevant 'homeland'.

2 The term *weyane* today implies 'revolution'. The original meaning of the term, however, stems from a traditional form of fighting in Tigray between two groups of youngsters from different hamlets or villages. Gebru Tareke writes that 'It [*weyane*] connotes organised resistance and a spirit of oneness. In practice, the popular sport provided the youngsters with the opportunity to demonstrate to their peers their potential as fighters and leaders. It also taught them the notion of group solidarity, hence the adoption of the word as an ideological expression of the rebellion' (Tareke 1996). The TPLF revolution which started in 1975 took the term second *woyane*, in order to draw the historical parallel to the first Tigrayan rebellion under Haile-Selassie.

3 See, for instance, the 'official' history of the TPLF struggle, *TPLF's Popular Struggle (1975–1991)*, (original in Tigrinya) published in 2000 by the TPLF, under the section 'National question in northern Ethiopia (Tigray)', pp. 20–9.

4 The TPLF argued that the political contradictions in Ethiopia were based on the repression of nationalities, thus one needed to liberate the nationalities in order to build a socialist state. The EPRP argued that the contradictions were class-based, and that one needed a class struggle to build a socialist state.

5 At least, this is an interpretation that is based on the policy's stated objectives. Opposition discourse rejects this objective, and claims that the ethnic policy was introduced in order for a minority (the Tigrayans) to divide and rule the country, a topic I return to in Chapters 7 and 8.

6 Quote taken from Solomon Inquai's paper 'Key Determinants of the Ethio-Eritrean Crisis, 1998', 5 December 1998, posted on the web-site of the Ethiopian Government's Press Spokesperson (http://www.ethiospokes.net) (my emphasis).

# Four

## Alternating Enemies
## & Allies
### Ethnicity in Play

In the past, Eritreans were our brothers and friends. Eritrea was our asylum area where we went in times of hardships, and vice versa. We were also tied to Eritrea through bonds of marriage. Today, however, they have invaded our land and we have now come to know that the Eritreans are really our mortal foes and enemies. (Tigrayan peasant, February 1999)

The very nature of Ethiopian identity, of the Ethiopian self, has been bitterly contested both on the battlefields and in discourse with competing versions of past and future. (John Sorensen (1993: 17)

With the outbreak of war, the bilateral relationship between Eritrea and Ethiopia changed from that of allies to enemies overnight. The alteration in the formal relations between the two states immediately influenced the notion of a wide range of collective identities in the region. This chapter explores how the outbreak of war shaped a Tigrayan discourse on identity, inspired by popular perceptions of history and culture, and influenced by official rhetoric and policies. As such, it demonstrates the palpable potency of ethnicity and its manipulative and flexible qualities (Wilmsen and McAllister 1996). The chapter is thus about the creation of images of enemies and friends, the construction of histories (past and present), and the formation of collective identities (self-ascribed and ascribed to others), from the point of view of Tigrayans.

There are different perceptions of what Ethiopia is and entails, as eloquently phrased by John Sorensen: 'Ethiopia, in a famous phrase, has been seen as "a museum of peoples", but it is also a warehouse of images, a repository for obsessions and projections of various identities both from within the region and from without' (1993: 3). Prior to the EPRDF takeover of power in 1991, the dominant ideas of Ethiopia were those promulgated by the 'Amharised' state (a Greater Ethiopia view), and

61

those espoused by the political fronts challenging the Amhara-dominated state, i.e. the EPLF (a colonisation discourse), and the TPLF and OLF (an ethnic discourse of state oppression). Conflicts over images, histories and identities are struggles for power and efforts to define social and political realities. Those who control the definition of the relevant other also decide how, and against whom, the war should be fought: namely, who rightfully belongs to Ethiopia, and who does not.

This chapter will examine the effects the Eritrean-Ethiopian war had on the conceptualisation of inter-ethnic relationships within, and beyond, the *Habesha* (Abyssinian) realm. By tracing the question of *who is the enemy*, one discovers the extraordinary malleability of Abyssinian allegiances and alliances. Indeed, this is so much the case that people who used to be recognised as mass murderers of innocent Tigrayans were, ten years later, perceived as saviours and close allies. First, the Tigrayan self-ascribed identity will be explored, as exemplified through traditional poetry and key Tigrayan concepts of character. Secondly, Tigrayan relations with Eritrea will be discussed, in order to explain how the Tigrayan notion of Eritrea shifted from friend to enemy. Subsequently, the Tigrayan notion of the Amhara will be addressed and the reverse process of turning the Amhara from enemy to friend. Concluding the chapter is a section on whether Tigrayan representations of the Ethiopian polity have changed as a consequence of the Eritrean-Ethiopian war.

## Poetics of identity and resistance: defining and declaiming Tigrayanness

Local perceptions of identity, war and resistance are expressed in a multitude of forms – oral and written, prose and poetry – and contain a variety of meanings – facts and fiction, coherent and irrational. Local sentiments on hotly political issues may either contest the official narrative or endorse it. Depending on political content, the opinions may be expressed through various strategies, in order to safeguard the actor from possible retaliation. James Scott (1990: 18-9) has analysed different strategies of expression by a subordinated peasantry, and distinguishes between four categories of discourse. The safest and most public form of political expression is that which seemingly endorses the official narrative presented by the power-holders and takes as 'its basis the flattering self-image of elites'. However, there may be slightly different connotations within this public expression that may facilitate representation of interests diverging from the official one. Examples of such incidents within the Eritrean-Ethiopian war are many, since some actors could refer to EPRDF policies and established practice prior to the war and thereby argue against some of the new policies inspired by the war. These examples were in particular related to the way in which the constitutional rights of 'nations, nationalities and peoples' appeared to undermine the national cohesion of Ethiopia, which, to a certain degree, was antithetical to the strong nationalistic drive created by the policies of the war.

The second and sharply contrasting form of political expression is that of 'hidden transcript', as phrased by Scott. This is argument taking place off-stage, out of sight of the power-holders, and voicing opposition to the officially sanctioned narrative. Many of my informants, who opposed the war or escaped recruitment, would fall into this category, since their voices could be heard only in the shadows of secluded, private, arenas outside the control of EPRDF officials or informers.

A third realm of subordinate group political communication lies between the first two categories. This is a narrative form of disguise and anonymity that takes place in the public sphere but is deliberately designed to have a double meaning or in some way hide the identity of the actors. This category of expression is traditionally termed *kinea* – or 'wax and gold' (*sam-ennã warq*), which has developed into a form of art in the Abyssinian highlands through centuries of peasant resistance to the feudal lords. This is a use of language with the purpose of cultural socialisation, political control or resistance (see Gelaye 2000; Levine 1965b; Molvaer 1995). It is a form built on two semantic layers, the figurative surface meaning of the words is called 'wax', and their more or less hidden, actual significance is the 'gold' (Levine 1965b: 5). This capacity of language is in particular used by peasants to express political resistance towards traditional landowners and political elites.

Finally, the most explosive realm of politics is when the hidden transcripts become public and the conventional official narrative is ruptured. When this happens, argues Scott, the power-holders must immediately repress these expressions and sanction the actors, otherwise the hegemony of power will rupture, which will lead to further subversive words and acts. This is what happened in Hadiya in Southern Ethiopia during the May 2000 general elections, which took place simultaneously with the last military offensive during the war, and to which incident I shall return in Chapter 6 (see also Tronvoll 2001).

## WORDS OF WARS

As noted in the previous chapter, the TPLF used the medium of poetry and songs to communicate its ideology and revolutionary *raison d'être* to the peasantry. The *poetry* as such is not, of course, the central issue here, but the *poetics* of resistance is, as its properties appear in all kind of symbolic expressions (Herzfeld 1997: 22). The spirit of resistance reflected in the old TPLF revolutionary songs was also carried onwards in new songs and poems created by the TPLF/EPRDF cultural troupes and bands during the Eritrean-Ethiopian war. In particular, themes related to Tigrayan heroism and enemy images were popular.

One of the most popular singers in Tigray was Girmay Haile-Selassie.

He joined the TPLF in 1980 as a fighter and was wounded in 1989 in a battle against the Derg. Towards the end of the struggle in 1990, he was recruited as a member of the *Selam* ('Peace') band that was organised and founded by the TPLF. The band was composed of disabled veteran TPLF fighters and was very active and popular in Tigray. Girmay Haile-Selassie was thus quick to compose a new song when the Eritrean war erupted, playing on well-known themes from the 17-years-of-struggle, but put in the new context of enemies and friends.

> Heroism is my inborn character;
> And thus also my identity.
> I am the doer of miracles in a fierce and heroic battle,
> he [Eritrea] has provoked me today
> wanting enmity and feud as in the old days.
> It is unthinkable [to surrender],
> I am ready to confront him
> as I have made an oath with my blood.

Three important topics in Tigrayan consciousness are emphasised in the song; heroism as a Tigrayan identity-marker; warring and invincibility; and the tradition of enmity with Eritrea. Let me elaborate on the last aspect first. 'He has provoked me today, wanting enmity and feud as in the old days', depicts the Eritrean invasion of Badme as a parallel to old feuds and battles. This vague mention of old feuds refers to the layers of conflict which have spanned the Mereb River throughout the centuries. During feudal times, the ruler of *Medir Bahir* ('the land on the sea': the Eritrean component part of the Abyssinian empire) was in a constant power struggle with the ruler of Tigray, which, at infrequent intervals, erupted into skirmishes and feuds between the nobility of two Abyssinian provinces. Later on, the Italian army tried twice to conquer Tigray from their bridgehead in their Eritrean colony and with the help of Eritrean colonial troops. In the eyes of the Ethiopian people, the Eritreans were perceived to be traitors during the Italian attack on Ethiopia in 1896 (ending with the decisive battle of Adwa) and during the occupation of Ethiopia (1935–41), when over 50,000 Eritrean troops under Italian command helped to put down Ethiopian resistance. Furthermore, in modern times, the line 'enmity and feud as in the old days' refers to the breach of relations between the TPLF and the EPLF from 1985 to 1988, during which the Eritreans stopped the transportation of relief aid into Tigray across EPLF-held territory. Just weeks after the Eritrean invasion of Badme in May 1998, a Tigrayan friend of mine explained:

> This shows the true character of the EPLF. They betrayed us in 1985 and they betrayed us now. We should never have trusted them after they tried to kill us all by cutting off our supplies of relief food during our struggle. The Eritreans have always been deceitful.

Returning to the song, we see that the two other aspects highlighted are Tigrayan warring and invincibility, and heroism as a natural part of Tigrayan identity. Here we touch upon some crucial elements in Tigrayan self-identity, termed as *habbo*, which deserve a closer description.

## *'Habbo* equals 'Tigrayanness'

The term *habbo* is one of the key terms used by Tigrayans when discussing issues related to their collective identity (see also Rosen 1975: 55; 1978).[1] *Habbo* refers to a specific human quality of determination and integrity, a quality which is particularly important in difficult situations. Another word used to explain *habbo* is *ma'anta* which literally translates as 'intestine'. In English a corresponding metaphor of 'guts' for 'courage' and 'resilience' explains some of the qualities associated with *habbo*. An elderly man in Mekelle interpreted the concept of *habbo* in the context of the Eritrean invasion in the following manner:

> *Habbo* has been with us since ancient times, during the time of our fathers and forefathers. It has a specific meaning in the Tigrinya language. It is something that initiates you to do something. This is especially manifested when a foreign enemy like *Shabiya* invades your country. Our fathers and forefathers have fought and preserved the country from foreign aggressors driven by *habbo*. Likewise, I will also do the same and may go to the war front inspired by *habbo*. *Habbo* therefore means courage.

A person with *habbo*, the *habbonya*, goes after what he wants and is unswerving in the pursuit of his goals. *Habbo* is primarily a quality associated with men, although female TPLF fighters during the 17-years-of-struggle were also described as having *habbo*. A *habbonya* is respected and admired in the local community for being a determined individual, willing to face any obstacles. The context that requires *habbo* is conflict-ridden and usually involves disputes over land and land rights. The objective might be to protect one's own land or land rights from encroachment. However, *habbo* is also required to protect and defend one's honour or kin and to protect one's people, other Tigrayans, from outside hostility. A Tigrayan intellectual explained to me that *'habbo* has thus been used throughout history as a sort of ethnic identifier, a character trait we Tigrayans pride ourselves in having and that we suspect other Ethiopians lack, or have less of'. A frequently heard saying describing this is *Amhara habbo yebilun*: 'Amhara don't have *habbo'* (Rosen 1978).

*Habbo* was often described by Tigrayan peasants as *the* factor which would help secure an Ethiopian victory in the war against Eritrea. Teame, a villager from central Tigray, explains Tigrayan reactions soon after the Eritrean invasion:

This [the invasion] has caused a deep anger and frustration among the Tigrayans in particular. We know the Eritreans and we know each other [the other Ethiopian groups]. We don't need any military assistance from the Amhara, Oromo and other peoples. Tigrayan *habbo* is sufficient for fighting the Eritreans, whom we know very well in fighting. We are, however, currently facing some unorthodox experiences at the battlefront where non-Tigrayan fighters are captured by *Shabiya* [Eritrean forces] and surrender voluntarily to them! (Personal communication)

Implicitly, Teame criticises the soldiers from the other ethnic groups in Ethiopia for lacking *habbo*, and thus surrendering when the fighting gets too tough. I asked if he meant that soldiers from other groups are not good fighters and that Tigray can take care of the war on its own. Teame hesitated, and understood that he had to be careful not to alienate other Ethiopians from the war.

I don't mean that Ethiopia is not also their country, so it's a national concern and responsibility to jointly defend the country. However, we Tigrayans are nearer to the front and we have a profound history of struggle and heroism, so we only need economic assistance from the others. Otherwise our *habbo* and cult of heroism is way superior to the Eritreans and we don't need the issue to take a national dimension. The issue is not too complicated; we can handle it ourselves. (Personal communication)

The Tigrayans pride themselves on being the best soldiers in Ethiopia, often referring back to the battle of Adwa, which was fought mainly with Tigrayan troops on the Ethiopian side. The TPLF, being a pure ethnic resistance movement, capitalised on this 'uniqueness' of Tigrayan resistance during the 17-years-of-struggle. The TPLF organ *Dimtsi Weyane Tigray* wrote, after a Derg offensive in November 1982, that the 'people of Tigray are proud of their Tigrayanness. When they are provoked, they react angrily and instantly like a leopard. This is what objective history writers cannot deny' (cited from Abbay 1998: 123). The emphasis on their own fighting abilities sometimes led to ridicule and belittlement of the fighting spirit and capacity of other ethnic resistance movements fighting the Derg, like the Amhara-dominated EPRP and the Oromo front, OLF. Thus, when the new Eritrean-Ethiopian war erupted in 1998, many Tigrayans were surprised that the TPLF/EPRDF government called for a national mobilisation against Eritrea. At the beginning of the war, people were heard arguing that 'we managed to topple the Derg, the biggest army in Africa, so we can also manage to crush the Eritreans,' when soldiers from Somali, Gambella, Amhara, Oromo, Afar, etc, started to come to Tigray. Berhane, a veteran fighter from the first *weyane* explained to me: 'Let them [other Ethiopian peoples] only send us the money and we will do the fighting alone. What advantage will it give us to count more corpses?'

Although the fighting spirit was high during the 17-years-of-struggle, some Tigrayans stated that this time around (during the Eritrean-Ethiopian war), the *habbo* was even stronger. An elderly peasant from the outskirts of Mekelle explained:

> The present *habbo* is even greater than that of the past because Eritrea and Ethiopia were one and the same country. But now, they have shown their contempt for us by stating that they are better than we are and taken our land. They showed overconfidence in themselves. As a result, Ethiopians had the feeling that they could not submit themselves to Eritreans. Let alone Eritreans, not even to the Italians. So all people of Ethiopia came together and fought against the invaders. The people of Ethiopia defeated the Eritrean army based on our spirit of *habbo*. (Personal communication)

Two issues are important in this explanation. First, the war is seen as a conflict between 'brothers', i.e. from 'one and the same country'. The war erupted since one part – the Eritreans – wanted to position itself above Tigray/Ethiopia in the internal power-play for political hegemony, a classic reason for war in Abyssinia. Secondly, the explanation points to the fact that this war was not only politico-culturally inspired, but also involved a struggle over land. This made *habbo* even more relevant. It is in land disputes that *habbo* is an essential quality to possess, independent of the level of conflict (i.e. between individuals, lineages, villages, *awrajas*, regions or countries). Land is understood as an integral part of one's identity in the highly territorialised Abyssinian highlands (Clapham 1996b; 2001; Hoben 1973; Tronvoll 1998). Encroachment on land is thus also perceived as an attack on identity and selfhood.

The quality of *habbo* is also communicated through poetry, and many of the traditional Tigrayan poets have been inspired by the Eritrean-Ethiopian war to write new poems to strengthen the Tigrayan spirit of resistance and help establish and cement new enemy-images. Even diaspora Tigrayans wrote such poems, and a Tigrayan settled in Saudi Arabia contributed the following parable to the *Wayen* newspaper (a TPLF organ) in July 1998:

> Agame is the maker of history and miracle;
> Agame, who thwarted his enemy's conspiracy;
> Agame, who laid the ground for the development endeavour;
> The Chauvinist *Shabiya* [EPLF] had gone ill on mere vengeance against Agame's development.
> They [the *Shabiya*] said Badme is ours;
> An unheard-of [strange] tale,
> Don't fool yourself – Badme is not Hanish;
> Badme is Tigrayan land and land of *Habesha*.[2]

Agame is the district in Tigray which lies across the border from highland Eritrea, and is traditionally the area in Tigray that has the closest links to Eritrea. Agame is also one of the districts in Tigray that has been heavily involved historically in the feuds and divisions surrounding the *awrajanet* phenomenon – Tigrayan infighting. However, 'Agame' is also used by the Eritreans as a derogatory term to describe the Tigrayans. It is an insult that implies that you are 'primitive, dirty and backward in culture and habits', as an Eritrean friend expressed it during my fieldwork in Eritrea (1991–3). The above poem thus clearly expresses the Tigrayan quality of *habbo*. Furthermore, Agame (i.e. Tigray) has developed an industrial infrastructure, which has taken market shares from traditional Eritrean industry. Many Tigrayans believe that the reason for the Eritrean invasion is to crush this infra-structure (Negash and Tronvoll 2000: 30-45). The line which says that 'Badme is not Hanish' refers to the Eritrean-Yemeni dispute over the small Red Sea Hanish archipelago, which Eritrea took from Yemen by force in 1995.[3] The poem ends with a somewhat contradictory remark, that Badme is both Tigrayan land and 'land of *Habesha*', emphasising both an ethnic and national consciousness (see below on *habesha* identity) – an ambiguity of identity and a clash of symbolism familiar in a Tigrayan politico-historical context.

## *WEYEN*: TIGRAYAN UNITY AND RESISTANCE

Contradictions between a parochial focus and base of mobilisation, and one that has ethno-regional or national aspirations, is also inherent in the Tigrayan *awrajanet* phenomenon. As described earlier, *awrajanet* refers to the competition and infighting between the various Tigrayan districts and entities of descent over political hegemony during historic times, as well as today. The TPLF revolution managed to unite the various dis-tricts (*awraja*) of Tigray under one ethno-regional umbrella of Tigrayan-ness, thus temporarily disbanding the *awrajanet* phenomenon during the time of the struggle (1975–91). However, the Tigrayan notion of allegiance to locality has endured, although in a muted form, during TPLF/EPRDF rule (from 1991 onwards). When the new war with Eritrea erupted, it was essential that the Tigrayans stood united (as in *weyane*) in their resistance towards the invader. Just three months after the outbreak of hostilities, a verse addressing this issue was printed in the TPLF organ *Wayen*, contributed by a Mekelle resident called Haile-Selassie Beyene. Called 'What did he [the son of Tigray] say?', it stressed the need for Tigrayans – from all districts – to stand united against the invaders.

> What did he say? The son of Shire [in western Tigray].
> When Badme was invaded!
> Has the son of Welqeit [also in western Tigray] also heard?
> That unbelievable evil [*Shabiya*/EPLF] has come on to us.
> What did the son of Axum and Adwa say [north Tigray]?
> When *Shabiya* harassed their homestead
> What did the son of Tambien [central Tigray] and Agame [eastern

Tigray] say;
What about [the sons of] Erob and Zalambesa [north-central Tigray],[4]
alongside Badme.
What about the entire Endarta [Mekelle and environs]:
When it was reported to him about the border invasion.
What about the father of *Weyane*; the country of Wajerat[5] [southern
Tigray];
The symbol for all Tigray.
What did he say when hearing about this incident?
Agents of destruction are the people of Raya [southern Tigray].
What did they say last?
The people of Tigray as a whole;
Their word is always one and the same,
and it has been implemented without delay and without even taking care
of his cattle:
He prepared his shields and marched to the front line.[6]

The verse illustrates the need of people from all parts of Tigray to
join ranks and defend their homeland. The Tigrayan fighting spirit was
reflected in many songs and poems composed during the war. A local
poet from southern Tigray (the district of Raya), nicknamed Wedi Raya,
wrote the following poem after the battle of Badme and the victorious
Ethiopian 'Operation Sunset'.

Lo and behold!
*Weyen*; they [EPLF] allege that you are demobilised and [have] become
weak;
And yet you have become the mower with bullets,
You have plunged from the front like a diver,
You, architect of the splitting tactic have divided like a plough,
You dressed the naked with gun powder,
You fed the hungry with bullets,
You smashed them like a pumpkin and shocked them with gore.
The mothers of Tigray have given birth to a good boy,
Who is not greedy in worldly matters [life]
And made us drunk on bullets instead.

The poem refers first to the EPLF's initial claim that the TPLF and
the Tigrayan unity and spirit of resistance (*weyen*) had become weak, so
Eritrea would easily win the war. This impression changed after 'Operation Sunset', in which the Ethiopian forces regained control over Badme
by splitting the Eritrean defence lines in an out-flanking manoeuvre. The
Badme battle (and the subsequent Tsorona offensive) was probably the
biggest military battle in the history of Africa since the Allied forces
pushed Nazi Germany out of north Africa during World War II.
Moreover, it is probably the most remarkable military achievement in
recent war history. But the human costs were extraordinary high with
possibly as many as 20,000 troops, mostly Ethiopians, lost during the

four-day offensive. The line 'who is not greedy of worldly matters' is fitting to describe the level of self-sacrifice exhibited by the Ethiopian forces – or rather their military commanders who gave the orders. It is important to notice, however, that the poem refers to *Tigrayan* resistance and unity, and not Ethiopian. It was Tigrayan mothers who 'gave birth to a good boy' who was not 'greedy of worldly matters' and willing to die for his homeland. Ethiopian unity and sacrifice are not mentioned. The poem focuses on the Tigray-Eritrea, or rather the Tigray-Tigrinya (Eritrean highlanders) relationship as the relevant adversaries in the war. The extraordinarily vivid language used to describe the carnage on the battlefield, where the two former comrades-in-arms slaughter each other in thousands, helps to re-configure the status and image of Eritreans as 'friends, allies and relatives' into the category of 'outsider/alien' turned 'enemy' in the eyes of the Tigrayan people. The pursuit of revenge is always a motivating factor in wars, and particularly so when it finds resonance in local cultural expressions.

## *Henay mifdai*: 'to obtain revenge'

Another element of *habbo*, or goal to which *habbo* is applicable, is revenge. Rosen writes that 'if someone has had a piece of land taken from him, he will fight not only to get the land back but also to get even with the person who took it from him' (Rosen 1975: 55). A Tigrayan is *habbonya* just as far as never giving up pursuing his cause in any case involving land, no matter the absolute value of the land or the cost and sacrifices paid. The *risti* (land right) is considered sacred and represents not only potential material resources, but also a place of belongingness. Whereas personal land disputes take the form of litigation, there is another sort of vengeance framed by the peculiarly Tigrayan expression *henay mifdai*: 'to obtain revenge' or 'retaliation'. The general implication pertains to someone who has a personal vendetta to settle – usually a blood revenge against a person who has killed a close relative. The following Tigrayan proverb told to me by an elderly Tigrayan captures the necessity for a person to seek *henay mifdai*: *Henuia zefedi wedi adgi*, meaning 'a person who does not seek revenge is the child of a donkey'. A comparable Tigrayan proverb is: 'An attempt to attack is tantamount to being attacked, so revenge must be taken' (Koraro 2000: 112). An elderly man from Mekelle described the purpose of *henay mifdai* as follows:

> If you are beaten by someone, your brother should pursue *henay mifdai*. If you are killed, your brother should kill. In the past, this revenge extended to the seventh generation and resulted in the spread of local banditry. Even today such a practice is still possible. People related by blood up to the seventh generation may become a victim of revenge. Unless your brother avenges your blood the neighbours will ridicule him. His friends

will ask 'What sort of man is he if he does not avenge his brother's blood?' People will not respect him. He will often be insulted and thus will not comfortably dare to eat *injera* in front of close relatives and friends in the wake of such comments; because it is a disgrace for him to be considered womanish. (Personal communication)

The symbolic, historical understanding of *henay mifdai* refers to the Tigrayan desire to wreak vengeance on their Amhara oppressors who, from a Tigrayan point of view, have taken advantage of Tigray throughout history (Berhane 1994; Rosen 1975). The Amhara-dominated feudal system extracted levies from the Tigrayan peasantry to such an extent that they were living in destitution. Moreover, the Tigrayan nobility and landowners, as well as the region itself, were discriminated against by the central government, a system of oppression and discrimination which was carried on throughout the reign of Emperor Haile Selassie and during the Derg regime. The first *weyane* can be understood as a collective expression of *henay mifdai*. No longer would the Tigrayan peasants accept the devastating taxation system and the exploitive capacity of the feudal system. As we know, Haile Selassie managed to crush the first *weyane*, but a lingering sentiment of resistance was sustained in Tigray, flaring up again some 30 years later.

Rosen writes that, 'The implications of *henay mifdai* and *weyane*, as core symbols for all Tigrayans, stem from their relationship to the particular historical events and social conditions from which they arose and to which they provide meaning' (1975: 57). The implications of *henay mifdai* are partly inspired by the nature of Tigrayan-Amhara relations over a considerable period. As mentioned earlier, for long periods the Tigrayan elites were preoccupied with fighting each other in order to gain control over the political centre of the region (*awrajanet*). These enmities and divisions were severely exacerbated, if not directly provoked, by the divide-and-rule policies of the Amhara Emperors. As a consequence of this long-term instability, many Tigrayans spoke of seeking revenge (*henay mifdai*) and the need to unite and fight (*weyane*) with determination and resilience (*habbo*) in order to break free from the long-standing Amhara domination to secure their land holdings and place of belonging (*risti*). I shall examine later how these key Tigrayan cultural concepts are appropriate to describe the context of the recent Eritrean war. For now, let me close this section with a verse sung by an Amhara singer who is a member of the Amhara Development Association band at a performance in Mekelle during the war; which captures the essential sentiments of *henay mifdai*:

Unthinkable it is, abandoning an inch of land from Ethiopia;
It is impossible, it is truly impossible and a nightmare.
Fight them as vanguards and rear guards.
They [the Ethiopians] fell on to them [*Shabiya*] like a cliff [landslide];
And their hearts melted like wax.

71

# Eritrea: image of a friend turned enemy

The Tigrinya-speaking community straddling the border between Eritrea and Ethiopia has always been linked by common history and linguistic and cultural features, but simultaneously also divided by political machinations. This ambiguity of relations has, throughout history, made it possible for political entrepreneurs to manipulate the perceptions of each other from friend to enemy and back again, in periods of political turmoil. In the following I shall focus on how the official party and government rhetoric, and popular expressions, were formulated in order to recast the image of Eritrea as a 'relative' and ally into an 'alien' and enemy, as means of mobilising the Tigrayan (and Ethiopian) people against the invading Eritrean army.

Historically, the close link between *kebessa* (highland Eritrea) and Tigray entailed a natural alliance between the two regions if one of them was attacked. In his survey of highland Eritrea, Alemseged Abbay notes that all respondents claimed that they would support Tigray if a war broke out between Tigray and Amhara, and described Eritreans and Tigrayans as comrades-in-arms (Abbay 1998: 160). An elderly Eritrean peasant explained:

> Eritrea must support the Tigrayans out of brotherhood. No Eritrean wants to learn about the denigration of Tigrayans. When the Amhara devalued Tigray by calling it a poor and famine-stricken region that was of no value to Ethiopia, tell me which Eritrean was not hurt? The people of Seraye [district in Eritrea] were sickened when Tigray was denigrated by the Amhara mass media! Which Eritrean will tolerate his *Adi Abo* [fatherland] being humiliated? (Abbay 1998: 160)

During my fieldwork in highland Eritrea (1991–3), informants emphasised the cultural affinity between Eritreans and the Tigrayan people. However, despite sharing the same language and religion, and traditions of intermarriage and exchange labour, they also had their differences. An elderly Eritrean peasant, a former village judge and a soldier in the Italian colonial army, explained *Kebessa*-Tigray relations in 1991, immediately after the fall of the Derg regime and the EPLF takeover of Eritrea:

> We have always had close relationships with Tigray. We belong to the same church and speak the same language. People from Tigray have come to settle among us, to work here, or to marry. Thus, the Tigrayans and *Dekki Kebessa* [Eritrean highlanders] will always be close. But, we have also had our problems with Tigrayan rulers. Historically, they wanted to control us, something we resisted. Also during our struggle [Eritrean war of resistance 1961-91], it was a period of animosity between our two fronts [1985-88]. So, although we have much in

common, you never really know the inside of the hearth of the Agame [Tigrayans]. (Personal communication)

The statement manifests the ambiguity between cultural relatedness and political differences which has characterised Eritrean-Ethiopian relations over the centuries. Nevertheless, the close cultural relationship across the Mereb helped to strengthen the political alliance between the EPLF and the TPLF in their common struggle against the Derg regime, in particular during the first decade of the TPLF revolution (1975–85): an alliance that in turn entailed an allegiance between the people and the political fronts. In 1999, during the Eritrean-Ethiopian war, I asked Hassan Shifa, at that time the security chief of Tigray, a TPLF Central Committee member and a veteran liberation fighter, to elaborate on this point:

I think war as such makes its own impact on every aspect of life of the people. Generally, the Eritrean and the Tigrayan people have come from the same root, having the same language and the same culture. The only difference is, if you take the highland of Eritrea and Tigray, the fact that they [the Eritreans] have been colonised. Apart from that, what you have to understand are the common links of marriages, relations and trade. Well, in practice, if you pick any Eritrean and go to his roots two and three generations back, he will tell you he is from Tigray. And if you take somebody from here and trace to the second or third generation he will say he has some connection with those people in Eritrea. The only difference is the ideology, the way of thinking that colonisation brought to Eritrea. This attitude has its own effect on people-to-people relations too. (Personal communication)

It is important to note that Hassan Shifa emphasised the Italian colonisation of Eritrea as the 'difference that makes the difference' between these two peoples. The same perception was also harboured by ordinary Tigrayans *and* the Eritrean political elite and people. Colonisation brought modernisation to Eritrea, which led to a process of development that created a gap between the 'modern and developed' Eritrea and the 'backward and stagnant' Tigray (cf. Negash 1986).

It was not only the top TPLF cadres who expressed sentiments of cultural closeness to Eritrea, but also lower-level officials. Iyasou Goshu, nicknamed 'Wode-Goshu', deputy district administrator in Wuqro, offered the following explanation to me.

We had a long history of cooperation [with the EPLF], militarily and politically. During the days of the armed struggle we were fighting and cooperating for a common political objective. Twenty years back I myself was sent to Eritrea and fought there for one year. We had close co-operation. I witnessed my colleagues fighting together, dying together, and being buried together in the same grave. Taking all this into consideration, I never had the slightest doubt that this state of cooperation and brotherhood would continue, and not take the form it has now. (Personal communication)

In order to facilitate a political and military mobilisation against the new enemy, it was essential – from the point of view of the TPLF/ EPRDF – to redefine the Tigrayan-Eritrean relationship. The kin-relatedness between the people of Tigray and highland Eritrea had to be recast into a different paradigm, and the political alliance between the two representative organisations (the TPLF and the EPLF) had to be dissolved.

## FRIENDS OR ENEMIES?

On the occasion of Eritrea's celebration of its formal independence on 24 May 1993, Meles Zenawi (the TPLF chairman and at that time president of Ethiopia) greeted independent Eritrea with reference both to the military alliance between the EPLF and the TPLF and the political allegiance between the people and the governments.

> I know you have wounds because I know your wounds either from nearby or from afar [and] because I know that similar wounds exist on my back and on the backs of my comrades. I will not ask you to forget the past. It is something that cannot be forgotten because it is educa-tional. However, *we should not scratch our wounds. You should not scratch your wounds.* The worst is gone. The worst is buried.
>
> We did not bury human beings [the Derg] alone. We have also buried ideologies and outlooks. We have buried hegemonic and chauvinistic outlooks, too. Therefore, we cannot forget the past so that it can teach us lessons; we remember our wounds so that we can learn from them; but we should not scratch them; we should not dwell on them. Let bygones be bygones. We have commenced a new chapter. In this new chapter, we shall not build a wall at the Mereb.[7]

In his speech, Meles aligns Eritreans and Tigrayans in a common experience of suffering, in their fight against the Derg regime. As they had fought together against Amhara repression, they should now build the peace together as friends and allies. No wall should separate the two peoples on each side of Mereb (the border river between Eritrea and Tigray). I quote this particular speech by Meles with a special intention in mind. The expression *'don't scratch your wounds, and we won't either'*, became a local saying in Tigray after the outbreak of the new war in May 1998. Several people remembered the occasion of Eritrea's independence and the way Meles attended this event. 'But,' they claimed, 'Eritrea started to scratch its wounds, and we were forced to do the same.' A trader in Mekelle added to this statement: 'It was foolish to build a good house [developing Tigray], so long as one had a robber as a neighbour. First you have to get rid of the robber!'

Prior to the outbreak of the war in May 1998, the official rhetoric from the TPLF was not hostile towards Eritrea or the EPLF. Quite the contrary: the Eritrea/EPLF was portrayed as a close friend; an ally

Ethiopians needed in order to develop their own country. For instance, the *Wayen* newspaper (a TPLF organ) did not carry any anti-Eritrean articles prior to May 1998, and no official statements or interviews with TPLF cadres could detect a change of relations between the two countries or the emergence of new enemy images.[8] After the collapse of the Derg regime and up to the time the new war started, the new 'enemies' of Tigray were poverty and underdevelopment. Parallel to the 'war' against poverty, however, the official TPLF rhetoric continued to reproduce and sustain the old enemy image of the Derg and the Amharised Ethiopian state. Even after the war started, these old enemy images were sustained in *Wayen*. Paradoxically, however, the EPLF was still portrayed as a comrade-in-arms against the Derg even after the Eritrean-Ethiopian war began. In the regular column 'Our Struggle', even after May 1998, descriptions of old battles against the Derg army were vividly painted by TPLF fighters who participated in the 17-years-of-struggle in alliance with the EPLF.[9]

## CONSTRUCTING ENEMY IMAGES

Immediately after the Eritrean invasion of Badme in the second week of May 1998, the Tigray regional president Gebru Assrat read a statement of mobilisation of the old TPLF army to the regional council of Tigray:

> In order to defend against the invading force of the Eritrean Government which has violated our sovereignty and independence, all members of the army should be mobilised forthwith. The interest of our people and our government is to urge the invading EPLF force to withdraw from the occupied territory without any pre-condition or delay. This is the only way for peace and the choice remains only in the hands of the EPLF leadership.[10]

His mobilisation call was also broadcast on local radio and TV. Gebru concluded his statement by stressing: 'The current burning issue is to safeguard your country!  Protect your country! Safeguard your border! Safeguard your freedom!'

The next time Gebru Assrat appeared in public was at an official gathering in Mekelle on the occasion of the seventh anniversary of the EPRDF's takeover of the government on 28 May 1998, only three weeks after the call for mobilisation. This time around, the rhetoric had hardened and Gebru was coming out strong against the EPLF regime, calling them by the old term *Shabiya*. It was immediately after the war broke out that the two governments started to call each other by their old guerrilla names – *Shabiya*[11] (EPLF) and the *Weyane*[12] (TPLF). The purpose of this change of terminology was, for the EPLF, to undermine the legitimacy of the EPRDF government. By calling them *Weyane*, it was implicitly stating that the Ethiopian government was composed only of TPLF fighters and had support from Tigray alone, i.e. an oppressive minority government. Similarly, when the EPRDF termed the Eritrean government *Shabiya*, they drew attention to the fact that the Eritrean government did not have a legitimate, democratic basis, but was still basically a military front, i.e. a dictatorship. Gebru Assrat stated:

> *Shabiya*'s dream is boundless. ... By refuting and repulsing their dreams let us stride along our path to development. It is advisable and wise that our neighbours understand our stand and genuine interest in peace. If, however, they were to say to us 'Let them be diverted [from the path to development],' this is something that we shall never accept. It is impossible! We had declared right from the beginning [our priority] for peace, development and democracy. For this we will pay any kind of sacrifice. Even if the war takes spans of generations. No force can invade us! Impossible! No one should dream of invading us! *This is because Ethiopia means 'anti-invasion'. Ethiopian means one who dies for his honour and fights for freedom and independence.* You have seen this week how all Ethiopians from Moyale [southernmost point of Ethiopia on the Kenya border], to people in Gode and Wardier [Ethiopian Somalis] have felt sad and condemned the act of aggression. They [the Eritrean leadership] might have wrongly felt that the confrontation is only with the people of Tigray whom they undermine most. That is not the case. They had made a wrong evaluation. They should know that they are now facing the entire Ethiopian population.[13]

This speech represented a decisive breach with the paradigm of friendship and alliance between Eritrea and Ethiopia, a paradigm introduced and sustained by the coming to power of the EPLF and the TPLF/EPRDF in 1991.[14] The speech introduced more than just one paradigmatic shift. Gebru Assrat is also rescinding the decade-old EPRDF paradigm of the discourse on the ethnicity of Ethiopia. For the first time in Tigray since the fall of the Derg an Ethiopianist rhetoric is heard: 'This is because Ethiopia means "anti-invasion". Ethiopian means one who dies for his honour and fights for freedom and independence.' The eruption of war launched two shifts: first, redefinition of the Eritrea-Ethiopia relationship from friends to enemies; and secondly, redefinition of the status of 'Ethiopia' in national politics, or, in other words, subduing ethnicity in governance and stressing the nationalist discourse instead.

Gebru continued to belittle and ridicule the EPLF leadership in his speech, by making fun of Issaias' rhetoric of war. But, at the same time he was also cautioning his own people and Ethiopians in general not to fall into the trap of hating all Eritreans. The official rhetoric tried to distinguish between the EPLF leadership and Eritreans in general, as formulated by Gebru Assrat.

> The hidden interest of the EPLF leadership is to interrupt and displace us from the rapid development victory we are achieving. Their interest is to make us poor. We will not accept this. We pursue our development and defend our sovereignty simultaneously. Especially this generation of

youngsters should be ready for any sacrifice. When we are now in a better position, we should never allow any one to urinate on us. However, having said this we too should not be the victims of prejudice and superiority. The source of our strength is not prejudice. Our strength is not hatred of other people. If we too develop feelings of chauvinism [like the *Shabiya* leadership] and prejudice, there is no reason why we will not be doomed to failure. We have to like and respect the Eritrean people. We should not develop hatred of people as a result of worthless propaganda [of *Shabiya*]. I say this because I am observing symptoms and tendencies. The Eritrean people should not also be misled and be victims of their own chauvinistic sentiments. Especially you Eritreans who are in Ethiopia! *You are our brothers and the Ethiopian people are your brothers.* Their aims are your aims. You should not be guided by your leader's prejudice. Feelings like: 'we are the superior!', 'we are the civilised!' and so on should not exist. All people are equal, but when they are oppressed and subordinated, they have power and may even explode what they had buried. Thus, bearing this in mind, we should work hard not to break the link between the people of Ethiopia and Eritrea, for the wish of the Eritrean leaders is to separate the two people.[15]

Although Gebru Assrat was introducing a brand-new rhetoric of enemies and friends, the ambiguity of the relationship between Tigray and Eritrea still lingered in the sense that in one context Eritrea and Ethiopia were enemies, while in another they were still friends and relatives. However, the explicit reference to the Eritrean leadership as an enemy, and the general warning to the Eritrean people not to follow their leaders, marked a clear breach with the notion of the state of Eritrea as an ally. The ambiguity of Eritrea – being, to a certain degree, both an enemy (the leadership) and a friend (the people) – was also stressed by others, particularly in reference to the common destiny of war for Eritreans and Tigrayans. Sitting in a *soha bet* (traditional beer house) some few kilometres south of the war zone in central Tigray in the summer of 1999, I asked the hostess how she felt about the war, which had lasted for over a year, and the fact that they were getting help from the Amhara to fight their old comrades-in-arms, the Eritreans:

Yes, we used to fight together against the common enemy, but now they have become our enemy and we have to fight them. It must be remembered that we, Tigrayans and *Shabiya*, used to fight together against the Derg. We shared their blood, we were buried in the same grave. But then they became independent and *Shabiya* adopted a chauvinistic (*tim k'heity*) attitude of saying that 'the Tigrayans are backward, poor and far behind us'. 'We are developed and civilised, and they will depend on Eritrean resources.' 'They have nowhere to go and must rely on Eritrean produce.' 'The Tigrayan cannot go anywhere other than to Eritrea as a day labourer.' But then they become frustrated when Tigray showed a remarkable boost of development during the last seven years. That's why they *scratched their old wound.* (Personal communication)

The elderly hostess of the beer-house had lived in the village all her life and grew up in an area which relied on the close connection with highland Eritrea, both in terms of personal relations and employment opportunities. She knew that these relations had been politically rescinded by the EPLF – a situation that she hoped would be revised after the war was over. A neighbour of the hostess was listening in on our conversation, and she added her own opinion:

> It is sad to see friends of the old days destroying each other now. Our desire and dream was to see the old friendship remaining intact and to fight against an external enemy, as we did in the past. But now the war has broken out only because of conflicting interests. The war is something imposed on us, and we don't like it. ... We come from the same people with the same historical and cultural traditions, linked to each other through marriage and kinship. But this link is now threatened and cut as a result of the leadership of Issaias [Eritrean President]. ... But I hope that relations will be restored after the overthrow of *Shabiya* and the coming to power in Eritrea of *Demhai* [Democratic Movement for Liberation of Eritrea, an Eritrean opposition movement supported by TPLF]. (Personal communication)

For the sake of clarity, I asked her: 'So your conflict and animosity is towards whom?' She replied confidently: 'The problem is Issaias [Eritrean President] and *Shabiya*. We have no animosity towards the Eritrean people.' The shift from perceiving Eritrea/EPLF as a friend to seeing it as an enemy was thus not only subscribed to by the party officials, but also by ordinary Tigrayans. Like Gebru Assrat and the TPLF, the peasant woman hesitated to turn all Eritreans into enemies, and expressed an ambiguity of attitude when she tried to distinguish between the Eritrean leadership on the one hand, and the people on the other.

## THE AMBIGUITY OF ERITREA

In the first phase of the war, the TPLF emphasised the close historical relations between the Tigrinya-speakers north and south of the river Mereb. A special editorial comment in the first issue of *Wayen* after the outbreak of war, called for reflection on the joint history of struggle.

> The links between the people of the two countries are interwoven and numerous. These links also have a long history; and more recently, a history of joint struggle against the Fascist Military Junta of the Derg. In that struggle both people emerged strong from their joint sacrifices, both people have in the days of the armed struggle bled, died and been buried together on one front line and in one grave and have repulsed a number of invasions and finally succeeded together.[16]

The same point was also emphasised by Hassan Shifa, the TPLF security chief, a year later in an interview with me. He presented a quite philosophical reflection on the Tigray-Eritrea relationship in the midst of war in June 1999.

The war has its own impact, the hatred is not so developed as in Rwanda's case, or Burundi's. The people here are sensible even though there are some emotions. The hatred doesn't amount to anything evil. That is the essential thing. And this shows you that, even though there are emotions nowadays, one day we shall be together again. I mean you can't take Eritrea and put it beyond Sudan. Or you can't do the same with Ethiopia. The land will be there – the people will be there – and we will pass as governments. The generations will pass. Whether you believe it or not the EPLF cannot eliminate the Tigrayan people. Nor can we eliminate them. ... I think the emotionality you see in the region differs from individual to individual. We are both peoples whom nobody can separate. The generations can pass. The governments can pass. But Eritrea will be there. Ethiopia will be there. (Personal communication)

Not all TPLF cadres managed to view the Tigray-Eritrea relationship in such a reflective vein. Many veteran fighters harboured a personal feeling of betrayal by the EPLF that influenced their way of conceptualising the new Tigray-Eritrea relationship. This was also manifested in a change in the official rhetoric and terminology in the party organs from the end of June 1998. A specific war incident promoted the dichotomisation of the warring factions, and painted Eritrea with the language of hatred. At the beginning of June 1998, Eritrean fighter planes bombed an elementary school in central Mekelle resulting in many dozens of casualties. This incident ignited an old hatred, and both political statements and oral traditions were used to stigmatise the Eritreans as enemies. After the bombing, *Wayen* and other TPLF organs began to call the Eritrean government a 'fascist regime', thereby establishing a link between the EPLF and Fascist Italy's invasion of Ethiopia in 1935. This was also reflected in traditional poetry, aimed at defaming the Eritrean President Issaias Afwerki and the EPLF. A poem entitled 'Whom should I name you after?', written by a Tigrayan in the diaspora, became popular in Mekelle during the summer of 1998.

Do you [Issaias Afwerki] like to be called Hitler or Mussolini?
Whom do you want to be named after, you small Graziani?[17]
What is all this hotchpotch?
Why don't you learn history and get the support of your people?
He who does not know the interest of his people and does not learn history,
He who is jealous of others and is never fed up with war;
He who is chauvinist and does not accept his mistakes;
He who does not listen and is a 'stone-head' of the north,
Adiabo[18] is not Hanish,[19] so don't feel proud,
There is a yardstick measurement that will bring you down to your limit,
Whom should I name you after? At any rate don't feel proud.[20]

Gradually, the language of war replaced the initial hesitation and ambiguity of classifying Eritrea as an enemy. The former multi-stranded and multi-faceted relations across the river Mereb, binding the two people together in a common framework of sociality and identity, were replaced by a unilateral attitude of enmity.

## PERSONAL STORIES – PERSONAL ENEMIES

On 5 June 1998 the escalation of violence reached its climax with an Ethiopian bombing raid on Asmara airport and Eritrean retaliation. The Eritrean leadership claimed that they had aimed at military targets, but it was Ayder Elementary School in downtown Mekelle that received a direct hit. During two sorties, 58 pupils and civilians were killed and 185 injured by cluster bombs.[21]

The killing of innocent children was an act that instantly helped classify Eritrea as a mortal enemy. A twelve-year-old girl recalled the moments of terror, as described in a commemorative publication:

> Minutes before the air bombardment, I was attending class along with my classmates. At the end of class our class monitor told us to clean up the room and we started cleaning. As we cleaned, we heard the sound of an approaching aircraft and we all went out of the classroom. As we ran, I was hit on the arm, leg and side. I didn't realise I was hit then; it was only after seeing blood all over me that I started to cry. I was running even after being hit. Later, I fell unconscious and don't know who took me to the hospital. ... It is Issaias who has sent the planes to kill us – the innocent children. (WIC 1999: 10)

The event was described in detail in all the Ethiopian newspapers and publications, both government-controlled and opposition-friendly. They were as one in condemning the Eritrean air-raid and portraying it as a deliberate heinous act perpetrated on civilian Tigrayans. The deputy headmaster of the school, Habtu Girmai, expressed a view shared by most Tigrayans.

> Nobody had imagined that such a heinous crime could be committed against innocent school children and the civilian population, as there was no trace of a military or quasi-military establishment anywhere in or near the area. The sight of dismembered bodies and disembowelled intestines strewn all over the place was horrifying and disgusting. (WIC 1999: 12)

At the first commemorative anniversary of the event, the school director, Gebre-Mariam Gebre-Selassie, proclaimed that the children who perished in the bombing raid were considered to be Tigrayan martyrs.[22] This incorporated the incident as a significant event in the history of the Tigrayan struggle, eliminating the feeling that the children had died without cause and labelling their deaths as appropriate sacrifices for the overall, and ongoing, revolution. This was also emphasised by the local people of Mekelle. I visited the school compound in June 1999, and the neighbours flocked to recall their pain and loss. 'My daughter was killed here by the Eritreans. I shall always hate Issaias for what he did, but she died in a good cause', explained a middle-aged man to me. 'She died for Tigray and her country, and she has been revenged by our *tegadelti* [TPLF fighters].'

The attack on Ayder also inspired the Tigrayans to go to war, in order to seek *henay mifdai* – 'to obtain revenge'. An elderly Mekelle resident explained:

> You see, when the students in Ayder School came under attack from Eritrean war planes everybody's blood boiled. When *Shabiya* attacked us the attack came at an unexpected time and place. After that bloodshed, we got angry and went to the warfront to avenge the blood of the little children. ... This is *henay mifdai* at its best. The [Eritrean] barracks were destroyed, their armaments were also destroyed. Compared with our casualties at the Ayder School, more Eritreans died, vehicles were burnt down and there was a loss of property. ... We forced the invaders to retreat and *regained our place*. (Personal communication)

The last point – 'we regained our place' – suggests the importance of re-establishing the correct order in the socio-political hierarchy between Eritreans and Tigrayans. By retaliating and destroying and killing even more Eritreans, the Tigrayans felt that they had restored their position at the top of the hierarchy and obtained hegemonic control. Furthermore, after the Badme offensive in February 1999, in which Ethiopia reclaimed the land invaded by Eritrea, the people of Mekelle felt that the Ayder incident had been avenged. One woman, Yalemsra Alemayehu, whose daughter had been killed in the bombing, explained her feelings to an Ethiopian news agency.

> At the beginning I was filled with a very deep sorrow. The depth of my sorrow was more than one can imagine. This is because I lost my little child who was only eight years old and was studying in this school in grade two. Her name was Birtukan Amare. Now I can say that my wound is healed. I can't tell you how delighted I was when I heard that Issaias' army had been destroyed at Badme. Among my neighbours, there were three young men who joined the ground forces to defend our country against the enemy. Before they left, they came to my house and told me the following: 'Don't cry. Feel strong! We will show you immediate retaliation on the war fronts. We will never try to kill children like the soldiers of Issaias. Instead we will destroy the killers of children.' Now according their promise, they showed me the humiliating defeat of Issaias' army. So now I am very happy, more than I can say![23]

Retaliation (*henay mifdai*) became an important driving force in stigmatising Eritrea as the enemy. In a statement issued by the regional government in Mekelle, the Ayder bombing was compared by the TPLF with the Derg's bombing of Hawzen in June 1988 in which about 2,000 civilians were killed.[24] The Hawzen massacre is the single most gruesome event during the TPLF's 17-years-of-struggle, and the official, national holiday of

81

Martyrs' Day on 22 June (15 June Ethiopian calendar) commemorates this event. By drawing a parallel between the Hawzen massacre and the Ayder bombing, the TPLF also made a direct link between the Derg regime of the past and the EPLF regime of today – a paradox, since the EPLF was a partner in fighting the Derg.

## CONTRADICTORY PERCEPTIONS OF ENEMIES AND FRIENDS

During the war, I was constantly puzzled by the contradictory statements made by both officials and ordinary Tigrayans in classifying Eritreans as both 'friends' and 'enemies' – a contradiction sustained even after the battle of Badme (end of February 1999). One day I talked this over with the owner of the hotel I was staying at in Mekelle, and asked him how the war could be possible, in view of the close relationship between the people of trans-Mereb:

> Well, all Eritreans are the same, they have this … [looking for words] top-down attitude. They think they are superior. Since the Italians colonised them and developed their country, they have always looked down on us. When our people went to Eritrea for manual labour, we were told that we were primitive and backward, since we were walking behind donkeys. And they were running behind automobiles! All Eritreans have this attitude. I can't understand why. Are they proud of having been colonised? Don't they know that all people are equal? But we showed them at Badme! Even though Issaias said that the sun would not rise again if they should leave Badme, we won. And as you see, the sun is still rising. (Personal communication)

I raised a concern about the costs of the war, and whether it was worth it. The hotel owner replied:

> It is sad about all the destruction. We should be concentrating on developing our economy and our resources instead. The villagers are suffering both here and in Eritrea. We are so close, historically and culturally. We are one people, and the Italian colonisation should not manage to divide us. We all have relatives in Eritrea, but with Issaias's crazy politics, everything is destroyed. Like Milosevic in Yugoslavia, and because of his politics, the whole country is being bombed to pieces. (Personal communication)

In the same conversation and minutes apart, my informant had first delineated a boundary of identity distinction for Eritrea and his acceptance of war, while in the next sentence he established cross-boundary connections by stating that Tigrayans and Eritreans are 'brothers', one and the same in terms of identity, and said that he resented the war. This contradiction could be observed in many discourses and social fields in Ethiopia. In a survey I carried out in Wuqro area, a number of similar examples were gathered. A Tigrayan described the Eritreans in the following manner: 'An Eritrean is always Eritrean! They are blind and emotional people who support their leaders even if the leaders take a wrong path.' However, later he explained that:

> It is only fear of Issaias that has kept the Eritreans silent. Otherwise, in their heart they do not support the war of Issaias for they would benefit greatly from friendship with Ethiopia. It is the EPLF leadership and particularly Issaias who is to be blamed for the conflict. (Personal communication)

The following opinion was expressed by an elderly man:

> If we are to reintegrate Eritrea with Ethiopia as it has been before, that is good and we like to see the Eritrean people continue to have close relations with us [after the resolution of the conflict]. However, if we are not to re-occupy Eritrea, why should we have a relationship with them? We don't want them! (Personal communication)

A middle-aged woman was clear in her opinion to start with: 'I was not really happy with the independence of Eritrea right from the outset. I would have liked it if Eritrea had continued as the child of Ethiopia as before.' Later, however, she stated: 'There is nothing Tigray needs from Eritrea except peace.' A trader in Mekelle offered this opinion some days after the bombing of Ayder school in Mekelle:

> They [Eritreans] have massacred our people! What more grave evil are they to commit against us other than this? What kind of healthy relationship can we have with them after this bloodshed? Meles and Issaias who were the best of friends are even lodged in a fight and separated. This is the end of the world! (Personal communication)

Later in the evening, however, he told me in confidence that:

> If Issaias, who is the main obstacle and source of the problem, is eliminated, there is no reason why we can't continue our previous good relationship with the Eritreans. Our glorious friendship, which was tested in the heated armed struggle to overthrow the Derg, may be renewed. Who knows? (Personal communication)

The contradictions of histories, discourses and epistemologies are a common experience for many researchers on Ethiopia (Aspen 2001: 250; Bauer 1989: 224). Our aim must be to develop an analytical framework that will accommodate them, a point I shall return to later.

It is difficult to grasp fully the transformation of the perception of Eritrea as a friend turned enemy. The historical and cultural connections between the people in trans-Mereb join them together in one context, but the histories of colonisation and war separate them in another. Common experiences of terror and war during the Derg regime created a community of fate between them during one period, but political ideologies and machinations divided the spirit of oneness in another. In June 1999 I offered a lift to two young Tigrayan soldiers returning home on leave from the Zalambessa front line. They explained their war frustrations:

> We asked you for a lift from Negash to Wukro. You were kind enough to give us that – a good favour indeed. But what would you feel if we crushed your car, throwing a big stone at it, after we reached Wuqro? A feeding hand should not be beaten. The same applies to *Shabiya*. We did much to help *Shabiya* to gain independence. The invasion has become their pay-back. (Personal communication)

The strong feeling of uncertainty and insecurity made people doubt their old notions of who the enemy was and who their friend was. In this context of ambiguity, Tigrayans even accepted the drive to deport all Eritreans and individuals with mixed Eritrean parenthood (elaborated in Chapter 7). During one of my stays in Mekelle, I was awoken at three o'clock in the morning at the hotel by TPLF security hammering on the door. They were randomly checking the identity of every hotel guest in Mekelle, looking for Eritreans. The continuous deportations of unwanted Eritreans began in 1998 and even *ferenjies* had to succumb to closer scrutiny of 'non-Eritreanness', as the security officers explained to me in the darkness of my room during a room-search in the middle of the night. The deportation of Eritreans had an enormous socio-political effect on Ethiopian perceptions of Eritrea *and* Ethiopia. However, the war not only created new enemies, but also new friends.

# Amhara:
## the image of an enemy turned friend

A second group of relevant others with whom the Tigrayans traditionally contrast their identity, other than their relationship with the *kebessa* Eritreans, are the Amhara. Alemseged Abbay explains that 'while it is their subjection to the Europeans that the *Kebessa* remember, it is their subjection to the Amhara at the end of the nineteenth century that the Tigrayans remember. This difference is manifested in their perception of historical enemies' (1998: 153). Not only the Tigrayan peasants, but also the Tigrayan traditional nobility and leadership regarded the Amhara ruling elite as enemies, since they were each competing to control the other through the position as *negus negast* (emperor). *Ras* Alula, Emperor Yohannes's 'ethnic brother' and strong man in Tigray, complained to an Italian journalist about the loss of power to Amhara in 1889 (after the death of Yohannes at the battle of Metemmah against the Mahdists):

> This country [Tigray] is ours, and if we submit to Menelik it is because we became very few after Metemmah ... I have my master who is the son of King Giovanni [Yohannes], why should I look for another in

Scioa [Shoa, i.e. Amhara]? ... Tigre cannot be a servant of Scioa, because our people are soldiers [meaning developed/modernised], while the Shoans fight only against people armed with spears [meaning backward]. (Quoted from Erlich 1986: 42)

Some scholars claim that the Tigray-Amhara relationship cannot be analysed within the conventional framework of Amhara domination and hegemony as interpreted by the TPLF. Teshale Tibebu (1995) writes that it is the historical setting of the Ge'ez civilisation – composed of both the Tigrayan and Amhara peoples – that has been hegemonic and has 'suppressed' other groups in Ethiopia. Within this civilisation, Tigrayan nationalism is, according to Teshale Tibebu, basically a compound of aspirations for political hegemony and struggle against Amharic *linguistic* oppression. Tigrayans have sustained a sense of 'superiority-in-seniority over their historical juniors, the Amhara. The Tigrayans feel that they are the direct descendants of Aksumite civilisation, as opposed to the Amhara who have been 'bastardised' (Tibebu 1995: 174). In this regard, concludes Teshale Tibebu, the Tigray-Amhara relationship should be considered as a 'sibling rivalry' or as a competition between 'brothers'.

No doubt the Tigrayan othering of the Amhara reflects a politico-historical conception of the Amharas as representatives of the centralised and oppressive state. Such an understanding of Amhara ruling capacity is also partly a self-ascribed perception, captured in the classical Amhara proverb: *Amara yazzal inji aytazzezim* – 'the Amhara is to rule, not to be ruled'. All the groups within the Abyssinian/*Habesha* realm, that is highland Eritrea, Tigray and Amhara, are component parts of a 'sibling-rivalry dynamic system'. The internal political play driven by the respective elites, both within and between these three groups, explains much of the dynamics of war and conflict in Ethiopia/Eritrea. Although the *Habesha* can be said to have dominated the other ethnic groups in Ethiopia, as argued by Teshale Tibebu, the internal power play within the *Habesha* groups also led to relations of domination and subordination for long historical periods between Amhara and Tigrinya-speakers, a point largely neglected by Teshale Tibebu.

Some scholars claim that it is difficult to talk about any specific basis of the Amhara identity, since the Amharas are not defined by a common descent from a single ancestor (Clapham 1988: 24). Rather than descent, the Amhara have mostly been identified by others and by themselves in relation to a specific locality or geographical entity, the main ones being Shoa, Gondar, Wollo and Gojjam, and subsequent sub-entities at lower geographical levels (comparable to the identity perceptions among the *kebessa* Eritreans, see Tronvoll (1998)). Some argue, however, that the Shoans are different from the other *Habeshas*, and have a distinct history and ethnic identity (see Salole 1978). None of these complexes forms anything like a corporate unit with which people 'identify deeply and remain steadfast loyal', as described by Donald Levine (1974: 117). As such, it is the plasticity and manipulative quality of Amhara identity that is most noticeable and is defined situationally as a socio-cultural category, rather than ethnic distinctions: 'On the ground, in social interaction, this means that any person, whatever his exact origin, who claims to be an "Amhara" and to whom others react behaviourally as though he were an "Amhara" is sociologically an Amhara' (Shack 1976).

Historical records tell us that the Tigrayan-Amhara relations of the nineteenth century were tense and conflict-ridden (Taddia 1994). What is important for the present analysis is how this relationship became relevant in the manifestation of a Tigrayan national-political identity at a later stage. As noted above, the TPLF found it opportune to present the Amhara during the reign of Emperor Menelik II as a category of relevant others for the Tigrayans, since Menelik betrayed Emperor Yohannes who was of Tigrayan descent (Abbay 1998: 193). Moreover, the socio-economic marginalisation of Tigray during the reign of Haile Selassie and the perceived political repression of Tigray by Shoan Amhara are other factors utilised by the TPLF to distinguish the Tigrayans from the Amhara ruling elite (Young 1997). At first, the TPLF presented the Amhara as a collective enemy of the Tigrayan people. It was towards the end of the struggle in the mid-1980s that the TPLF started to distinguish between the oppressed peasants of Amhara on the one side, and the rich peasants and ruling elite on the other, since the Amhara broad masses were needed in the fight against the Derg army beyond Tigray region. The TPLF thus reclassified the broad, poor Amhara masses as allies and not enemies of Tigray. Iyassu, a veteran TPLF fighter interviewed by Jenny Hammond towards the end of the 17-years-of-struggle, illustrates this differentiation: 'Formerly we considered all Amharas our enemies. Our people used to say of even the poorest Amhara, although he is poor, his heart is dangerous. But we don't now – we believe that only the exploiters are our enemies' (Hammond 1999: 181).

## TIGRAY-AMHARA:
## POLITICAL ALLIANCES IN AN ETHNIC DISGUISE

The distinction between the Amhara elite and peasants was internalised by all TPLF senior cadres towards the end of the 17-years-of-struggle. In an interview with Jenny Hammond in 1991, TPLF leader Meles Zenawi explained the task of differentiating between the Amhara suppressing structures and the Amhara suppressed masses.

> The hatred, the suspicion, that some of the fighters have a bias against the Amhara as a people, ... has to be handled in a different way. It comes from a people who have been on the receiving end of oppression. It must not be shouted down. The roots of this suspicion must be explained. You don't overcome suspicion by saying the oppressed Amhara is your friend.

You have to show him how the process of oppression works, the role the oppressed Amhara plays in this and what suffering in different ways the Amhara has gone through because of the class structure. ... The best way to undo the past is to undo the structures and to replace it with a new relationship based on equality and respect. (Hammond 1999: 238)

This framework of understanding is very much acknowledged within the context of a new war. I asked Wode-Goshu, the deputy *woreda* administrator of Wuqru, how he felt fighting his old comrades-in-arms the EPLF with the support of his old enemy the Amhara. His answer was a clear correction to the implications of my question. 'To begin with, we have never declared and thought that the Amhara people were our enemies. We have always been clearly defining our enemies. It was the Amhara ruling class, not the entire Amhara group who had been our historical enemies.' Subsequently, Wode-Goshu continued to elaborate on how the new war had created new enemy images, or rather re-activated old enemy images. In his own words:

After 1991 the former TPLF or EPRDF army was reintegrated and demobilised in order to form a multinational army. This led the Eritreans to believe wrongly that there is no strong Ethiopian army, with a TPLF contingent. And it was perhaps this wrong miscalculation and under-estimation that led Eritrea to invade Ethiopia. However, the EPRDF has a particular political scheme and art or ability of organising and *mobilising people against its classical enemies*. This was extensively done during the last seven years [1991–98], and the EPRDF has gone far into the hearts and minds of all Ethiopians. Above all, the last seven years of EPRDF rule have proved that Ethiopian nationalities were the beneficiaries of their own development. Secondly, as a tradition and culture itself, Ethiopia had never passed through the history of colonial occupation. Moreover, there is not as such a page in our history that shows Ethiopia invading and violating the integrity and sovereignty of others. However, if we are invaded and encroached upon, the Ethiopians do not have the shoulders to carry that yoke. For instance, the Eritreans, economically and militarily, do not exceed us. In fact, they are even far inferior to us. Thus, the fact that our history is a history of sovereignty and honour, and the fact that Eritrea is such a tiny country, filled with excessive prejudices and chauvinism, have created a conducive ground for Ethiopians to display their unity and stand together against the enemy. (Personal communication)

The response captures a shifting perception within two fields: first, a shift of enemy images from the Amhara elite to Eritrea, and secondly, a changing notion of what Ethiopia is and should entail, from the point of view of Tigray. As a veteran senior TPLF fighter, the tone and content of Wode-Goshu's response is, at surface value, surprising since he so strongly emphasised the great Ethiopian tradition of sovereignty and integrity, in very similar language to that the Derg used in their fight against the EPLF and TPLF a decade earlier. He was not alone in stressing this Ethiopian greatness, and the whole renewed EPRDF rhetoric was calculated to play on these sentiments, as will be discussed later.

The TPLF socialisation of its fighters stressed the ideological understanding of the struggle, and the importance of defining and identifying the enemy. This ideologisation was also impressed upon the peasantry, in order to justify the struggle and gain support. Jenny Hammond noted the following conversation she had with three Tigrayan farmers in February 1991, just a few months before the Derg regime collapsed.

> 'What do you think now of fighting alongside Amhara people as comrades?'
>
> 'When we say Amhara,' said Seyoum Gezai, at once removing the sting, 'we don't mean ordinary Amhara. They are oppressed. We mean the Amhara administrators, the feudal system, the ruling class.'
>
> 'When we send our children to Shewa,' added Gebrehiwot Kiros, 'it doesn't mean we are sending them to fight against poor Amhara. We have a common enemy, Mengistu Hailemariam, who is the oppressor of the people.'
>
> Tadesse Ayele also wanted to have his say: 'We are not against anybody. We are against oppression – we want to bury oppression. We are not against any nationality. *Whoever is our enemy, we do not care.* We fight for our liberation and that's why we send our people to central Ethiopia'. (1999: 323, my italics)

According to these farmers, the 17-years-of-struggle was a war against oppression, disconnected from the geographical terrain and local identities where the war took place (after the liberation of Tigray). The new war with Eritrea was also a war against oppression, both foreign – in the sense that Eritrea was a separate country – and also domestic, since the Eritreans were also considered to be part of the *Habesha* cultural sphere. But simultaneously the war was also rooted in territories and against a people and their political leadership. Thus, the war did create a shift of perceptions among the Tigrayans on how they perceived themselves and their allies. It not only shifted the Tigrayan perception of the Amhara, *but also how the Tigrayans thought the Amhara perceived them*. This important distinction was brought to light by an elderly hostess in a *shoabet* (beer house) in Negash after I questioned her about her views on the relationship to the Amhara today, in contrast to under the Derg:

> There is a dramatic change, a big difference. In the old days, the Amharas never used to know our identity (*men'nenetena*). … Because the *Weyane* and *Shabiya* were fighting against them and they used to think of all Tigrayans as if they were fighting for secession (*min'nesele*), hating the other Ethiopians. (Personal communication)

Her answer reflects the notion that all 'Tigrayans' – i.e. all Tigrinya-speakers on both sides of river Mereb – are the same people, although two different political movements, the TPLF and the EPLF, lead them. Since they were fighting a common enemy, they were also categorised as one group by the adversary. I asked her to explain how this relationship was understood in the present context of war:

> The course of the struggle ... which the TPLF had carried out and its victory over Mengistu, had clearly demonstrated to the Amhara that we are powerful. Now in view of this, Issaias happened to be a dictator and tyrant, a Tigrayan [EPLF] Mengistu, thus the Amharas who had developed a trust in the Tigrayan [TPLF] political leadership and a strong nationalism ... decided to side with the Tigrayans [TPLF] against the tyrant Issaias for unity and integrity, correcting the old wrong stand on the Tigrayans [TPLF]. (Personal communication)

She manages in a remarkable way to distinguish between a Tigrayan ethno-historical identity embracing all Tigrinya-speakers in the trans-Mereb on the one side, and Tigrayan political identities represented by the EPLF and TPLF and divided by the state border, on the other. Although the cultural-historical identity links the Tigrayans with the *Kebessa* Eritreans, the current politico-Tigrayan identity links them with the Amhara in order to fight the politico-*kebessa* identity. As such, it illustrates the salient feature of an identity boundary – as the theoretical argument of this study advocates – that it distinguishes in one context and connects in another.

In the same vein, I discussed the contradiction of a cultural-historical identity and a political identity in the trans-Mereb with two young farmers turned soldiers on their way to the front in June 1999, asking them who was siding with whom, and what alliances had been made in this war in contrast to the war of resistance against the Derg regime:

> Definitely, it was we Tigrayans and the *Shabiya* people who overthrew the Amhara people [in 1991]. But, when *Shabiya* took control over Asmara in May 1991, there were more than 100,000 Amhara soldiers who were mistreated by *Shabiya*.[25] Their backs were beaten, they lost their property, including golden ornaments. Fingers were cut to take the rings. Having passed through this misery and inhuman treatment, they happened to pass through Tigray heading back south. On their way, all Tigrayans gave them all the necessary assistance, providing them with food, clothing, etc. since they also were Ethiopians. By then I vividly remember most of them saying with one voice: 'this Tigray country [people] is good'. Then when the invasion took place, our former enemy, the Amhara, sided with us to take revenge, because they harbour a deep grudge against the Eritreans. (Personal communication)

The two soldiers emphasised the political context of war and the definition of an enemy, as the primary reason for forming alliances. A common enemy joins together a temporary alliance. However, as soon as the enemy is defeated, the alliance is suspended, until a new enemy is defined and a new alliance is established. I was surprised by the frankness of the answer and followed up with a question of cultural relatedness in relation to political alliances: 'Even though you speak the same language as the Eritreans and have the same culture and religion, do you feel closer to the Amhara?'

> Yes, we have similar, and sometimes even the same, cultural ties, history, language and religion. More than with the Amharas, we are strongly linked through marriage bonds with the Eritreans. However, a marriage bond is a mere thread if there is no understanding and peace between the two people. (Personal communication)

Acknowledging the intimate cultural relationship between the Tigrinya-speakers in Eritrea and Tigray, the young Tigrayans nevertheless rejected an allegiance built on cultural relatedness and opted for an alliance based on political pragmatism instead. As such, ethnicity, as in cultural relatedness or distinctions, did not emerge as a determining factor in defining who is and who is not the enemy, and in establishing alliances and allegiances during the war.

A similar interpretation of history and understanding of events was confirmed by many of the peasants of Tigray. For instance, an elderly farmer from Selassie village outside Wuqro said:

> The Eritreans, like the Tigrayans, were heavily dominated and used to suffer under the yoke of the Amhara since the days of Haile Selassie. However, like us they took control over their capital in 1991. Nevertheless, they soon caused the deportation of many Amhara from Eritrea. Not to mention the destructive and cruel inhumanity they inflicted on the Amhara soldiers, killing them, looting their property and even taking the gold out of the teeth of their corpses. Now the Amhara people are siding with us against the Eritreans just to revenge all this.

As communicated in these statements, the ethnic discourse presents only the surface intention (the 'wax' in Abyssinian rhetoric), and not the deeper, hidden meaning (the 'gold'). What these people were really talking about was the construction of new and the abolition of old political allegiances and alliances. Basic questions like 'Who is our enemy?' and 'Who is our supporter and friend?' in the political context of war, were taking priority over issues of cultural relatedness and ethnic affinity. However, since the ethnic discourse is hegemonic in contemporary Ethiopia due to the EPRDF's policy of ethnic federalism, the enemy/friend categorisation was also cast in an ethnic categorisation of 'Eritreans' as the enemy and 'Amhara' as the friend. Alternative discourses of enemy images could have used categories of regional identities (an Ethiopian historical discourse), class (an Ethiopian revolutionary discourse), or political identities (a Western liberal discourse). Some may argue that a class perspective would be most appropriate in order to understand these dynamics, in view of the 'feudal' history of the country.

However, although the language of class struggle, rulers and sub-ordinates, has been used to describe the ethno-political uprising against the imperial order of Haile Selassie, in a contemporary context, class, as in a Marxist economic understanding of the term, does not carry any explanatory value, as shown above.

# Re-emerging *Habesha* identity

The Tigray-Amhara and Tigray-*kebessa* Eritrea relationships can be inter-preted within idioms of kinship and sibling rivalry. Actually, one can possibly distinguish the Tigray-Eritrea relationship as a kin-based relationship and the Tigray-Amhara relationship as an affine one. This distinction is made clear in several of my informants' expressions. In a conversation I had with the *tabia* (neighbourhood) chairman in Negash, a veteran TPLF fighter, the close identity between Tigray and Amhara was clearly articulated.

> The TPLF at first had a narrow political objective of creating an independent state of Tigray. However, this idea was found to be improper and otherwise impossible after it was openly discussed. The people understood that independence [of Tigray] would not be viable. Since then the TPLF had never in its history declared its enmity with the Amhara people, as a people, but only with the Amhara ruling class. For the Amhara and Ethiopian peoples, Ethiopia means Tigray! Ethiopia without Tigray is no more Ethiopia. *Bakka* (final)! Eritrea we could let go, but never Tigray. Believing this, the non-Tigrayans have emotionally backed and sided with us in the war against Eritrea, so as not to lose Tigray, which is an integral part of Ethiopia. (Personal communication)

In order for many Tigrayans to make sense of the sudden shift of allies and enemies, the new paradigm had to be rooted in history. Amhara was given legitimacy as an ally when the new context of war was interpreted within a *Habesha* (highlands) framework. As an elderly Tigrayan peasant explained: 'What I know about Ethiopia is that it consisted historically of *habesha*-land. Somalis, Gurage and I don't know what, are not ours and have never been ours.' As described earlier, *habesha* land is historically made up of the Amhara and Tigrinya-speaking peoples – the Orthodox Christian civilisation. The ethnic groups of the lowlands and at the fringes of Ethiopian territory are not considered to be 'true' Ethiopians, in the eyes of the *Habesha*. Donald Levine explains that:

> Despite the pervasiveness of regionalism among Amhara-Tigrayans, however, some sense of a truly national consciousness seems to have been present at least since the fourteenth century. This manifests itself through references to a national ethnic community; through the agency of a national monarch; and above all through the organisation and minis-trations of a national church. (1974: 118)

With the colonisation of Eritrea and its subsequent independence, the Tigrinya-Eritreans have been excluded from the *Habesha* realm in the eyes of the EPLF. (Lowland Eritrean groups, for instance the Afar, may still, however, categorise the *kebessa* Eritreans as *Habesha* Abyssinians.) The *Habesha* identity was – and is – not a hegemonic identity, but rather a supra-identity on top of local and regional identities. Gebru Tareke explains the historical relevance of the *Habesha* identity by emphasising its overlapping and fluid quality:

> Historically, it is possible to speak of double or even triple consciousness and loyalty. In relation to one another, Abyssinians tended to identify themselves with their respective locality or region to the exclusion of others, as in Aksum versus Agame or Tigrai versus Gojjam. But in relation to the surrounding people and all foreigners (*ferenji*) from far beyond, the Amhara-Tigrinya-speaking Ethiopians regarded themselves as belonging to a supra-region, supra-ethnic community which they called *Habesha*. (Tareke 1996: 36)

Although such a framework helps to explain the closeness between the two former enemies of Tigray and Amhara, the *Habesha* identity also created confusion and contradictions regarding the explanation of other relations of allegiance and enmity. Consider how a Tigrayan peasant, former soldier in the Derg army turned TPLF member, explained it:

> The Tigrayans and Eritreans were one and the same people. We as Tigrayans feel that Gondar is our country (*addena*), Gojjam is our country, Wollo is our country, Shoa is our country. The area beyond this is overseas [i.e. not ours]. But we have a closer proximity and ties with the Eritreans. The Eritrean highlands were part of *semien*-Ethiopia (northern), together with Tigray, Wollo, Gojjam, Gondar and Shoa. We have long historical ties and we have displayed our unity before at the battle of Adwa. (Personal communication)

Since a traditional *Habesha* identity also included the *Kebessa* Eritreans and excluded lowland, non-Orthodox Ethiopia, it did not work as an appropriate explanatory framework to legitimise the full set of changes of allegiances and enemies in the Eritrean-Ethiopian war. However, the main new alliance and friendship between Tigray and Amhara was rooted historically in the *Habesha* realm, and thus obtained a historical-cultural legitimacy among the Tigrayan and Amhara peoples.

# Imaginings of Ethiopia from Tigray

The war inspired a twofold process of collective identification of self (Tigrayans) and others (enemies and allies), one feeding into the other. First, the new context of war implied a sudden shift of political alliances which were draped in an ethnic categorisation of friends and enemies, building on cultural-historical traditions. This re-making of alliances also entailed a re-positioning of Tigrayanness as a category of collective self-identification in relation to the new set of relevant others, both enemies and friends. This complex process of identity re-categorisation was fuelled by the violence of war, inspired by popular poetry and traditional sentiments, and endorsed by official rhetoric and policies. It involved notions of ethnicity and matters of politics, but also issues of class and sentiments of kinship. As such, the identity-formation process in Tigray during the war had characteristics similar to that of ethnogenesis, since boundaries of identity have referents to personal consciousness, social interaction and cultural symbolism. This implies that the boundary of identity is essentially contestable. People have different experiences, life histories and preferences, thus their understandings and interpretation of the boundaries of ethnicity differ. Newer theories of boundary mechanism open up to consider the 'affordances' of boundaries for social activities (Barth 2000; Cohen 2000). Cross-boundary activity might be just as salient a feature of boundaries as creating distinctions and separateness. The ethnic boundary of Tigrayans was flexibly applied in both these capacities, to create a distinction with the *kebessa* Eritreans, and at the same time to re-establish a connection with the Amharas. These options were selectively and pragmatically explored by the Tigrayan community in order to make sense out of the identity chaos created by the war.

Let me pursue the development of processes of identity formation in the wake of the Eritrean invasion one step further. Since the invasion was regarded as a threat to both Tigrayan territory and politico-cultural autonomy, the Tigrayan political elite responded appropriately and mobilised both militarily and culturally against the new enemy. The occupation of Badme, Zalambessa and other territories inspired two ethno-cultural processes among the Tigrayans in general: first, a process of self-reflection on the two issues of 'what makes us distinct from *Kebessa* Eritreans', and 'who are our natural friends and allies in the fight against Eritrea'. These reflections in turn stirred a new dual process of self-identification and identification of others. First, a Tigrayan ethno-political consciousness was created to establish a cultural distinction and political division between the two Tigrinya-speaking blocks straddling the Mereb River. Parallel to this one could observe the re-emergence of a 'Greater Ethiopia' nationalist discourse that facilitated the shift of Amhara from 'enemy' to 'friend', which in turn helped the Tigrayans to create and re-establish natural bonds of alliances/allegiances with other Ethiopian groups in order to obtain support in the war against Eritrea.

The second process inspired by the outbreak of war was a dual response to the Eritrean land encroachment. First, the Tigrayan authorities issued a political rejection of the encroachment and mobilised their army in order to reverse the invasion militarily. However, a demotic response to the encroachment found legitimacy in cultural notions of land and the handling of land disputes. Such a blatant grabbing of land was a violation of both individual and collective notions of *risti* rights. This obliged the Tigrayan people to join ranks in the spirit of *weyane* in order to seek *henay mifdai* – retaliation. *Henay mifdai* was the traditional and locally anchored driving force for the Tigrayan population to contribute its efforts and resources in order to take back the occupied land. The Tigrayan notion of *habbo* (courage) motivated the able-bodied men actively to seek *henay mifdai*, by participating in the war against the invader. The notion of *henay mifdai* also helped to mobilise the broad civil society in the fight against the Eritrean invasion: women baked *injerra* and prepared food for the troops, youngsters helped in gathering wood and carrying equipment, elders gave money or kind to the troops, etc. The two processes stirred by the Eritrean invasion – a self-reflection on Tigrayan ethno-political identity, and the pursuit of *henay mifdai* – fed into and reinforced each other as the war developed and followed its course. This clearly illustrates that the war inspired a collective expression of Tigrayan identity within one discursive field; an identity which was projected in relation to the state as the representation of the hierarchical political order (see Alonso 1994; Williams 1989). In this sense, the ethnogenesis observed in Tigray during the war can be viewed as a product of state formation in which the Tigrayans were competing for political, social and material resources vested under the state. In this manner, the Tigrayan ethnogenesis was a strategy to achieve collectively what could not be obtained individually.

In the chaos of war, Tigrayan perceptions of what Ethiopia was also changed. The war gave legitimacy to the reappearance of a 'Greater Ethiopia' sentiment among the Tigrayan population – a sentiment antithetical to the ideas of the Tigrayan revolution (1975-91) and to the new official state ideology of ethnic federalism of the EPRDF. The Tigrayan discourse on Ethiopia and what Ethiopia meant for Tigrayans had shifted into a view diametrically opposed to what was usually expressed prior to the war. Ethiopia was no longer an artificial polity held together by state coercion and without any emotional content. After the outbreak of war, Ethiopia was perceived as a saviour and guarantor of the continued existence of independent Tigray, and no longer understood as a threat to Tigrayan autonomy and identity. This is a significant shift of perceptions of identity. A young man from Negash on his way to be recruited to the army, said:

I know there are a variety of different nationalities living in Ethiopia: Tigrayans, Amhara, Oromo, Afar, Kunama, Saho, Gambella, and so on. What links us together is that we are all Ethiopians. Nowadays, a Gambella is here with us on the front line, which is an indication proving to me that he is an Ethiopian. *Actually, it is as simple as that; an Ethiopian is one who fights Eritrea.* (Personal communication)

94

The shift of perceptions of Ethiopia among Tigrayans was not only grounded in war and the making of alliances and allegiances based on common experiences as comrades-in-arms. The changing set of perceptions was also given legitimacy by historical and cultural continuity. The notion of a 'Greater Ethiopia' was found wanting among the Tigrayan peasantry itself. An elderly man living in the outskirts of Selassie village gave a surprising response to my question about how he felt about Eritrea:

> I don't know what [independent] Eritrea is. What I know is that Eritrea is Ethiopia. My fathers and forefathers have taught me and shaped me that Ethiopia is under one *dagna* [united under one 'judge', i.e. king]. We never know and still I don't know of a country called Eritrea. Eritrea is for me the same as when it was called Hamasien,[26] administered under the Ethiopian imperial crown. I don't know when 'Eritrea' became 'Eritrea'. I think it was in the 1990s, the mystery of which I don't really know. (Personal communication)

The two views presented here on how Tigrayans perceived *Kebessa* Eritreans – as friends and relatives in one context, and as arrogant enemies in another – are not necessarily mutually exclusive; rather, they represent the complexity of the relationship between the two peoples. For the Tigrayans, Eritrea represents both 'familiarity' and 'snugness', (through intermarriage and trade relations); 'arrogance' and 'superiority' (as employees or manual labourers, and as 'developed' during the Italian colonial period); and 'betrayal' and 'enmity' (by historically helping the Italians in their war against Ethiopia on several occasions in the late nineteenth century with their colonisation of Eritrea; at the battle of Adwa; and with the Italian occupation of Ethiopia in 1935, in addition to the Eritreans' own machinations during the struggle when they cut the relief aid to Tigray; and lastly with the attack on Badme). Being aware that ethnicity is constructed in social interaction where cultural differences are communicated (Eriksen 1991), it seems clear that the Tigrayan–*Kebessa* Eritrean relationship may be an illustrative example of such an encounter of differences. Furthermore, the concrete formation of ethnicity is observable in the minutiae of everyday practice – in the routine encounters between representatives of different social, cultural and political positions (Barth 1994). And who is more likely to meet and communicate differences than neighbours such as Tigray and *Kebessa* Eritrea? Boundary construction and communication of ethnicity does not necessarily involve strangers. On the contrary, explains Barth (1994), it involves adjacent and familiar others living within the same encompassing system of social interaction, in which issues of shades of distinction are more prominent than hegemonic and exclusionist views of the other.

Concurrently, however, the apparently paradoxical perception of *Kebessa* Eritrea among the Tigrayans is also symptomatic of the intrinsically problematic relations between Tigray and Amhara, and between Tigray and the greater Ethiopian sphere. A Tigrayan is also related – in terms of history, religion and tradition – to the Amhara, but Tigrayans also consider the Amhara, or at least the Amhara elite, to be their historical enemies. It needs to be stressed that when the two views appear side by side, and a clear contradiction is emerging in the perception of what *Kebessa* Eritrea is or implies, or Amhara is or implies – from the point of view of Tigray – one needs to be more analytically sensitive towards the context of these contradictions in order to see the distinctions that are made between the people of *Kebessa* Eritrea or Amhara, and their rulers (both historically and contemporarily). This distinction reflects a parallel process of identification, one as a 'cultural-ethnic' being (stressing links of kinship with Eritrea and affinity with Amhara), the other as a 'politico-ethnic' supporter (stressing distinctions of politics with Eritrea and class with Amhara). The process of re-identification can be illustrated as the following:

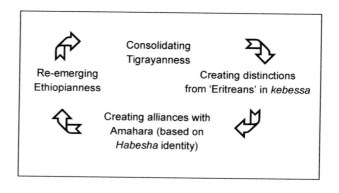

We have seen in this chapter how the Eritrean-Ethiopian war has influenced the perception of a Tigrayan identity, an identity that is formed, *inter alia*, in contrast to an Eritrean and Amhara identity, and in relation to *Habesha* and Ethiopian supra-identities. An ethnic discourse was prominent in the rhetoric of war in Tigray, and the war itself had an impact on the renegotiation of ethnic perceptions of the self and the 'other(s)', as well as on the formation of alliances and allegiances. Although ethnicity might appear to be given and natural, essential and primordial, in the eye of the beholder, this analysis has shown that the empirical reality is different.

# Notes

1 Rosen writes that Tigrayans have many self-ascribed traits which, in their own eyes, distinguish them from other Ethiopian groups. Generally, these characteristics are positive and favourable to their own self-image. Examples of such concepts are: *astewi ali*, meaning 'intelligent and quick learner'; *felat*, meaning 'philosophically reflective and clear-thinking'; *mehur*, meaning 'learned in many things'; *luba*, meaning 'generally quick and nimble-witted; *nefa'e*, meaning 'smart and mentally adroit'; and *gworah/tenkwel*, meaning intelligence (Rosen 1975).

2 *Wayen*, 24 Sene 1999 EC (8 July 1998 GC).

3 In 1998, an international court of arbitration granted Yemen the sovereignty of the islands.

4 Two other border areas occupied by Eritrean forces during the invasion.

5 This refers to the first *Weyane* revolt of 1943. It was started by the people of Wejerat in Southern Tigray.

6 Printed in *Wayen*, 20 Nehasse 1990 EC No. 309, 23 vol. (27 August 1998 GC).

7 *Haddas Ertra*, No. 77, 27 May, 1993, p.4, quoted from Alemseged Abbay (1998), my italics.

8 We know, however, from my earlier work together with Tekeste Negash on the origins of the war, that Eritrea–Ethiopia relations had started to sour already in the mid-1990s. From our unique studies in the archives of the Ethiopian Foreign Ministry, we discovered that the two countries had difficulties in implementing the Asmara Pact – the comprehensive bilateral agreement of cooperation between independent Eritrea and Ethiopia – already from the mid-1990s. This growing tension between Eritrea and Ethiopia was, however, kept hidden from the public discourse and did not affect official relations or enemy images. For a more detailed description of the Asmara Pact and its hampered implementation, see Negash and Tronvoll (2000).

9 See, for instance, *Wayen*, 26 Tiqemit 1990 EC No 269, 22 year (6 November 1998 GC). It should be noted, however, that other non-party publications, like *Zemen*, did publish certain Eritrea critical articles during the Fall of 1997 just prior to the outbreak of war.

10 *Wayen*, 12 Genbot, 1990 EC No. 295, vol. 23 (20 May 1998 GC).

11 'Popular' in Arabic, i.e. the 'popular/demotic front'.

12 As explained previously, the term has come to be understood as 'revolution'.

13 *Wayen*, 27 Genbot, 1990 EC No. 297, Vol. 23 (4 June 1998 GC), my emphasis.

14 Prior to Gebru's speech, on 13 May 1998, the Ethiopian Cabinet (Council of Ministers) had issued a formal statement on the Eritrean invasion. This statement, however, emphasised first the long-term cooperation and friendship between the two governments and the peoples of Eritrea and Ethiopia, before it criticised the Eritrean invasion in formalistic phrasing. Clearly, the terminology used is intended for foreign consumption and is not aimed at domestic mobilisation.

15 *Wayen*,27 Genbot, 1990 EC No. 297, Vol. 23 (4 June 1998 GC), my emphasis.

16 *Wayen*, 12 Genbot, 1990 EC No. 295, Vol. 23 (20 May 1998 GC).

17 Graziani was Fascist Italy's colonial governor of Ethiopia (1936-41).

18 The district where Badme is located.

19 The Red Sea islands taken by force by Eritrea from Yemen in 1997 and granted to Yemen in November 1998 by an international arbitration tribunal.

20 *Wayen*, 27 Genbot, 1990 EC No. 297, Vol. 23 (5 June 1998 GC).

21 The numbers vary slightly according to different sources; see, for instance, the report issued by the Ethiopian Ministry of Foreign Affairs, *Violation of Human Rights and Humanitarian Law by the Eritrean Regime*, March 2000 and the report by Walta Information Center (WIC), *Ayder: An in-depth report on the massacre of school children in Tigray, Ethiopia*, October 1999, published by Walta Information Center.

22 'Ayder School Commemorates June 1998 Bombing, Honours Student Martyrs', Ethiopian News Agency, 5 June 1999.

23 'Events planned to commemorate anniversary of Ayder bombing', Walta Information Center (http://www.waltainfo.com/conflict/basicfacts/1999/may/fact7.htm).

24 See '47 civilians killed in Eritrean air raid', *Ethiopian Herald*, 7 June 1998. On the Hawzen raid, see de Waal (1991).

25 The Derg army in Asmara was left more or less intact when the Generals fled the city just before EPLF troops entered the city on 24 May 1991. It is important to note, however, that these Tigrayans classified the Derg army as an 'Amhara' army, although the soldiers were recruited from all Ethiopian ethnic groups, and the largest segment was probably Oromo (in view of the demography of the country). The same collective categorisation was also made by the Eritreans during their war of liberation. My informants in Eritrea during my fieldwork there always spoke of the 'Amhara' enemy, equalling 'Amhara' to 'Ethiopia'.

26 Hamasien was one of the districts (*awraja*) of highland Eritrea, but it was also used as a term to describe the *kebessa*.

# *Five*

## *War Behind the Front Lines*
### Individual Approaches

> Repression and resistance generated at the national level are often inserted into the local reality in culturally specific ways. As a result, phenomena that anthropologists have often viewed as results of local processes take on entirely new meaning when viewed in relation to more macro-level political change. (Nordstrom and Martin 1992: 5)

The Tigrayans seemingly accepted and adapted quite quickly to the new war situation and the radical constraints it implied. People continued to support the TPLF in words, by joining the military, by participating in rallies in support of the war, and with voluntary contributions in money or kind to the war-front. The whole population condemned the Eritrean invasion and apparently accepted the shift of perception of Eritrea from friend and ally to enemy and alien. If we delve beneath the public discourse, the official rhetoric and everyday poetics, however, a different picture emerges. At an individual level people acted and reacted differently to the new war situation: some were supportive of the war, others negative; some determined, others reluctant; some willingly contributing, others rejecting; some volunteering recruitment, others escaping the draft; some admiring and loyal to the political leadership, others antagonistic and treacherous. These different and contradictory positions also influenced the perception of 'who is the enemy?' in the eyes of individual Tigrayans. Yesterday's liberators become today's suppressors; friends and kin who once were considered to be unshakeably like-minded change their views and positions on vital matters; last year's brother-in-arms is the current enemy; today's confidants become next week's informers. There are shifts the other way around, too. Past perpetrators of crimes may turn into present human rights defenders. Enemies become friends, superiors become equals. Individuals living in destitution or with lost illusions turn into determined citizens fighting for the common good (Nordstrom 1997). Old divisions and schisms are forgotten and new alliances and partners are made. To manifest one common and sustained 'significant other' – or, to follow the guiding metaphor of this study, an 'enemy' – for people to identify against in such a turbulent context, is quite impossible. By way of illustration, let me refer to a conversation I had with a farmer from eastern Tigray. Haile Berhane is 60 years old. He is the proud father of eight children, of whom two have been TPLF fighters since 1985. He has somehow internalised the notion of a constant shift in ethnic-based political alliances:

'Since I had contributed two of my children to the 17-years-of-struggle long ago, I was not required to contribute more. Indeed I feel proud of not being asked this time. But they joined the warfront voluntarily anyway.'

'Has the new conflict changed your daily life?', I followed up.

'Yes, I'm seriously affected. It's as if someone is snatching or taking the food I was supposed to swallow. Moreover, my children are not beside me for support, because of the war. As a result, I'm not getting the proper assistance a father is supposed to get,' he said grudgingly. 'We were very happy in the old days, though. Then we had one king and one crown for both people [Ethiopia and Eritrea], and this is how it should be. Even a cow will not be sent alone to grass without a cowherd. But now we have given them [Eritrea] independence and allowed the cow out to grass on its own. However, it turned out to be impossible to do that, and hence created a problem for us, leading to the present terrible situation.'

I asked: 'Is highland Eritrea (*kebessa*) historically part of Tigray?'

'Yes, the Eritrean highland is historically part of Tigray. Our children, our sons and daughters, even when they quarrelled with the family, used to go to Eritrea and work there and later come back to a better position and with a good amount of money for the family. They did this because the highland was more of a kitchen for all of us to use. Today, however, even those who have gone are unable to come back and we don't know their whereabouts.'[1]

'Tell me', I said, 'how has the historical, cultural and political relationship between the Tigrayan and Amhara people been?'

'Well, the history of the Tigrayan people and the Amhara was basically a history of political disobedience. Haile Selassie at the head of the Amhara people tried to impose Amhara domination over Tigray. We refused and revolted in 1943, during the first *Weyane*. His successors also tried to show their supremacy over us in the name of the Amhara people. We revolted and achieved what we are now, the second *Weyane*. Thus, to me there was no long and deep cordial cultural or historical relationship between the Tigrayans and the Amhara.'

I challenged him further on the shifting ethnic alliances. 'Today, the Amhara you used to consider as an enemy are behind you in the war against Eritrea. How do you view this?'

Haile explained: 'The Eritreans like the Tigrayans were heavily dominated and were used to suffering under the yoke of the Amhara since the days of Haile Selassie. However, like us they took control of their capital Asmara in 1991. Nevertheless, they soon caused the deportation of many Amhara from Eritrea. Not to mention the destructive and cruel inhumanity they inflicted on the Amhara soldiers, killing them, looting their property and even taking the gold out of the teeth of their corpses! Now the Amhara people are siding with us against the Eritreans just to avenge all this.'

I told Haile: 'For me as a foreigner, even though I have read Ethiopian history, it is confusing to see the constant shift of alliances. One day Eritrea and Tigray are fighting the Amhara, today the Tigrayan and Amhara are fighting the Eritreans, and tomorrow we might have another change in alliances. Why is this so?'

'Although we have shifting alliances, the people do not change,' Haile begins. He continues, 'The Tigrayans were fighting the Amharas, who were supported by the Eritreans. Now the Tigrayans are supported by the Amharas in our fight against Eritrea, and it's not surprising. Moreover, the reverse again might be true tomorrow! It is the same people, but passing through historical changes and shifting kings [i.e. political contexts]. When we were fighting the Derg, that was the time the Amharas were killing us, inflicting all kinds of suffering on us, throwing all kind of bombs on our pasture and farming lands. We never used to think that the Derg would come to its demise, and that the torrential rain would stop. Nevertheless, God has shown us the death of the Derg and the defeat of the Amhara by us. No sooner than this the Amhara who were our yesterday's mortal foe and enemy are siding with us against the Eritreans. Therefore, who knows what tomorrow will bring? Maybe the Eritreans who are fighting and killing us today will come to us in peace tomorrow?'

It is obvious that a shifting political landscape in the trans-Mereb area influenced the creation of enemy images and the identification of significant other(s) with which to contrast a Tigrayan – and/or an Ethiopian – identity. This in turn led to the fragmentation of the Tigrayan population into political and sub-ethnic alliances (*awrajanet*) and the emergence of a number of individually perceived significant others.

In this chapter I shall focus on individuals supporting the war and absconding from it; people who volunteer for the front lines, others who run away; in order to illustrate the complexity of individual preferences and actions during wartime. Just because there is war, the plurality of interests and choices as exercised every day under 'normal' circumstances does not cease to exist. In one sense war destroys culture, but concurrently it also becomes part of and constitutes sociality. War and violence are experienced differently and the new cultural web of significance spun out from the war is perceived differently from individual to individual.

# Celebrations of war

War does not only bring sadness and despair. War may also inspire and motivate a war-stricken population. Also festivities and celebrations are common events and forms of expression during wartime, events which represent the 'celebrations of war'.

On 5 June 1999 a peculiar celebration took place in Mekelle, the capital of Tigray, demonstrating the mixed and contradictory feelings created by war. It was the first anniversary of the Ayder bombing in which Eritrean fighter-jets bombed Ayder elementary school in Mekelle, killing 58 children and adults. As already mentioned, the raid sparked off Tigrayan hatred of Eritrea and all Eritreans. The mood of the participants in the commemoration was festive and not solemn, a fact that puzzled me. The cheerful response from a mother, whose child had been killed in the bombing, may explain the *raison d'être* behind the celebrations of death: 'I'm happy today and do not show sorrow for my dead child. I have been compensated at Badme!' She was referring to the battle of Badme in which Ethiopian forces recaptured the Eritrean-occupied territories at the cost of many casualties, both Ethiopian and Eritrean.

Not one household has been left untouched by the war in Tigray, in terms of recruitment to the army, economic constraints, injured or killed family members, displacement, political distress, and so forth. Despite these circumstances, many people joined in the celebration of war and rallied in support of the government's representation of the enemy. Fekadu Woldie, a Tigrayan poet, expressed his support in a poem entitled 'We are on your side', published in *Wayen* immediately after the battle of Badme:

> We greet you *abba hayet* [cubs, i.e. TPLF] the hero,
> Master of war and crusher of enemies.
> They provoke you to fury and consequently
> Everyone becomes the victim of your inflicting hand.
> Tigray is supporting you and the people [are] at your back.
> The son of Tigray, you have all virtues and truth.
> Your mortars shake the mountains and
> Your machineguns cause the hills to tremble.
> Beat your enemy and mutilate him.[2]

## INDIVIDUAL CONVICTION, PERSONAL SACRIFICES

Although people's livelihoods were directly affected by the constraints imposed by the warlike situation, many offered their full support to the war effort. For instance, Miriam, in her early forties and the chairman of the local branch of the Women's Association of Tigray (WAT) in central Tigray, came forward as a relevant role model. She lived in a small hut made of rocks and mud, and crowded with children of various ages, some her own, others friends of her children. Although she had been responsible for her own household since she was 18 years old, when her newly married husband went off 'to the jungle' (to join the TPLF), she had borne and raised eight children. Her husband joined the struggle while she was carrying her first child and was a front-line fighter throughout the struggle. He was demobilised three years ago, and was adapting to civilian life for the first time in his adulthood, when the new war erupted. He rejoined the army immediately as a front-line fighter. Miriam was once again left alone with the children and the sole responsibility for the household.

'Are you afraid that your eldest son will be sent to the front line?' I asked her.

'I don't have the slightest fear', she responded. 'It's rather I who encourage him to decide and he has made up his mind. In fact, the first round of recruited youths is ready and will be sent off tomorrow. However, my son is allocated to the second batch that I hope will not be far away.'

'Why do you want your son to go to the front line when your husband is already there?'

'Yes, it is true that his father is at the front line, but our son is basically born to stand up for his mother country. Therefore, if he did not decide to defend the country, on whose soil could he then stand? I was three months pregnant with him when his father joined the *Weyane* 19 years ago. It was only in 1987 that his father came home and met him for the first time. Our son has an obligation to continue the struggle as his father does', she explains in a sombre voice.

Her steadfastness and national conviction that seemingly make her willing to sacrifice both her husband and her eldest son at the war front surprised me. I was curious to learn more about her earlier wartime experiences and background.

'What did you feel at that time when you were a young bride three months pregnant and your husband went off to the field?'

'When my husband left me he didn't tell me where or why he was going. For almost a year I was ignorant of his whereabouts. However, after a year, news came to me that he was with the *Weyane*. Since then I used to go and visit him in the liberated areas when I had the opportunity.'

'How did you react when you heard that he was alive and with the TPLF?', I inquired.

'I was shocked and had a mixed reaction of happiness and sadness. I could not believe that he was alive. So I decided to go and visit him without telling anyone and, outsmarting the Derg, I managed to cross the front lines and reach him.'

'Did he explain why he had left you without telling you about it?'

'When I reached him he told me all the reasons why he couldn't inform me in advance. He said that he had been a clandestine member within the TPLF rural cell network, and that he was secretly communicating with the front from the time before we were married. In the meantime, however, he had heard a rumour that the Derg would jail him. As a result he decided to leave me and join the *Weyane* in the field. He avoided telling me this decision, for fear that I would be disturbed.'

Miriam explained her background in a straightforward manner. How could she apparently feel so detached from her own personal hardships during seventeen years of war and being alone raising her children?

'During the years of the struggle when your husband was in the field, you had to manage your household by yourself. How was that?' I asked.

"Nowadays, if your husband has gone to the battlefields, the local *baito* [administrative council] will take care of all the agricultural activities and other social assistance. Indeed there is no problem. In those days, however, it was very difficult. You could only stagger on by yourself. Nevertheless, my husband's family was helpful and I lived near enough to get immediate assistance from them.'

'Are you afraid for your children's and your own well-being because of the war?'

'We know that a cruel and powerful enemy is in front of us. We know that the enemy could inflict all possible miseries on us. However, we are in a state of war and these things happen in wars. We [the women] are even insisting on going to the front line to fight, side-by-side with our brothers', she says determinedly.

Apparently, Miriam had no difficulties in accepting the new war and the need for Tigray to mobilise resources, both in manpower and in kind, to fight it. She not only felt comfortable with the nationalistic rhetoric and the creation of the EPLF as the significant other, but was also actively participating in the process herself. As the local chairman of WAT, she toured the area visiting female-headed households to give support and addressing public gatherings to encourage people to give donations to the warfront. However, when I asked her directly about her feelings towards the Eritrean people, she hesitated and stated:

They are our brothers. There is nothing wrong with them, but by snatching children and throwing them into the burning fire, this man [Issaias Afwerki, president of Eritrea] has decided to watch the two brothers destroy each other.

Towards the end of our conversation, Miriam modified her previous stand somewhat and homed in on the significant other. Instead of casting it in cultural or ethnic terms, identifying all Eritreans, she described it in political terms as the EPLF and its leadership only. Thus, the cultural and kinship affinity to the Eritrean highlanders (*Dekki*

*Kebessa*) was restored. The majority of the rural peasants had difficulties in distinguishing between the EPLF political leadership and the Eritrean people as such. However, peasants more closely associated with the TPLF, as local *baito* administrators, mass organisation representatives and peasant militia, did emphasise this distinction. They had received more political training and more information regarding the official interpretation of the war, making them capable of differentiating the enemy from a hegemonic, unilateral view into various sub-categories.

On my way home from Miriam, my driver – a veteran *tegadelai* (resistance fighter) – recited some sentences from an old TPLF song from the days of the struggle, in honour of this strong woman:

We see their footprints in the dust.
Did they pass by –
Our children?
The sound of distant firing
Guides our footsteps
As we bear them food.

We hear the distant firing of their guns
And we must follow.
Be strong, our children!
We are bringing food and drink to you.
Can a needle sew without thread?
Can children fight without their mothers' support?

The mothers of Tigray gave tremendous support to the 17-years-of-struggle, a support they also rendered during the Eritrean war. While the male household members usually contributed money, labour or pack animals to carry war supplies, the women contributed food (baking *injerra*) and labour. Although some households claimed that these contributions were imposed on them by the government, it seems unlikely that it was an officially sanctioned policy. Enormous social pressure was put on individuals to contribute money or kind to the war front, rendering it almost impossible for people to deny contributions for fear of harassment, humiliation and social ostracism. So a certain historical parallel to the first *Weyane* can be drawn regarding the way recruitment to the cause was secured, as noted by Gebru Tareke:

It is apparent that ridicule and threat were used in recruitment and that many who might have preferred abstention took part in the uprising for fear of intimidation, isolation, humiliation, and social ostracism. Regardless of the method of recruitment, the disciplinary rules were fairly effective. As long as each peasant family was prepared to give one *injera* (pancake-like bread) or its equivalent in *hambasha* (bread) or *tihinni* (flour) a week, no punitive measures were taken against it. (Tareke 1996: 117)

The support given by the mothers to their sons on the front lines was instrumental in sustaining the Ethiopian war offensive. The support, however, often had a double connotation. At a meeting in one *woreda* to prepare dry food for the army, a woman claimed to have sent two of her sons to the front and 'urged them to die for their motherland'. Subsequently, she encouraged all Ethiopians to make historic sacrifices for the war effort, concluding by declaiming the following verse:

Let us follow them and die!
When he [the Ethiopian army] swallows them [*Shaibya*] like a vulture [*amora*];
Let us follow them and die.
What house, what child, what kinsman and what country is left for us [without them]?

The 'waxen' interpretation of the verse might be the display of sacrificial support for the war. However, the 'golden' interpretation might be a desperate plea for help expressed by a mother being separated from her sons, and claiming that without them her life was not worth living.

### THE SYMBOLS 'IN THE AIR'

Walking in the streets of Mekelle a few days after I spoke to Miriam I suddenly noticed how some fellow pedestrians were pointing at the sky, cheering and smiling. Over my head, two Ethiopian fighter jets made loops and 'pirouettes' in the air. I stopped a young boy and asked him what the pilots were doing and he replied cheerfully: 'They are celebrating the start of a new offensive against *Shabiya* and a successful bombing raid on Eritrean positions.' The new offensive did not come as a surprise. Earlier that week rumours had spread about the hospitals in Mekelle being cleared of patients. Elderly and sick civilians were discharged to vacate beds for new war casualties. In their own language of war, the Ethiopian fighter pilots were communicating to the Tigrayan people that the enemy was under attack and that they could take part in the ritualised celebrations.

The Ethiopian air force were generally celebrated as heroes in Tigray since they created havoc with the Eritrean defence lines. A few years earlier, however, during the Tigrayan struggle, the air force was considered the 'devil in the skies' and the most feared instrument of terror of the Derg. I was surprised at the heroic status of the pilots, and intrigued by the paradoxical political irony which they represented. The Derg air force received substantial help, both in terms of infrastructure and advice, from Russian military advisers. Some even claim that Russian pilots were instrumental in the Hawzen massacre, in which about 2,000 Tigrayans were slaughtered during a bombing raid on market day. During the 17-years-of-struggle, the TPLF regarded the Russian military assistance to the Derg as neo-colonialism and imperialism. When the new war erupted in 1998, however, both Ethiopia and Eritrea purchased new military equipment from Russia, including new fighter jet planes (Sukhoy 27s and MIG 29s respectively). As part of the purchasing agreement, Ethiopia (and Eritrea) received assistance from non-official Russian military advisers and pilots, who once again participated in the warfare in northern Ethiopia; their new local partners being their old enemy (the TPLF and the EPLF).

The Russian personnel in Tigray were housed at the guest researcher flats at Mekelle University and in the best hotel in town, the Hawzen Hotel. The Hawzen Hotel is owned by a Tigrayan from Hawzen, who named this hotel in memory of the massacre. I frequently dined at the hotel, in order to try to get in contact with the Russian personnel, but they avoided both local and foreign guests. They usually occupied a big corner table in the restaurant and talked only to Ethiopian military liaison personnel (probably the same interpreters as the Derg used for the very same purpose). While sitting at the next table to the Russians, I asked a Tigrayan friend of mine how he perceived the situation.

> It is truly a paradoxical situation. The Russians used to be our most feared enemies ... The Hawzen massacre is particularly remembered, and those gruesome acts will never be forgotten by Tigrayans. But now the situation is turned upside down. We have new enemies today, and new friends too. So in order for us to fight the Eritreans effectively, we also need assistance from the Russians. We know that they have good military knowledge. The Eritreans are using them as well! But I can tell you that I am happy that very few Tigrayans know that we have Russian military advisers with us in this war. If it became known, it might create protests. (Personal communication)

### THE RECRUITMENT FESTIVAL OF WUQRO

Immediately after the outbreak of war in May 1998, a military recruitment campaign was launched in Tigray and elsewhere in Ethiopia. Old TPLF fighters were the first to rejoin the army and to be sent to the front lines. After the first round of fighting came to an end in June 1998, a second round of recruitment was carried out during the fall and winter of 1998/99, in order to prepare for 'Operation Sunset', or the 'Badme offensive' of February 1999. These two conscription campaigns were carried out by administrative orders, without much fuss. The third time around, however, in the summer of 1999, the authorities in Tigray launched huge recruitment festivals at district (*woreda*) level, in order to boost the support of the Tigrayan people. When I heard rumours of the forthcoming event in Wuqro, I made plans to join in the festival, which was staged at the main outdoor stadium in the town.

On my way to Wuqro I gave a lift to an elderly peasant, Hailemariam, and we started to chat about the war. He had three sons at the front. One of them was a former TPLF fighter; the other two had been in the peasant militia during the struggle. He was proud of his sons, and told me about a trip he had just made to the Zalambessa front line to visit them:

While I was there, I was provided with a separate room in a guesthouse. I was furious and refused to accept it. I told them to give me a gun, and that I ought to spend the night in the trenches like the other soldiers. Knowing my spirit, they accepted my request. I was given a gun and subsequently spent the night in the trench. I felt proud and was extremely touched by the organisation, readiness and spirit of our army, as well as the heavy and modern artillery of the Ethiopian army. (Personal communication)

Hailemariam was annoyed that the Ethiopian army delayed an offensive on this front line, recalling the successful 'Operation Sunset' at the Badme front line some months earlier.

The army has been pushing for quite a long time to dislodge the enemy, and they are heard to say that Zalambessa is inferior to Badme. It is you [referring to me as a party/government official, since I was travelling in a four-wheel-drive] who is delaying and killing the fighting spirit of the army. ... Once you beat a snake on its back, you should not leave it before you make sure that its head is crushed.

The strong nationalistic stand and uncompromising position of Hailemariam turned out to be praised by the local district officials. Two days later he was honoured with a certificate at the big recruitment festival at Wuqro stadium, and, since he had sent three sons to the front line, he was presented as an example to follow.

The festivities started early in the morning of 12 June 1999. Slowly the stadium filled with thousands of spectators, who found seats on a gravel slope on the east side of the field. At around nine o'clock we could hear chanting from afar which gradually increased. Covered in a dust cloud, several hundred young men jogged into the stadium, singing:

We will not, we will not, we will not,
We will not break the trust of Hayelom.[3]

You youths, you energetic youths,
This is the time for you to flock to the training centre.

The hero has stood up, the hero has stood up,
Saying 'never' to *Shabiya*.

A group of women followed the youngsters, singing and carrying posters with the slogans: 'We will repeat the dramatic victory scored by Operation Sunset'; 'Let every citizen join hands to dislodge *Shabiya*'; 'We will not allow our nation, whose integrity and sovereignty is left to us intact, to be invaded by *Shabiya*'. In high-pitched voices, the group of women sang:

You on the front line;
You the destroyer;
You are not alone.
Your brother is coming to assist you!

A bus full of front-line fighters in uniform followed thereafter, and the popular EPRDF *Salem* music band started to play as the fighters entered the stadium. The soldiers disembarked from the bus and joined in the dancing and singing, screaming: 'Go, go, go to turn Issaias into ashes!' and waving posters with the slogan 'We will not break the trust of our martyrs'. After a while, all kinds of people – women and men, young and old, fighters and peasant militia, town clerks and bar-women – were crowding the field between the bandstand and the spectators, dancing, singing and cheering. Once in a while, one verse or one slogan could be heard through the tremendous cacophony of voices and music:

Powerful is EPRDF, powerful is EPRDF, powerful is EPRDF!
Victorious! Victorious! The *Weyane* Tigray is victorious!
Victory will come to the *Weyane*, so as to reverse *Shabiya*'s invasion!
Let us be united and stand together.
*Woyen*[4] brave, *Woyen* brave, who will dare now to stand before you!

At 10.45 in the morning – after the stadium had filled to the brink and the field in front of the spectators was packed with young recruits from various villages and districts nearby, their parents, spouses and children, etc., – the deputy chairman of the district, Iyasou 'Wode' Goshu, called for silence and spoke:

Dear guests and gentlemen, as well as volunteer recruits. This is a special occasion for the people of Wuqro to display their determination to eliminate the *Shabiya*. Making this introduction I want briefly to state the aims of this mass rally. While the people of Tigray and Ethiopia were blindly engaged in development activities the *Shabiya* regime invaded us. Our government has been trying to resolve the problem diplomatically and has gone a long way towards exposing the *Shabiya* regime internally and externally. However, *Shabiya* who have determined right from the onset to divert us from our development paths refused to accept a peaceful resolution to the crisis. We have, as you know, liberated a vast territory along the western border through 'Operation Sunset'. However, as you will know, we still have territories not yet liberated. We have therefore decided to liberate the territories and thereby destroy the *Shabiya* regime once and for all, and so make sure that the regime will not dare to dream of turning its face back to Ethiopia. You are here to join the army which is making history at the front. Today is a special occasion when we give and make oaths to our people that we are ready to throw *Shabiya* into its grave. You volunteers – from this hour onwards you are soldiers. And from now on you have to abide by total military discipline. I am confident that you will respect and keep the trust of your people and government. I wish you great success.

The deputy chairman's speech was received with jubilation, as the thousands of spectators, soldiers and soldiers-to-be roared their support for the war against Eritrea. A number of speeches by lesser officials, elders and mothers followed. A high school teacher proclaimed:

109

Nations and nationalities will fight for you [Ethiopia] until the last drop of blood, against the enemy who came crossing the Mereb river. They were foolish to awaken us from our sleep. If they decided to commit this tragic mistake, I'm here determined to fly like a bird and [create] lightning to break the sky.

A *shimagile* (elder) focused on the culturally perceived distinctions between *Kebessa* Eritreans and Tigrayans, and the relationship of inferiority/superiority:

They say to us we are Agame, without knowing what Agame means. Agame is a thorny tree: do these people know that these sharp thorns are here to pierce them? How courageous they are to dare to invade us, while the worms are still eating our martyrs' bodies [i.e. the recently killed, meaning the end of the 17-years-of-struggle].

The elder was referring to the 'Agame' stigma projected by *Kebessa* Eritreans on to Tigrayans, as a label for 'backward', 'uneducated', 'dirty' and 'deceiving'. The following *Kebessa* Tigrinya pun illustrates the perceived derogatory qualities of the 'Agame': 'Are you an Agame – or are you a human being?' Many Tigrayans were also referring to the fact that the Ethiopian army after the Badme battle discovered a little note on many of the dead Eritrean soldiers reading: 'All things are good in this world, but living with an Agame is bad!'[5] The continued Eritrean use of this old derogatory term provoked the Tigrayans who became even more determined and motivated to go to war.

After the many speeches came the ceremony of presenting certificates of honour to citizens who had excelled in various fields of national defence, among others Hailemariam, the elderly farmer to whom I had given a lift. The festivities closed with a long session of songs accompanied by the *Salem* band, to enhance Tigrayan ethno-nationalism or Ethiopian nationalism, and inspire people to join the war against Eritrea:

By defending us from *Shabiya*'s invasion,
We will accomplish our development projects. We shall win!

Our identity is peace.
We paid everything, (to get) you peace.
There is nothing superior to peace.

*Gomera, gomera* [army],
You demolish like a volcano,
You are serious and cannot be manipulated.

Hundreds of youths danced in front of the stage, and the police started to drive them back with long sticks in order to maintain crowd control. Everybody joined in a final song, concluding the recruitment celebration:

The avenger of Mekelle
The avenger of Ayder [the school which was bombed]

My country Ethiopia – feel proud now.
You have been compensated at Badme.
They [Eritreans] call it heroism, they call [their army] heroes.
Yet it was demolished and destroyed at Badme.
While they were being destroyed and were retreating,
They claimed to have captured tanks.
While they are being driven by the flood at Badme,
They said it was a strategic retreat.[6]

The half-day recruitment festivities had an impact on perceptions of the war and the collective obligations they entailed. The festivities were a collective manifestation of Tigrayan *habbo*, a display of courage and determination to confront an enemy. The show emphasised the presentation of all Eritreans as an enemy, and not only the EPLF political leadership. By drawing on cultural distinctions of superiority/ inferiority between the *Kebessa* Eritreans and Tigrayans (as in the Agame example), the ceremony helped to identify the Eritreans as natural enemies of Tigray.

Later on in the evening of the same day, I ran into the elderly peasant Hailemariam again, and invited him to join me for some food and *araki* (local liquor). As we were entering the restaurant, the deputy party chairman of the district was leaving and exchanged a few words with Hailemariam, out of earshot for me. While enjoying our food, Hailemariam was suddenly reluctant to talk about the war and the recruitment festival, saying only: 'I'm an old man, what do I know?' He subsequently admitted: 'I am not comfortable with the situation because the deputy chairman was unhappy because he saw me enter this restaurant with you. He warned me not to talk much. I'm sorry I can't feed you more [information].' Hearing this, I cut our conversation short and bade him goodbye, in order not to jeopardise his status. I was, of course, aware of the suspicious eye of the TPLF observing me – usual for a country at war. A similar incident happened a few days earlier when the *tabia* (neighbourhood) administrator of Negash prohibited two young soldiers from talking to me, and sent them away on an assignment instead. For the TPLF and the military authorities, stopping any ambiguity surrounding the issue of support for the war coming to the surface was an important mission, an ambiguity which should not meet the eyes of a foreign researcher and, more importantly, enter the minds of the Tigrayans themselves. Events such as the display of the Ethiopian air force and the recruitment festivities helped to rationalise the war and internalise the new enemy images.

# Subverting the war

The few scholarly publications on the TPLF and its relationship with the Tigrayan people tend to describe it as a 'symbiotic affair'; the Front is the 'people' and the 'people' are the Front (Firebrace and Smith 1982;

Hammond 1990; Hammond 1999; Peberdy 1985; Young 1997). The TPLF has in general been portrayed as a political front with absolute backing from the Tigrayan people. Although there were some critical views of the lack of pluralism and democracy in Tigray in the post-1991 period (Tronvoll 1995; Tronvoll and Aadland 1995; Aalen 2002b), it was not until internal dissent within the TPLF surfaced at the beginning of 2001 that the TPLF's relationship with the Tigrayan people was openly questioned. Prior to the dissent movement, all opposition and criticism was suppressed and the civilian population of Tigray was nervous and intimidated by the TPLF's coercive potential. I remember sitting in a small *bunnabet* (coffee-shop) in Mekelle in May 1995, discussing the upcoming elections and politics in general with two Tigrayan friends. One of them, a student at the regional college, confided to me:

> This is not like Addis, you know. We talk a bit about politics and elections at school with close friends and at home. But the TPLF is everywhere, so we are careful what we say. ... Even now, when it is only the three of us sitting here, I have a fear inside me talking with you about these issues. Everyone is watching everyone else, and when people see me talking to you it may create difficulties for me later after you have left Mekelle.

Based on my experiences in Tigray prior to the Eritrean-Ethiopian war, it came naturally to me to question the seemingly unanimous support of the Tigrayan people for the TPLF. Could it be that dissenting voices on the ground were once again overlooked in the chaos of war and under the strict political control over foreign journalists and observers? Since I was able to move relatively freely within Tigray during this period, talking to people from all walks of life and accompanied by an independent Tigrayan researcher/field assistant, I was able to access hidden transcripts of dissent (Scott 1990); since it is vital to listen to voices at the grassroots in order to understand the contradictory processes of identity formation during war.

Let me illustrate these contradictions by telling the story of Hiwut Hagos, a woman in her mid-fifties from a village a few kilometres south of the main front line at Zalambessa. She had been very welcoming and open towards us during our many visits to her rather ramshackle home. We also visited Hiwut's daughter, who was in her mid-twenties and lived by the roadside, where she had turned her one-room cabin into a *bunnabet*. Quite often we enjoyed a cup of strong, delicious Ethiopian coffee together with Hiwut and her daughter.

> 'You have had a lot of experience and have lived through difficult times and wars. Could you share some of your experiences with me?', I asked.
> 'What is war?', she replied. 'I've seen many things in my life. I've been through a number of wars, but I've found them useless for me. In an earlier war I lost one of my sons. I'm now left with only one son, and now they [TPLF] are pressuring me to give them the only son I have left. I spend the night praying and holding the 'pillars' so that they will

not cave in on me. My husband is in his bed sick and blind. My daughter's face is turning bony. Not because she can't find anything to eat, but because they have denied us our only surviving son. He was a hope for 'our face and the eye for us'. He has been recruited to the training centre by force, and they will take him tomorrow!' she cried. 'We shall surely miss him. This is a big blow to the family.'

Our conversation was interrupted by a new customer coming in, and we changed the subject and started to chat about everyday things with him, until he finished his coffee and left. Soon Hiwut's son joined us, back from a meeting with the local administrator who had told the youths of the area to get ready to leave the military training centres early the next morning. Hiwut was in tears.

We are seeing him off, weeping and crying. There is nowhere to go. They're pressuring us and even those who were not willing to go will be forced to. They argue that 'your country is invaded' and there is no one to defend it other than you.

I felt sorry for the old lady; her destiny reminded me of the many stories I had been told in Eritrea during my fieldwork there, about how the EPLF forcefully recruited youths from the villages when they had lost many in battle.

'When he leaves, I shall have several problems,' Hiwut explained. 'Who will farm my land? Who will look after me? I shall be left like "dry wood" [useless] with my blind husband. You see our physical bodies only, but they are mere containers. We are like living dead.'.
'Are you offered any help from the *baito* (local administration)?'
'Yes, the local community will give me some assistance. But under no circumstances could it be compared with what my son could do for me.' She stopped talking, looked straight at me and asked bluntly:
'Why are you asking me such simple questions when you very well know the effect of this war?'
I was taken by surprise by the sudden change in our conversation and tried to ignore her question by replying with another:
'What kind of changes will this war bring to Tigray and you?'
'There is nothing we can get from the war, except we are being destroyed and are dying like flies', Hiwut answered. 'Don't press me to say anything further while you can actually see what is going on! The rain doesn't seem to stop. The clouds are still looming, our children are being called on from day to day and this doesn't seem to have an end.'

We sat in silence for a moment. How could she possibly understand why I was asking her all these questions, when I was not able to do anything for her and the pressure she was under? Did she think that I didn't care, since I was not offering my help to her as an influential *ferenji* (foreigner) in her eyes? For me to complain to the local administrator about the recruitment of her son was a lost cause, but did she understand that? These thoughts were spinning round in my head, as four huge trucks loaded with grain-sacks from the World Food Programme passed northward-bound on the road outside. I asked myself whether the relief aid was going to the displaced farmers or to the soldiers at the front line. After a while I dared to ask her about her lost son, and what had happened to him. She looked at me sadly and said briefly:

'He was forcibly recruited to the Derg army and served there for six years. He was killed in action in 1991 fighting the TPLF, only two months before the peace came.' Hearing this, I fell quiet once again and didn't know how to continue without being too intrusive. After a minute or so she continued:

'It was only in the last five days that I decided to get some money by working as a daily labourer in the communal water and soil conservation scheme. It used to be my oldest son who looked after us. He was the breadwinner. But then the Derg took him. Now the *Weyane* are taking my youngest son by force, darkening the household once again. I don't even have a single chicken in my house. Neither are we benefiting from the grain aid package. They are taking him and killing the household', she said bitterly.

'But aren't households which contributed sons to the 17-years-of-struggle excused?' I asked.

'I have never contributed a son before to the armed struggle', Hiwut explained. 'The only son I have left is this one. I cannot cut him into two pieces and give one piece to them before, and reserve the other piece for me now! It's unfortunate I happen to only have one son left', she said resignedly.

'But your oldest son died in the previous war too? What is the difference?'

'Yes, whether on the wrong or the right side, I have sacrificed a son in the struggle too. They should have seen that. But who dares to speak out now?'

I could not argue with her about that. It was, of course, impossible for her to raise such a question under the circumstances. Instead, I tried to get her to explain who the enemies in the war were.

'Who is fighting with whom? Whose war is this?', I asked.

'What can I say? Both [EPLF and TPLF] are destroying for their own "ego" and I see that we [the ordinary people] are being destroyed. The war is being fought between the two elephants, Meles and that terrible man Issaias. Meanwhile, they are finishing off the people.'

'Is it a war between Eritrean and Ethiopian people, or is it a war between the political leaders?'

'The two leaders are the operators in this war, but they are using the people as firewood. This is the reality. I do not want to hide that, to say anything but the truth from the bottom of my heart.'

In Hiwut's view the TPLF was just as much an enemy to her survival as the Eritrean forces. The TPLF had killed her oldest son and was now taking away her youngest son too. For her the war was not about some disputed territories and the national integrity of Ethiopia. It concerned her personal survival and the well-being of her family. Up to then, the TPLF had brought her only sorrow, and there was no need for a distant country as an enemy image or 'significant other', while the TPLF was so much closer.

## COERCION, CONSCRIPTION AND CONSTERNATION

Looking more closely at the younger generations of Tigrayans with no prior personal experience of the resistance struggle also reveals a mixed picture, with some expressing dissent from the hegemonic TPLF/ nationalist discourse. The most important group whose confidence the state needs to win during wars is the young men who are supposed to fight and defend the country's honour and sovereignty. It was vital for Ethiopia's survival that the Tigrayan youth should be compliant to the politics of war – but were they?

During the summer of 1999, one year after the war started, I visited a friend's house in the outskirts of Mekelle for supper. I noticed a young man in the house whom I had not met before. I asked my friend who he was. My friend was somewhat reluctant to introduce us at first, but after some hesitation he called the young man over and told me he was his younger brother. My friend explained:

'I know you are interested in how we Tigrayans think about the war with Eritrea, and how we cope with the present terrible situation. I will let my brother tell you his story, but you must promise me to protect our names and identities. The government must not know the reason for him being here with me!'

I, of course, agreed to this condition, and sat in silence while his brother told me why he was staying in Mekelle.

'I usually live in a small village close to Shire, where I till my land to support my family. One day the village administrators called about 300 of us to a meeting. They had our names on a list. We were told that we should help at the war front at Shimboko. Many of us did not want to go, but we had no option. If you objected, you would be put in jail until you had paid a fine of between 25 and 400 birr. And if you did refuse to go and would rather pay the fine, you would be called to the front at a later stage anyway. At the front line we were carrying ammunition and water to the soldiers who were lying in the trenches. And on our way back we brought with us the dead and wounded. It was a terrible job, and there were dead and injured people all over. Sometimes, when the soldiers saw us coming with supplies, they would come and meet us, so we did not have to go all the way to the trenches. But often they did not come, and we were forced to go all the way ourselves. Six of my friends from the village were killed and some 15 injured while we were working carrying supplies. We were not given any weapons or protection as such, but had to manage as best we could. But if we wanted a Kalashnikov we could just pick one up from the ground, because they were lying all over the place among the dead. Sometimes, some of the villagers who had been active in the 17-years-of-struggle took a gun and started to fight with the soldiers. I did not do that. I do not like fighting and just wanted to be safe,' he explained.

'For how long where you assisting at the front lines?' I inquired.

'After three weeks we were allowed to go back to our village. The ones who took a AK-47 and wanted to keep it had to promise to tell the *baito* administrators that they had taken arms, in order to be registered as local militia. When they heard that, most of them threw the rifles away, because if they are militia they can be called to the front line to fight at any time.'

'What happened after your return to the village?', I wondered.

'After I returned home to the village, I left for Mekelle some few days afterwards. There were rumours about a new offensive, which meant that we would be called out again to assist at the front line. I do not want to do that any more. I'm just a villager and do not know what is happening. I am afraid to live in the village because of TPLF conscription. Youngsters like me who have relatives in Mekelle or other towns in south Tigray have left our area to escape conscription.'

The young man had tears in his eyes as he was narrating the terrible experiences from the front line. After completing his story, he recited a verse TPLF officers had been repeating at the front, when the peasants dug graves for the dead Ethiopian soldiers. The dead Eritreans, both high-ranking officers and rank-and-file soldiers, on the other hand, were left to rot and feed the hyenas and other scavengers:

Let the hyena pass by, leave the hyena alone.
His stomach is bearing the top [Eritrean officers],
His burdens are so many [Eritrean soldiers].

The sentiments expressed in the above case are not unique to this one man. An old woman explained the procedure of recruitment as she perceived it:

'There is a recruitment programme going on now. All the youngsters are registered. They are asked about their family relations and whether they are married, their health, their weight [must be above 50 kg.], joint problems, their height [must be above 150 cm], educational background, etc. All men between 17 and 30 are registered and asked these questions. And they will be called to the military.'

'Is it voluntary?' I inquire.

'Well, it is not voluntary. They put pressure on the family and we are told that it is this generation's obligation to fight this war,' she admitted.

'What kind of pressure is put on the family?' I wondered.

'Family members will be imprisoned and our son will always be sought after. We will be pressured to take an oath that we will turn him in to the police if he comes back home.'

She drew a parallel with the notorious conscription campaigns during the Derg called *afessa* (sweeping-up), when all the young men were taken from the streets and homes and sent to the front. However, she made it clear that this time they were fighting a foreign enemy in order to protect their homeland, so the recruitment campaign was partly excused. Nevertheless, the painful memories of the Derg's conscription made her explanation ambiguous, and she recited a poem first declaimed by a mother from Gondar, describing the terrible years of forcible Derg conscription:

> They [the Derg] told us to give them youngsters and we gave them;
> They again told us to give grain and we gave
> They further told us to contribute money and we did
> Alas! God save us from these evils [the Derg]
> Before they wrapped up the earth itself like a piece of cloth.

The young man dodging the draft and the old mother cited above presented hidden transcripts of dissent in Tigray during the war. The official story, on the other hand, was a different matter. When the local TPLF administrators were confronted with the issue of recruitment, they were proud to present the official narrative of a unified and voluntary backing of the war. The chairman of Negash *tabia* explained the background to recruitment in his area during the summer of 1999:

> We are busy recruiting youngsters to the army from this area. We do not send youngsters from this area to assist in carrying supplies and wounded soldiers. That is the responsibility of the villages where the fighting is going on. We recruit people to the army for three-month training before they are sent to the front. We must prepare ourselves for a long-term perspective. Since 1991 we have sent 40,000 militia back to the villages [in all Tigray]. But this time we shall be preparing for the future, and to keep intact and remain a strong army even after the fall of *Shabiya*. This is also necessary because of internal conflicts, as we have seen with the OLF forces and EPRP remnants. Our military force will remain strong, in order to face all future enemies. (Personal communication)

The chairman was quite steadfast in his priority of tackling the war, and represented Eritrea as a clear enemy. However, even in the midst of the war, the Eritrean enemy image did not overshadow other lesser enemies, such as the OLF and the EPRP. In order to confront these enemies, the chairman had been over-zealous in his work of recruiting soldiers for the war.

> We have collected about 270 young men here from the *tabia*, although the quota from the central government is only 26 men. But we have to assess our potential for recruitment; therefore we register all 270 men in

117

order to prepare for the best possible force. This is also a political show-event. Even a weak neighbour, when mobilised, will show his strength. What is important is that this *tabia* Negash has contributed 420 youngsters since 1990 to overthrow the Derg. This *tabia* has a special record in providing fighters to the 17-years-of-struggle, while other *tabia* in the region contributed less than 300 and 200 people. (Personal communication)

The chairman expressed surprise at the fact that there were families which had not contributed any children to the struggle until now, and he explained how the selection of recruits would take place, who would be sent to the front (and probably die), and who would remain at home until further notice.

The *tabia* has come to discover that there are families which have not contributed a single youth from their family throughout the struggle until now. What will be done here now is that all the 270 youngsters registered will be presented in an open forum to each other. Thereafter the men themselves will thoroughly discuss and debate and finally decide among themselves whose family's son is to be sent to the war. They will discuss whether the family is poor or rich, sick, educated or whether it has contributed family members before to the 17-years-of-struggle. The whole idea is to inculcate a sense of responsibility among them, and that the youngsters themselves decide who should go and who should not go.

The day after my conversation with the chairman, I encountered a small gathering of mothers, fathers and wives in a rural community of eastern Tigray. In search of another local administrator in order to conduct an interview, my assistant and I were walking along a path that took us past a small cluster of mud huts and over a field of barley. We had been informed that the administrator would be in that area on some official business. We found him round the next bend, addressing a group of young men, who were in turn surrounded by small groups of older men. The women were standing a little further away, watching – fully draped in their *gabi*, a huge white cotton shawl. Observed from a distance in the morning mist, they looked like pillars of salt. As we came closer, I was puzzled, since we heard no voices or noise of any kind; everybody stood as if frozen, watching the central group of young men and the administrator who seemed to be giving them instructions in a muted voice. We immediately sensed that we ought not to be there. Hesitantly we approached an elderly man standing alone and inquired what was happening. He turned his head towards us and looked at me for a long time with an expression that conveyed the deepest pain: 'They are taking our sons away to the warfront', he finally uttered. Sensing a type of hostility towards us as outsiders violating their time of mourning, we quickly retreated. But the people's sombre poses, the quiet tears running down the faces of the women, the expression of fear in their eyes of future death and dismemberment of their loved ones, all in an atmosphere of total silence, were impressions which were imbued in us in a manner no writing can possibly communicate. Perceptions of duty to defend your country, as expressed by the chairman, are likely to be contested by individuals affected by such policies.

## THE 'ENEMY' AT HOME

This strategy of political consciousness-raising had been decided 'from above' and was implemented in the same way throughout the region. As such, the war and the conscription campaigns directly affected the whole Tigray region and all Tigrayans. People feared the war and the terrible consequences and personal sacrifices it entailed. The sentiments of war, however, were expressed in a variety of ways: some clear and positioned, supporting the government stand; some muted and indecisive; and others reluctant and protesting. As individuals digested the flow of information, and observed the local action taken by the authorities, they interpreted the war and made up their minds about it, about who 'the enemy' was for them. On my way back to Mekelle after the meeting with the Negash *tabia* chairman, I stopped at a petrol station. The driver began discussing the ongoing recruitment campaign with the gas-station guard and the pump attendant. The driver and the guard were sure that the call-up of the youth was just for awareness-building and preparedness. They did not believe that everybody would be sent to the battlefield. The elderly pump attendant, however, objected:

> Don't be foolish. Do not talk like this in front of me. I'm 57 years old and have lived through the previous times and the Derg and seen how things were operating. You two are talking like the cadres. Don't be politicians. It is obvious that these youths will be sent to the war-front to die!

The voices presented above did not belong to individuals trapped in the trenches at the front, and who had a clear and present 'enemy/other' just a few hundred metres away, dug in at fortified positions ready to kill. For military personnel and front-line fighters, few grey zones existed. They lived in constant fear of combat and engagement with Eritrean troops, leaving few options to interpret the situation in various ways. It was you against the enemy; if you didn't kill him, he would kill you. For the civilians living in the rural areas indirectly affected by the war, on the other hand, the perceptions were somehow more contradictory and blurred. They did not stand eyeball-to-eyeball with the Eritrean soldiers. Their everyday experiences were not of trench warfare and bombing, but of the struggle to cope with farming duties when most of the able-bodied men were at the front. They struggled to secure enough food for their children when evening fell. They were not harassed by Eritrean shelling, but by the local TPLF administrators who were pressuring them to give their sons to the front, or some food to the soldiers, or money to the displaced. For the peasants in Tigray and elsewhere in

Ethiopia, the war meant that the state was intruding into their household and private sphere, looking for resources to confiscate on behalf of a war very few people really understood. Thus, some did perceive an enemy much closer than the Eritrean soldiers at the front, namely, the Ethiopian state itself represented by the local administrator.

# Encounters with violence

Violence is not expressed in a dichotomy between the perpetrators as active and the victims as passive. Stereotypes of this kind blur the fluid, contested and negotiable manifestation of violence (Nordstrom 1995b) and, hence, how violence impinges on the formation of identities. Violence must be considered to be integral to the social and intrinsically part of the modern, translocal arenas of state bureaucracy (Broch-Due 2005). National narratives of war are created with the intention of enhancing the willingness of the citizens to participate in and make sacrifices for the war effort. However, since war and violence are perceived differently by different individuals, so also are the national narratives. Povrzanovic writes from the Croatian war theatre that:

> The variety of experiences and responses of civilians who are not recognised as victims tends to be overlooked. Croatian war ethnographers have been trying to express that variety and reveal that the national narrative and personal narratives on the war differ considerably and in some cases are scarcely compatible (Povrzanovic 2000: 153).

Allen Feldman (1991) explains that violence in itself is formative in shaping people's perceptions of who they are and what they are fighting for across space and time – a continual dynamic that forges identities as well as affecting them. Since each person's experience of war and violence is unique, and the expressions and characteristics of violence vary from village to village and from area to area, violence must necessarily influence every person's identity individually. Thus to concentrate only on the formation of a collective ethnic or national identity in response to collective violence might obscure the actual empirical processes on a micro level. It is important to critically assess and compare analysis from a 'collective point of view', with perceptions of individual actors.

## FORMATIVE IMPACT OF VIOLENCE

To find a person or household in Tigray untouched or unaffected by the histories of violence – past or present – is impossible. The grievances of each generation – their personal sacrifices and dead martyrs – are told and retold to each subsequent generation in such a way that contemporary narratives of violence and enemy images are always layered on a historical backdrop of old enemies and sacrifices. This tradition sustains the memory of the dead in society in such a manner that a social space for the martyrs is constructed among the living. Allen Feldman's explanation, based on material from Northern Ireland, seems appropriate for the Tigrayan context: 'The lineage of the dead and the sociation of the living – exist side by side as mirror images of each other. The synchrony of the two social orders is a tensioned trope of the immanent inversion of the living by violence, past and present' (1991: 66).

During my fieldwork in Tigray, nearly all my informants stressed the effect violence had on their everyday life. One farmer summed up the situation as follows:

> The conflict with Eritrea has absolutely brought many changes in our daily activities, changes which we are used to from the previous struggle. These changes are fear of being away from the family, fear of ploughing the fields because of fighter planes, fear of fetching water and firewood, fear of forceful recruitment to the army for our children, fear of destruction of material necessary for livelihood and fear of death and other injuries. (Personal communication)

A similar view was also confirmed by local TPLF administrators. Wode Goshu, the deputy *woreda* administrator of Wuqro, explained the impact of the war on the local community in the following manner:

> Prior to the war we were busy with development activities. Our daily language and vocabulary was development. As a result of the war we were forced to shift our talk and vocabulary. The situation we are now facing can be defined as two facts. First, since nothing comes before the motherland, we are wholly preoccupied with the war, mobilising all our human and material resources. Nevertheless we have not forgotten our development altogether. We are trying to handle it so to speak in parallel. However, if we are to choose between the two, we will and indeed we are giving more and urgent priority to the war. (Personal communication)

Let me present in more detail an extreme case of encounter with violence at the front line. Even under such circumstances collective violence may influence the formation of identities individually. In the shanty quarters of Mekelle, I met a troubled and scared young man in June 1999. He had just run away from military service at the front line at Shimboko, where he had experienced the carnage of war fought with modern weapons and ancient military strategies. I knew him through a common friend, and he was obviously very nervous about discussing the politics of the war with me. I asked him to describe life at the front. He hesitated somewhat, before conveying the anguish on the battlefields.

> There were many different nationalities fighting together in the same unit. But most were Amharas and Tigrayans. The best fighters, though, are the Gambella.[7] They do not fear anything. If they are surrounded they will keep on fighting until all are dead. I saw one Gambella bringing back two Eritrean captives, a girl and a boy, all by himself. He dragged

the girl by the hair and held the boy by the neck. But since the boy resisted a bit, he just strangled him to death right in front of me. He then pulled the girl on to his back in order to carry her back to his friends in the trenches so they could enjoy her. The girl was terribly frightened and was fighting him, biting his shoulder, pulling his hair and screaming for help in Tigrinya. So after just 20 meters or so the Gambella man gave up and threw her to the ground, stepped on her face and shot her through the throat. After that he just walked away towards the trenches to continue fighting.

I was, of course, aware of the gruesome incidents happening at the front lines, but this eyewitness account, conveyed to me in the shady back streets of Mekelle, made me shiver. I asked him how he coped with what he had witnessed. He replied:

I saw many terrible things, friends being shot or blown to pieces by artillery and land mines. After an intensive round of fighting, in which we managed to break through the Eritrean defence lines, the plains were filled with corpses and there were rivers of blood running in the trenches.

After a period of silence, I asked about his thoughts on fighting and killing his ethnic brothers, the Eritrean highlanders.

Although we speak the same language and are both Christians, we are forced to fight each other because of the politics of the *Shabiya* regime. But this should not affect how we treat the prisoners of war. I know that many terrible things happened to some of the Eritrean prisoners. In one instance, a Gambella fighter was ordered to guard around 20 captured Eritreans. But he wanted to be at the front line fighting, and not sitting idle. So, after a couple of hours, he became bored and killed all the Eritreans and went back to the trenches to continue fighting. Other acts, which are alien to us Tigrayans, are the collection of war trophies. Many groups from the southern and western part of our country have a tradition of cutting off the penises of the enemy men and the breasts of the enemy women, in order to prove their capability as fighters. This was also done by many at the front. I was shocked when I saw this. We should not do such things to the Eritreans, after all they are Christians too! Many of us Tigrayans reacted against this, but what can we do?

I knew from the ethnographic literature that the Afar, Guji and other groups in southern and western Ethiopia, for instance, had practised such customs during traditional feuding and warring (Abbink 2000; Lewis 1998: 168). Nevertheless, I was surprised to hear that the Ethiopian army allowed these traditions to be practised in a so-called modern war. The young man narrating this story felt a need to distance himself from his fellow comrades in arms who perpetrated these atrocities against the captured Eritrean fighters. The acts of violence established – in the eyes of my informant – a distinction between the Tigrayan and, in this case, the Gambella soldiers of the Ethiopian army, since the Gambellas performed uncivilised acts of violence against the common enemy. My informant even went so far as to include the Eritrean enemy within a common frame of identity based on Christianity and to some extent ethnic origin (being Tigrinya-speakers), and pointedly designated the Gambella as a relevant 'other'.

Violence is, of course, not only experienced by soldiers at the front. Violence permeates all aspects of society in varying degrees during conflict and war. More or less every household stated that the war and the fear of violence had brought about changes in the way it ran its daily activities. Most of these changes were related to the fear of Eritrean air raids. This fear was not unwarranted, in view of the personal experiences of war among the Tigrayan people, with many having family members or friends who were either killed or injured during the 17-years-of-struggle. During this struggle in the 1970s and 1980s, acts of severe violence — bombings, killings and armed fighting — were personally witnessed by the majority of the farmers in my area of study, who communicated an array of sentiments and perceptions of violence and its effects, a few of which are presented below. Some were concerned about the war's effect on agricultural production and market conditions:

> We do not pasture our cattle far from home. Markets are moved far away for security reasons. We do not feel free to go to them since we are afraid. Even at the beginning of the conflict, markets had started to be held at night [to avoid air raids]. As a result, some vagabonds are cheating people by exchanging some old [discarded and out of date] currency notes with new ones under cover of darkness ... The resulting depression in trade has driven many small merchants out of business, and deprived farmers of consumer goods and staple grains. (Personal communication)

Others emphasised the physical dangers of the war:

> We are afraid that Issaias has decided to finish us off and that he may send mercenaries to drop poison in our water wells, channels and sources. We therefore spend every night under bone-piercing cold and torrential rains taking turns guarding our water sources. We haven't really slept since the conflict started ... The nights are tense, long and often sleepless, as we listen for fighter-planes and trucks passing by carrying troops. (Personal communication)

The women and the elderly who were left alone in the household, while the able-bodied men were mobilised, stressed the constraints imposed on their livelihood by the conscription:

> Our male youngsters have all gone [to the front line]. Elderly and destitute people on their deathbeds are left. These people can't do any-thing. We even have a big problem getting enough people to dig graves and help in the funeral services.

My husband who is a peasant militia was initially exempted from

123

mobilisation to the front line due to old age. However, he has recently been included in the local militia which will serve as a support force operating alongside the regular military. He is now at the Zalambessa front.

It is true that many youngsters have expressed their readiness to defend the unity of Ethiopia, and fight alongside the defence force. However, the increased mobilisation has subsequently taken different forms. Some punitive measures are being taken against those who have resisted recruitment and their families, such as temporary detention. (Personal communication)

The issue of Eritrean betrayal of the long-standing relationships between the *Kebessa* and Tigray, was also pointed out: 'The wounds Issaias has inflicted [on us] will continue to burn deep in our hearts, and they will not heal.' The many personal stories relating to the different layers of war in Tigray suggest that violence should be perceived as an enduring social and political phenomenon manifesting itself within all aspects of social life. Reidulf Molvær writes provocatively about the Ethiopian 'culture of war', arguing that 'Ethiopian history has been full of wars, so much so that people may take it as the normal order of things' (Molvaer 1995: 148). Within such a context, violence has an essentialising effect on the formation of identities (Povrzanovic 2000: 154).

## LAYERS OF WARS – LAYERS OF ENEMIES

After May 1998, the Ethiopian government made a shift in its bilateral policies in reaction to the Eritrean invasion and identified the EPLF as a collective enemy for the Tigrayan group and for Ethiopians at large. Subsequently, political entrepreneurs (i.e. TPLF cadres) were encouraging the Tigrayans to form alliances with other ethnic groups, like the Amharas, Oromos, and so on, in order to mobilise against the new enemy. However, since different wars have swept over the trans-Mereb during the last decades, individuals have been forced into different personal alliances with the many warring factions operating in the area, be they the TPLF, Derg, EPLF or some other movements. The previously personal alliances influenced the attitudes towards the EPLF.

Teame Medhin may serve as an example of the point of violence and its impact on individual identity formation. Today Teame is a farmer and a strong supporter of the TPLF's war with Eritrea. However, some extracts from his intriguing life history tell us that it has not always been so. I met Teame not far from his homestead in Negash. I asked him to tell me about his background and the political situation he had been living under.

During the hardships in the late 1970s, my family and I had a difficult time getting enough food. At the same time there was political unrest in the area and *Weyane* and the EPRP were fighting each other here in Tigray, at the same time as they were fighting the Derg. I was struggling to acquire a living for my family, when I decided to join the army [Derg military]. At that time I did not have the slightest political conviction, know-how or understanding of the war; I simply joined them on the basis of the 'wheat-salary' we received as militia members. I believed we ought to stay in Ogaden to fight the Somali invasion of our motherland. After a while, however, in 1984 the Derg transferred us from Ogaden to Asmara via Assab and Massawa. We spent only one day in Asmara before we were taken to the front to fight *Shabiya* [EPLF] under the command of the Weqaw regiment. For one year I was fighting the Eritrean rebels before the Shabiya captured me during combat.

Teame subsequently told me about his time as a prisoner of war when he was kept in caves for almost five years. The conditions of imprisonment in the caves have ruined his lungs and he was constantly coughing and had difficulty in breathing. During this time, Teame said, he gradually developed a Tigrayan consciousness, since the *Shabiya* treated them more harshly than the Oromo prisoners.[8]

> The majority of the prisoners were Oromo and *Shabiya* frequently took Oromos out of the prison camps and gave them military training for later integration into the Oromo Liberation Front. As such, the Oromo prisoners were treated well, while the Tigrayans were under *Shabiya*'s strict control. *Shabiya* used to think that all Tigrayan prisoners were *Weyane*.

I recalled tales told by the many EPLF fighters I met in Eritrea during my fieldwork there in the early 1990s. The contrast between Teame's story and theirs was, of course, stark, both sides being influenced by the political situation during war; both then and now. However, the narratives also overlapped in their explanations of the shifting political alliances. Teame recounted his release from prison.

> In 1988 the *Shabiya* surprisingly allowed us to listen to the *Weyane* radio, which was a sign of a rapprochement between the two fronts. Subsequently *Shabiya* issued an amnesty decree for 13,000 prisoners of war, *Shabiya* told us that the Derg refused to negotiate with them for our release and hence we were mainly released because of the friendly alliance *Shabiya* tried to make with the opposition forces in Ethiopia. Thus, we were told that we would be sent to the TPLF liberated territories and thereafter we could decide to join whichever front we wanted.

We started to talk about the reasons why the new war erupted and Teame reflected upon the Tigrayan position.

> In some cases the *Weyane* cannot escape from taking historical responsibility for bringing the war on itself. It was the *Weyane* that gave Eritrea its independence and created favourable conditions for its growth, making military contributions to Eritrea and paying all sorts of political price for

it in Ethiopia. And still *Shabiya* invaded us! This has caused a deep anger and frustration among the Tigrayans in particular.

Teame continued to describe the Tigrayan fighting spirit (*habbo*) and the way this quality distinguishes Tigrayans from other Ethiopian groups. He then concluded:

> Ethiopia can obtain peace, liberty and territorial integrity if and only if the Tigrayans and Eritreans go to war. For Ethiopia to remain at peace the two peoples have to fight so that the political situation remains intact. Eritrea and Ethiopia can only live in peace if both of us are going to war. Because if we occupy Eritrean territory and continue the war in order to strive for more territory which is not ours, we will be defeated and destroyed. Likewise, if they dare to do the same, they will also face a similar fate.

I was puzzled that Teame, a farmer from a small village in Tigray, could hold such a Machiavellian attitude towards the power balance and politics. 'Has the relationship always been like this between Eritrea and Tigray?', I wondered. 'No, no,' replied Teame:

> This is due to a political confession we made to them recently. Since we gave them their independence just some years back, this problem is also new, something which has grown out of the current political situation. ... What is puzzling us and has become abnormal for us is the events of this year [i.e. the new war]. Otherwise there is no doubt that we [Tigrayans and Eritreans] are one and the same people.

Teame projects several different identities with correspondingly different enemies. Starting with being an Ethiopian during the Derg and serving in the national army against enemies of the state (i.e. first Somali, subsequently the resistance movements of the EPLF and the TPLF), he later recasts his identity more narrowly as a Tigrayan nationalist, defining Eritrea/EPLF as the major enemy, with other Ethiopian groups, like Amhara and Oromo, as minor enemies from which to distinguish his Tigrayan identity. Finally, Teame modifies his narrow Tigrayan identity, and defines it according to a trans-Mereb view, i.e. a greater Tigrinya identity within a greater Ethiopian identity sphere.

The above excerpts from Teame's life-history demonstrate that to adopt the boundaries of the collective as the main focus of analysis is to neglect the continuously shifting positions of individuals in and out of those boundaries. This is also in concordance with a point raised by Barth (2000) – that boundaries create affordances which are selectively and pragmatically explored. If ethnicity and nationalism are treated as tactical postures only, aspects of self-consciousness and the symbolic expression of group identity are ignored. Hence, we need to substantiate or contest a collective discourse on identity with individual biographies (Cohen 1994a).

# The fragmented enemy

Anthony Cohen has argued that 'when I consult myself about who I am this entails something more than the negative reflection on "who I am not". ... It is the symbolic expression of ethnicity which renders it multivocal' (1994a: 61). Just because a person identifies himself as Tigrayan rather than Eritrean, it does not necessarily mean that he is like every other Tigrayan. He does not have to sublimate himself in an anonymising 'Tigrayanness' in order to suggest that Tigrayans have something significant in common which distinguishes them from Eritreans. But, at the same time, there are internal distinctions among the Tigrayans too. Ethnic identity is expressed symbolically (ibid.: 62), masking the plurality of content in ethnicity. Viewed from an actor-oriented perspective – reflecting individual biographies and agencies – an ethnic group may contain a variety of ethnic expressions and relate to a number of significant others.

Recent anthropological research (cf., for instance, Bringa 1995; Conversi 1999) has shown that the boundary-based aspects of people's identities, particularly ethnicity, increase within the community as the effects of war and experiences of violence become more prominent in everyday life, progressively displacing people's individual interpretations of the multi-stranded and multi-faceted social relationships they have among themselves and with the other. In the end, people who formerly entertained multi-faceted social relationships may be driven into a position where they endorse new enemy images and stereotypes of the alien other. A socio-political process of dichotomisation and boundary-construction has thus reinforced and cemented a black and white stereotypification of the relationship between the in- and out-group, whilst at the same time having a homogenising effect within the in-group.

Based on the Ethiopian material presented so far, it would seem opportune to pause and reconsider this perceived given process of dichotomisation and boundary-construction as an effect of violence and war. Can it be that conventional ideologies of nationalism and/or ethnicity tend to over-emphasise the division of individuals into two mutually exclusive categories of 'insiders' and 'outsiders', demarcated by mutually polarised enemy-images? And does war really have a homogenising effect on the 'in'-group? The material presented so far indicates that identity-formation processes which take place during conflict are much more complex and ambiguous than was previously argued. Rather than only stressing common denominators of inclusion or exclusion in identity formation and the drawing of national and/or ethnic boundaries (or relying on one, or a limited number of, cognitive schema to make sense out of their surroundings), identity-formation processes draw on a range of individually perceived and experienced factors. Within local, regional and national discourses, processes of identity formation, negotiation and re-creation are taking place that involve a multitude of different actors: the state and government, military and party, intellectuals and NGOs, churches, community-based organisations, and so on. All these actors produce information that influences the formation of identities during times of war and conflict. However, the experience and perception of this flow of information is likely to vary from individual to individual, based on his or her localised context. Hence, the formation of their identities during conflict also takes on different expressions.

During conflict and war, the social and material processes are at their most influential, impinging dramatically on every household in the conflict zone, and may thus have the strongest potential to shape individual connections across collective boundaries (Barth 2000). Hence, during conflict and war it might be beneficial for the study of identity formation to focus on the individual rather than on the collective. Individual experiences of terror and violence influence people's understanding of the collective. Nevertheless, they might use collective forms to assert their identities, 'but we should not mistake these for uniformities,' as Anthony Cohen argues (1994b: 178). The collective, be it the ethnic group or the nation, and its boundaries signify different things to different actors. An individual's loyalty to the group is never so pressed and challenged as in times of war. Thus it is no wonder that the processes of recasting or reinventing the boundaries for the collective from the individual's point of view seem to be at their peak during war.

I discussed how the Eritrean-Ethiopian war influenced the discourse of Tigrayanness in Chapter 4, and, in the current chapter, individuals' perceptions of identity and violence. I shall now move up the scale and focus on the national discourse of identity. In order to obtain an overall understanding of the formation of identities in war, the investigation has to be consistent in its pursuit of the metaphor of 'who is the enemy' within a number of social fields and levels of scale. More particularly the following chapter discusses how the Eritrean-Ethiopian war has influenced and re-shaped the notion of Ethiopianness.

# Notes

1  Due to the outbreak of war, several thousands of Ethiopian 'guest-workers' in Eritrea were trapped on the other side of the front line, unable to go back to their homes in Tigray or elsewhere in Ethiopia.
2  *Wayen* 15 April 1999 (7 Miazia 1991 EC), no. 341, vol. 24.
3  Hayelom was the most famous TPLF general during the resistance struggle. After the fall of the Derg, he was killed in a bar-fight by an Eritrean in Addis Ababa.
4  *Woyen* is 'to be *Weyane*', i.e. united in struggle.
5  See article in *Wayen* 23 March 1999 (15 Megabit 1991 EC), No. 338, vol. 24.
6  During the war of liberation, at the end of July 1978, the EPLF was forced to order a

'strategic retreat' to the Sahel base areas in response to a massive Derg offensive, giving up most of the territories previously captured. This strategic retreat, although controversial at the time, left the EPLF army more or less intact to continue fighting after the offensive was over. It was thus in retrospect considered a wise military decision. The Eritrean retreat from Badme in 1999 was described as a 'strategic retreat' by Issaias, in order to associate it with his wise decision during the liberation war.

7   People from the Anuak and Nuer ethnic groups living in Gambella regional state in south-western Ethiopia.

8   Between 1985 and 1988 the TPLF and the EPLF had a breach of relations and were engaged in fierce 'ideological warfare' against each other that also influenced the treatment of POWs on each side.

# *Six*

# *Reconstructing 'Ethiopianness'*
## Competing Nationalisms

This war is important for Ethiopia. We needed it. Finally, Ethiopia is again an important entity for the government. With the coming of war, the EPRDF has been forced to subdue the politics of ethnicity and concentrate on enhancing the national spirit instead. The re-emerging feeling of Ethiopianness is thus worth the costs of war. (Ethiopian intellectual, 1999)

This chapter will pursue the metaphor of 'who is the enemy' within a national Ethiopian context of identity discourses. The aim is to shed light on the construction of Ethiopian national identities, and to see how these relate to the perceptions of identities as explored in the two previous chapters. It will be revealed that similar processes are also taking place within the field of national identity discourse; there is not *one* commonly subscribed to the understanding of *one* Ethiopian 'enemy' with which *one* homogenous understanding of national identity can be contrasted. Several competing, and sometimes contradictory, discourses of enemy images are produced and reproduced with contrasting notions of national identities. This is not, of course, a novel discovery. For instance, John Sorensen (1993) has also addressed these topics, concentrating on describing the 'Greater Ethiopia' nationalism and the competing discourses from the Eritrean and Oromo viewpoints (see also Sorensen 1992; 1998). Sorensen bases his analysis on the deconstruction of the Ethiopian polity and argues that it is a historical and political creation of the Amhara political elite. My material, on the other hand, disagrees with this deconstructivist notion of Ethiopia and suggests that 'Ethiopia' as an imagined community (cf. Anderson 1983) is indeed viable and continuously reproduced by both political elites and commoners from various ethnic backgrounds (including Oromos).

In order to understand the changes within the discourses on identity in Ethiopia caused by the outbreak of war in 1998, one needs to keep in mind the hegemonic EPRDF-driven identity discourse on the 'rights of nations, nationalities, and peoples' which was developed after they assumed power in 1991. The reconfiguration of the Ethiopian unitary state into an ethnic federation entailed a strong focus on ethnic groups, restraining the notion of Ethiopian cohesion and nationalism within all public discursive fields (such as policies of economic redistribution, industrial production, foreign investment, educational priorities, social welfare, cultural initiatives, etc.) (Abbink 1995; Tronvoll 2000; Turton 2006; Aalen 2002a).

This chapter uses the celebrations of public holidays commemorating histories of war and political transformations in Ethiopia as an entry point to explore the changing content of Ethiopian identity discourses. Thereafter follows an analysis of the celebrations of the Operation Sunset victory, the major Ethiopian military offensive to retake Badme village in 1999. These celebrations coincided with the commemoration of the 103rd anniversary of the battle of Adwa, in which the Ethiopian army crushed the invading Italian military force. The focus of analysis will be on the symbolic expression of nationalism during this commemorative celebration. I shall also argue that Operation Sunset might be interpreted as *henay mifdai*, the traditional Tigrayan concept of retaliation. Subsequently, an analysis of the official political discourse contrasting Ethiopia with the Eritrean 'other/enemy' will follow. The political discourse at the centre is contrasted with the national discourse at the periphery, exemplified in the case of Hadiya in southern Ethiopia, before I conclude the discussion on the competing expressions of Ethiopian nationalism.

# National rituals of war and revolution

All states celebrate national holidays commemorating historical events of significance to the establishment of the state and the formation of the 'nation'. Usually, these events are some epic battle or a politico-juridical act symbolizing the manifestation of statehood, like the reading of a declaration of independence, or the drafting of a constitution. Observance is expressed in standardised acts and performances and draped in symbols of power, which imbue the participants with ideas and feelings in relation to their understanding of nationhood. What is remembered on such occasions is the historical narrative of a community (Kertzer 1988: 46). We may term these commemorative events national rituals, meaning activity and behaviour of a symbolic character that is socially standardised and repetitive (Connerton 1989: 44; Kertzer 1988: 9). What is important to bear in mind is that these rituals are not fixed and permanent, but shift in relation to political changes and transformations of power, as during revolutions, wars, and coups d'état. New regimes re-create the nation in their own image in order to give legitimacy for political change, by re-inventing history according to their own ideologies (Hobsbawm 1983).

In this regard, Kertzer explains that through 'ritual aspiring political leaders struggle to assert their right to rule, incumbent power-holders seek to bolster their authority, and revolutionaries try to carve out a new basis of political allegiance' (1988: 1). This is an apt characterisation of Ethiopia, where, out of a total of 16 national holidays, *five* of them commemorate both past and contemporary battles, and the war sacrifices made by the Ethiopian nation and people.[1] These five important events in Ethiopian history, as interpreted and officially sanctioned by the current EPRDF regime, are:

- Commencement of the Tigrayan revolution/establishment of the TPLF (18 February)
- Victory of Adwa commemoration day (2 March)
- Patriots' victory day/Liberation day (5 May)
- Downfall of the Derg (28 May)
- Martyrs' day (22 June)

These five holidays reveal the changing politics of the creation and maintenance of enemy images in Ethiopia. The oldest event marked is the Adwa day, commemorating the epic battle against the Italian colonial army in 1896 when the imperial Ethiopian peasant army crushed the invading forces. Thereafter follows the Patriots' victory day, which commemorates the return to Addis Ababa of the Emperor after the Italian occupation (1935–41), and thus the restoration of the nation's freedom in May 1941 (see also Levine 1965a: 268). These two holidays were celebrated both during the Imperial reign and the Marxist-military rule of the Derg, and their observance today under EPRDF rule represents continuity with the past. Italy, or rather foreign forces represented by Italy, are seen as the enduring historical enemy of Ethiopia. As we shall see below, the Adwa victory commemoration of 1999 was a unique national ritual. It claimed a historical depth and continuity with the battle of the past and its legendary heroes, while simultaneously celebrating the 'second Adwa', the Ethiopian victory in the Badme battle in Operation Sunset in February/March 1999, thus establishing a direct link between the Eritrean-Ethiopian war and the defining moment in Ethiopia's past.

## COMMEMORATION OF MARTYRS' DAY

Ethiopia's troubled history is also marked by the commemoration of the victims of violence, Martyrs' Day. Haile Selassie first introduced the observance of Martyrs' Day after his return to Ethiopia at the end of the Italian occupation in 1941. The Italian administration had perpetrated several repugnant acts of violence against the Ethiopian population, but one event stood out: the massacre of 19-20 February 1937. On 19 February, two young men (paradoxically, in the contemporary Ethiopian context, they were Eritreans) staged an unsuccessful assassination attempt on the Italian Marshal Graziani in Addis Ababa. In response to the attack, the Addis Ababa Fascist Party voted in a pogrom against the city's population the same day:

> The slaughter began that night and continued into the next day. Ethiopians were killed indiscriminately, burnt alive in their huts, or shot as they tried to escape. Italian truckers chased people down and then ran them over, or tied their feet to tailgates and dragged them to death. People were beaten and stoned until dead. Women were scourged, men emasculated, and children crushed underfoot; throats were cut, people were disembowelled and left to die, or hung, or stabbed to death. (Marcus 1994: 148-9)

The Italian reprisals were not limited to Addis Ababa and the bloodletting became a national calamity. Altogether as many as 10,000 Ethiopians were massacred, and the date of 19/20 February (12 *Yekatit* in the Ethiopian calendar) was thus a convenient reference to the symbolic commemoration of all sacrifices and martyrs during the Italian occupation. The Derg regime discontinued the official observance of Martyrs' Day, but the EPRDF reintroduced it in 1991. However, the new government introduced a new date for the observance, 22 June, commemorating another event and a different set of martyrs. As described in detail earlier, the Derg air raid on the village of Hawzen in Tigray on 22 June 1988 was the most savage incident against the civilian population during the three decades of civil war in Ethiopia, in which approximately 2,000 Tigrayan peasants were massacred by the Derg air force (de Waal 1991: 258). From the EPRDF's point of view, it was an appropriate event to be commemorated, and was singled out to represent symbolically all martyrs in the war against the Derg regime.

The shift of Martyrs' Day from 19 February to 22 June,[2] from commemorating martyrs of foreign aggression to martyrs of domestic repression, is also a shift of enemy images: from the alien to the domestic enemy – the oppressive Amhara ruling class. Moreover, imbuing a massacre of people from one ethnic group – the Tigrayans – with the symbolic value to represent all Ethiopian martyrs, in a context where the contested current ruling elite is Tigrayan, will necessarily create a clash of symbols and confusion rather than national cohesion. As an Amhara teacher explained after the observance of Martyrs' Day in 2000:

> You know, the *Weyane* [TPLF/EPRDF] has good reason to commemorate the Hawzen attack and the 50,000 Tigrayan martyrs that were killed in the fight against the Derg. It is very understandable that the Tigrayan people will like to honour their dead. But, at the same time, it should be understandable for the *Weyane* that the rest of the Ethiopian peoples also want to honour their dead who lost their lives in the fight *against* the *Weyane*. Tens of thousands of Amharas, Oromos and Southerners were killed on the battlefields in northern Ethiopia, defending the Ethiopian state against the Eritrean secessionists and the Tigrayan rebels. We do not feel that our

concerns, our grief, and our martyrs are represented at the *Weyane*-organised Martyrs' Day. Let them commemorate Hawzen and their Tigrayan martyrs in Mekelle, and the rest of us can commemorate our martyrs in Addis on a different occasion! (Personal communication)

## OBSERVING THE CHANGE OF REGIMES

All three regimes – Haile Selassie, the Derg and the EPRDF – commemorated their coming to power and assuming formal authority over the Ethiopian state with a national holiday. As the Coronation Day on 2 November commemorated the throning of Haile Selassie I in 1930 (Marcus 1994: 132-3), the Popular Revolution Commemoration Day of 12 September celebrated the proclamation of the suspension of the Imperial constitution, the deposition of Emperor Haile Selassie, the dissolution of the parliament, and the establishment of the Derg with full governmental powers in 1974 (Tiruneh 1993: 70). Today, under EPRDF rule, 28 May is commemorated as the 'Downfall of the Derg,' and thus the coming to power of the EPRDF in 1991. This is probably the most important political commemorative event for the EPRDF government, and on 28 May 2002 the Ministry of Foreign Affairs felt it necessary to issue a statement explaining the meaning of May 28 for Ethiopians:

> May 28 marks a turning point in Ethiopia's history. The day marks the end of dictatorship in Ethiopia, and the beginning of the process of democratisation which has continued to be deepened over the last eleven years. The day also marks the laying down of the foundation for a new Ethiopia in which its nations, nationalities and peoples live in full equality and freedom. May 28 marks the beginning of the realisation of the right to self-determination in Ethiopia which is enshrined in full in the Constitution of the Federal Democratic Republic of Ethiopia. Unity in diversity, as the motto of the new Ethiopia, has contributed to the strengthening of the solidarity among the Ethiopian people which was so abundantly demonstrated in frustrating the Eritrean aggression against the sovereignty of our country.

Whether or not all Ethiopians have a similar understanding of the day, as expressed by the EPRDF, is, however, a different question. When I asked an Oromo friend at Addis Ababa University to comment on the observance of 28 May, he reluctantly stated:

> 28 May marks not so much the downfall of the Derg, as it does the coming of the EPRDF. It is a day signifying the shift from one type of dictatorship to another. The EPRDF is much more clever than Mengistu, who killed his opponents and violated human rights openly. The EPRDF does the same, but clandestinely. For that reason, the 28 May is not a day for us to celebrate, but to obey. (Personal communication)

Similar attitudes were expressed by many of my non-Tigrayan informants. Also the private press has picked up on this issue, and an editorial comment in the Amharic paper *Dagim Wonchif* mocks the 28 May commemoration.

> Sure enough, May 28 is a day of remembrance just like February 20 [the Fascist Italian massacre of 1937] and May 5 [the liberation of Ethiopia from Italian occupation], days when our noble ancestors were martyred for the cause of the Motherland. May 28 is remembered as the fateful day which spawned the agents of the massacre of the Ethiopian people. May 28 is a day to look back at the massacre of 60 Ethiopians at Areka (Wolayta), of 200 Oromo peasants in Hararghe, the hurling to their death of numerous Amharas into the Beddeno ravine in Hararghe, the recent killing of Oromo students and the latest massacre of demonstrators in Awassa.[3] Yes, May 28 is a day of remembrance just like any other day of remembrance in our history.[4]

The editorial associates the commemorations related to the Italian occupation of Ethiopia with recent events after the EPRDF took power in 1991. These are political incidents/small-scale massacres in which either the TPLF/EPRDF policy of ethnic federalism is blamed as the cause of the ethnic clashes, or the TPLF/EPRDF security forces are accused of deliberately clashing with civilian groups and demonstrators. By contrasting these two latter comments with the statement issued by the Foreign Ministry, the contradictory perceptions of enemy images become apparent; the officially sanctioned historical narrative of enemies is being rejected by civilian observers of the commemoration ceremony.

National holidays in Ethiopia are one means of many by which new regimes establish themselves as the legitimate representatives of the Ethiopian people and delegitimise the *ancien régime*. By marking certain political events as vital to the formation of the nation, the new regime(s) also presents an officially sanctioned enemy with which the redefined nation is contrasted. At the same time, these commemorative events and ritualised celebrations have cloaked emerging dictatorships and repressive governments and been used as symbols of democracy and popular participation in an attempt to inspire solidarity and uniformity among a wide range of people with vastly different perceptions of the whole political enterprise (cf. Kertzer 1988). Sometimes such holidays will, as time passes, accrue more and more symbolic value, as new political events are associated with these same dates. This happened on Adwa day in 1999.

# Operation Sunset, Adwa
## and the restoration of Ethiopianness

> A lot of confusion has been caused around the issue of Badme, with the TPLF insisting that Eritrea [should] pull out of Badme. But insisting on pulling out of Badme may be likened to insisting that the sun [should] not rise in the morning. (President Issaias Afwerki)[5]

The Eritrean President's rather arrogant remark on the status of the disputed village of Badme in the aftermath of the first Eritrean military offensive in July 1998 sparked a deep sense of anger and demand for retaliation among Ethiopians from all walks of life. Ethiopian government officials, politicians and intellectuals viewed the invasion as a violation of Ethiopian sovereignty, and Tigrayan peasants considered it as an offence against their inalienable *risti* rights to the area. Thenceforth, much of the rhetoric of war from both countries was concentrated on 'Badme'. Since very few academics, intellectuals or journalists had actually visited the area, a lot of what was written about the village and its environs was based on hearsay and speculation. Nevertheless, this small cluster of brick houses and mud huts acquired a symbolic value. Badme came to represent the crux of the war for both Eritreans and Ethiopians, and it was Badme that tens of thousands of Ethiopians and Eritreans were willing to die for. As a response to the arrogant statement by Issaias Afwerki, the Ethiopian government and defence forces planned Operation Sunset (*wefri tsehay araribo*), a military offensive that would prove him wrong and drive the Eritrean occupation forces out of the area.

## INSTIGATING WAR

The seven-month lull in the fighting between the Eritrean invasion in May 1998 and the Ethiopian offensive starting in February 1999 was used to build up the Ethiopian armed forces and to prepare the people for war. Every day, in the newspapers and on the radio and television, the preparation for war against the new enemy Eritrea was covered. Poems and songs about the new political situation were particularly popular, since they managed to capture and convey the re-emerging spirit of nationalism among the Ethiopian people. For instance, my informants often cited a verse printed in the Tigrinya newspaper *Wayen*, praising the Ethiopian defence forces. It was composed by Haileselassie Taferre, himself a soldier at the Badme front line. The title is 'The Trustee':

The trustee – one with a profound experience,
The one at the front lines of Badme and Sheraro, and in the Matewo's trench;
You have an appointment to harvest and mutilate *Shabiya* [EPLF],
To dig a hole and bury these arrogant men,
To teach them not to repeat what they did.
Prepare your trenches and strengthen your muscles;
To tear down and throw away their war drums,
To crush their swollen head like a balloon,
To announce your victories to the Ethiopian people.
Repeat the history from your fathers – strategy from Awaelom,
and spirit of heroism from the recent late Hayelom;
Combining it all to demolish these arrogant men,
Here, you are now carrying the trust of all heroes.[6]

What was particularly appreciated in this verse was its ability to link the current war with the mythological wars of the past, creating a continuity of enemy images which helped to legitimise the depiction of Eritrea as the present enemy. 'Repeat the history from your fathers,' the couplet announces, and refers back to the Adwa battle against the Italian army, with the reference to Awaelom, a noted Ethiopian military commander and strategist under Emperor Menelik in 1896. Subsequently, a connection to the *Weyane* revolution and the struggle against the Derg regime is made, calling on the spirit of resistance and the heroism of Hayelom, the most admired and respected TPLF general.[7] It was the combination of these historical qualities of war and resistance that would help Ethiopia in the new war against Eritrea.

Other songs and couplets focused on ridiculing the Eritrean leadership and army, on the one hand, and, on the other, praising the qualities of the Ethiopian army. A particularly popular media figure known as Merigeta Hailu (his original name is Shishay Hisha) is famous for his oratorical skills. He used to work as a medical nurse, but after the war with Eritrea started he was offered a full-time position on Ethiopian television, and was the most popular performer on the Saturday night show in which he displayed his poetic capacity:

*Gumaya, Gumaya, Gumaya*;[8]
The death of a fearful and cruel man does not matter,
We have warned you right from the beginning.
He who pretends to have become a bull [*Shabiya*],
has gone down to the plains of Badme,
*Weyane* have marched towards you,
what would now be your fate?
A long kept *tella* [local beer] has intoxicated the *wadal* [Issaias Afwerki]
Hence, forced him to say the sun will never set again,
which was a slip of the tongue!

*Wadal* can be translated both as a fat donkey and as a thoughtless person. This Tigrinya term bears an obvious negative connotation and is usually used as an insult when the physical capacity of a person is sharply contrasted with his/her mental ability. The Eritrean President Issaias Afwerki was a favourite figure depicted within such a context.

First and foremost, the songs and poems performed in the aftermath of the Eritrean invasion reflected the determination of the Ethiopian people to take up arms and confront the enemy. The time had come to quit talking and to show the determined spirit of unity and Ethiopianness. A song written by a certain Allene Abbay from the Central Hospital of Shire in western Tigray entitled 'We shall meet [in battle]' captures this sentiment.

You made a sudden invasion without our knowledge,
And turned our journey from development to war.

Our people have now mobilised against you as one;
to teach your arrogance a lesson in practice.
However, you are short-lived like summer mushrooms;
Whose chest is delicate and fragile.
We have tolerated them until now;
Let them now see our bravery.
We shall not speak much, let us rather meet there [at Badme].[9]

The time of talking was over, and, after nine months' preparation, the day of retaliation had arrived.

## OPERATION SUNSET

Early in the morning of Tuesday 23 February 1999 Operation Sunset began. In the two weeks prior to that, Ethiopian artillery and air force had bombarded Eritrean positions along the border. I was aware that something more serious was in preparation, since the few remaining foreigners in Tigray were ordered to leave the region in early February, and the whole of Tigray was declared a military security zone. The Ethiopian ground offensive was launched along the 100-km-long Mereb-Setit front, employing both mechanised units and infantry forces, assisted by the air force. The first Eritrean line of defence collapsed under the enormous Ethiopian attack, which employed more than 43,000 troops to advance on the Eritrean positions. The Ethiopian forces used the 'human wave' strategy in order to penetrate the dug-in and fortified Eritrean trenches. The Ethiopian troops had first to cross wide areas of Eritrean minefields, endure constant artillery shelling and, when approaching the trenches, run through intensive machine-gun fire in order to reach the trenches and man-to-man fighting. After repeated attempts, the Eritrean line was penetrated in several places by Ethiopian troops, and the Eritrean forces withdrew in disarray.

A Tigrayan soldier vividly described the carnage experienced on the battlefield: 'It was like the entrance to hell. Killed and maimed people were lying everywhere, and body-parts were scattered all over the area. The soil was coloured red with blood!' (personal communication). A hundred years earlier, eyewitness reports of the Adwa battle had a strikingly similar content, as noted by Prouty: 'The dead lay in heaps ... streams of blood turned into rivers ... and the enormous field of killing looked like some horrible chessboard where fate, with a merciless hand, had interfered in a terrible endgame' (1986: 158).

The second and third day the Ethiopian forces met fierce Eritrean counter-offensives which were repulsed. On the fourth day, 26 February, Ethiopian forces advanced into Badme village and regained control over this symbolic site. Operation Sunset had achieved its immediate goal, but the fighting continued for days, as Eritrea launched repeated counter-offensives in an attempt to regain the village.

Operation Sunset was the biggest mechanised battle on African soil since the el-Alamein offensive by the British forces against Nazi Germany in 1942, involving a total of 90,000 troops in one war theatre.[10] Moreover, it was probably the bloodiest battle since the Derg army's 'Red Star' offensive during the Eritrean liberation war. No confirmed casualty numbers are available from either side, but conservative estimates suggest that around 20,000 people were killed during the four-day offensive.[11] No wonder the epic battle of Badme and Operation Sunset instantly gained mythological status among Ethiopians, terming it the 'Second Adwa'. In the immediate aftermath songs were sung and poems cited in honour of the Ethiopian martyrs and the sacrifices of the heroic Ethiopian defence forces.

### CELEBRATING THE 'SECOND ADWA'

By coincidence or design, only a couple of days after the victory at Badme, the Adwa commemorative celebrations took place on 2 March. Hundreds of thousands of people flocked the streets of Addis Ababa, waving Ethiopian flags, dancing and singing in praise of both old and new Ethiopian heroes. The procession gathered first at Arat Kilo, the monument in honour of the martyrs of Adwa, and proceeded to Mesqel Square, in central Addis Ababa. The dancing and signing continued as more and more people gathered at Mesqel Square. Various ethnic groups performed traditional dances wearing customary clothing and weapons; elderly patriots from the Italian war and occupation had donned their old uniforms and were proudly marching the streets, while homeless street-children were screaming and cheering. The police estimated that about 500,000 people had assembled at Mesqel Square at the height of the celebrations.[12] Rather surprisingly, no high-ranking government official participated in the combined celebrations of the Adwa and Badme victories. Only Addis Ababa's chief administrator, Ali Abdo, greeted the crowds and made a speech claiming that Eritrea was living in a 'dream world in its desire to take part of Ethiopian territory'.[13] As I was watching the cheering crowds, an Ethiopian scholar and friend, rather puzzled about the absence of government officials, commented:

> Why on earth isn't Meles [Prime Minister] or Seyoum [foreign minister] here? They should have participated in the celebrations and praised the army. Considering that they lack popular support, this event would have been perfect for the EPRDF to capitalise on in order to become more widely accepted among the people. You bet, if this had been during the Derg, Mengistu would have made a spirited speech, imbuing us all with proud national feeling. But Meles hides in his office and a low-ranking cadre is sent instead. The lack of public awareness and political smartness of this regime still surprises me! (Personal communication)

In the afternoon the same day I had an interview with Yemane Kidane, popularly known under his fighter-name 'Jamaica'. He was chief of cabinet in the Ministry of Foreign Affairs, a veteran TPLF fighter and a senior EPRDF cadre. He was, of course, overtly enthusiastic about the Ethiopian victory; however, he explained that none of the top EPRDF leaders had addressed the crowds since he claimed that they were confident in their political and military position.

> We do not need it [the publicity]. Our people do not need such a reaction. They will see the fruit of the struggle because of our confidence. ... Now the task of the government is to conduct war. As Meles said, 'If it is war, it will be full-time war, and not a joke.' This is full-time war, so we give priority to that. (Personal communication)

The EPRDF government was present, however, through its cadre network. Several people in the crowd carried posters and banners with various slogans describing political positions and expressions of national sentiments. Many of these slogans and banners had been prepared in advance by local *kebele* (local administrative unit) committees composed of EPRDF cadres. The slogans may be interpreted as the explicit opinion of the government. One set of slogans established a direct link between the Badme victory and the Adwa victory over the Italians over 100 years earlier:

- The victory of Adwa was repeated at Badme!
- The victory scored by our fathers was repeated by our children!
- The youth have lived up to the historical legacy through a resounding victory!

Such slogans sustained the historical enemy images of Ethiopia, and views that Ethiopia has been – and always will be – threatened by foreign aggression; a country 'fenced by fire' as one informant described it. Another set of slogans focused more explicitly on the sovereignty of the nation and the defence of Ethiopian territory:

- We shall not expose our sovereignty to a deal!
- We will ensure our sovereignty through popular martyrdom!
- Our defence force is the source of our confidence!
- We have realised that we have both the strength and the inspiration to sustain our sovereignty!

These slogans implicitly criticised the OAU/UN-facilitated negotiations, which many Ethiopians judged as biased and unfair. Since, in their view, it was a victim of Eritrea's aggression, Ethiopia had a legitimate right of self-defence. But instead of receiving support from the international community, Ethiopia was treated on an equal footing with Eritrea and condemned for its use of force. After hostilities broke out on 6 February 1999, as a run-up to 'Operation Sunset', the UN Security Council adopted

Resolution 1227 of 10 February 1999, condemning the use of force and demanding an immediate halt to the hostilities between the two countries, in particular the use of air strikes. Moreover, the resolution also urged all UN member states to end immediately all sales of arms to Ethiopia and Eritrea, a clause that sparked particular rage in Ethiopia. Prior to the adoption of the resolution, the Ethiopian Ambassador to the UN, Duri Mohammed, addressed the Security Council to put on record his strong objection to this clause. Chiming that Ethiopia was a victim of Eritrean aggression, the ambassador referred to Article 51 of the UN Charter and a state's legitimate right of self-defence, and concluded: 'It is patently contrary to elementary principles and the sense of justice to place aggressor and victim of aggression on the same footing and call for the cessation of arms sales to both countries.' He continued by drawing a parallel with a traumatic historical event in Ethiopia's history:

> In this connection, we should recall how Ethiopia was treated by the League of Nations back in 1936 when the Organisation imposed an arms embargo on both Fascist Italy and Ethiopia knowing full well that Fascist Italy, the aggressor, was self-sufficient in arms while Ethiopia, a poor country, was trying to defend its sovereignty against a major European power at the time. History is repeating itself, Mr President.[14]

The same point of injustice was reiterated some days later in an official statement by the Ethiopian Foreign Ministry, expressing the implicit notion of Ethiopia being alone against the rest of the world.[15] The statement was repeated in both print and radio/television, and EPRDF politicians' redundantly lashed out against the UN,[16] establishing it as a new enemy image. The Ethiopian Parliament followed up, adopting its own resolution expressing 'its deep sadness and anguish' regarding the Security Council's resolution and elaborating in detail on the unjust position taken by the UN.[17] The political statements consolidated a feeling of common destiny for all Ethiopians; they re-established the notion of 'Ethiopia alone against the world' and only able to rely on its own peoples and resources in the fight against injustice. That the slogans displayed during the Adwa/Badme celebrations also included references to this event, came as no surprise:

- We condemn the unjust decision of the UN Security Council!
- UN Security Council resolution 1227 should be revised
- We oppose every foreign interference!

The main enemy image reproduced during the commemoration festivities was, however, the Eritrean leadership, with posters and banners displaying slogans such as:

- The swollen muscle of *Shabiya* has exploded due to Operation Sunset!

- Operation Sunset is the grave of *Shabiya*!
- The madness of *Shabiya* led to Operation Sunset!

In the crowds, even usually sombre and calm elders were screaming their anger against the Eritreans and cheering on the Ethiopian heroes. Several people I talked to asserted that Badme was just the first step. Next, the Ethiopian army would take Asmara and then proceed to Massawa at the coast. A young man told me: 'Nothing can stop our army. We are way superior to the Eritreans and now we shall rightfully take back what was lost in 1991 but which belongs to us. Eritrea will once more be joined to the motherland.' The statement shows a striking resemblance to a promise hailed by Ethiopian soldiers of Haile Selassie in 1935 before they marched against the Italian invading army: 'Never fear, we shall soon be at the sea!' (Marcus 1995b: 170). An Ethiopian colleague from the university made the following comment on the crowd's euphoria:

Ethiopia needs this victory. The people need this victory. We need to feel proud once again, proud of being first and foremost Ethiopians and not Amharas, Oromo or some other ethnicity as the EPRDF has forced us to identify as. This time we are Ethiopians first, and whatever ethnic background we have is not relevant! (Personal communication).

The official poster also picked up on these sentiments and contrasted the madness of the Eritrean regime with the great qualities and the bold character of the Ethiopian people:

- Heroism and conquering – unique symbols of Ethiopianism!
- Our unity is reflected by our victory!
- Unity is power!

Prior to the Eritrean–Ethiopian war, it would have been unthinkable to display publicly such slogans, since they ran counter to the ideology of the TPLF revolution and the EPRDF government's stated policy on ethnic federalism – the reconfiguration of the Ethiopian state and the reinterpretation of Ethiopian history. My companion at the Adwa/Badme celebrations made the following reflection in this respect:

I have been present here on this very square during the time of Mengistu and have heard and seen the same slogans as today. 'Unity' – 'Ethiopianness' – 'Heroism' were the key terms in most of his public speeches during the war against the northern rebels of the EPLF and TPLF. From the government's viewpoint, today's slogans and jubilee must be a paradox and contradiction, since we are celebrating what they fought against for 17 years! (Personal communication)

A young man, overhearing our conversation, interrupted, correcting my friend:

You must not be fooled and think that this celebration is an expression of government support. We are here to celebrate the defeat of our worst enemy, *Shabiya*. Always, when Ethiopia is attacked from outside, we put our internal differences aside, and stand united against the foreign aggressor. But, as soon as the foreign enemy is beaten, we turn our attention back to our internal issues. So, although we have *Shabiya* as number one enemy, we have the *Weyane* as number two enemy. After this war is over, we shall again direct our efforts to ousting the *Weyane* government. (Personal communication)

The notion of shifting enemy images is not only a historical phenomenon, but also contemporary reality. The participation of Ethiopians from all walks of life in the combined Adwa commemorations/Badme celebrations could be interpreted as strong support for the EPRDF government in its war against Eritrea, but this may be a misinterpretation: 'We are here celebrating the defeat of the Eritrean army, not to give support to our government,' explained one of the many Ethiopians I spoke to during that day. Others declared support both for the war and for the EPRDF: 'Thanks to our government, we have managed to drive *Shabiya* off our territory and taken revenge for their betrayal!'

As a symbolic action and ritual the celebration is multivocal, rendering it possible to accommodate different understandings and political positions in the same event (cf. Kertzer 1988). In order to analyse these positions, it is vital to distinguish between absolute support of hostilities against the common enemy Eritrea, and hypothetical political support for the EPRDF government. Since the masses viewed Eritrea as the main enemy, a temporary allegiance to the EPRDF government was accepted in order to stand united against the primary enemy. But, at the same time, this was a fragile allegiance, held together as long as the foreign enemy was a threat to Ethiopian sovereignty. After that, new enemy images would be given priority, and new allegiances and alliances would be formed as has been the Abyssinian practice for centuries.

OPERATION SUNSET AS A METAPHOR OF *HENAY MIFDAI*
As already mentioned, *henay mifdai* is a local Tigrayan tradition of retaliation to land loss, designed not only to get the land back, but also to get even with the person who grabbed it. As such, *henay mifdai* incorporates and builds on several other key Tigrayan cultural concepts, such as *habbo*, understood as 'resilience' and 'courage to confront a challenge and/or adversary'; *weyen*, 'to stand together against the enemy'; and *risti*, the inalienable right to usufruct of land and the notion of belonging. The symbolic significance and historical understanding of *henay mifdai* are in reference to the Tigrayan desire to obtain vengeance against their Amhara oppressors and overlords who, from a Tigrayan point of view, have taken advantage of Tigray throughout history. In a contemporary context, *henay mifdai* can as such be understood in reference to Eritrea's

143

economic exploitation of Tigray and Ethiopia after the fall of the Derg (see Negash and Tronvoll 2000, p. 30-46), and the need of Tigray and Ethiopia to wrestle their way out of this exploitative grip.

In the aftermath of 'Operation Sunset' slogans were shouted, songs sung and poems recited, all describing the epic event and depicting Eritrea as the mortal enemy. However, there was more to these songs than met the eye, and if one examines a set of songs one can identify a pattern of allegorical content that plays on the notion of *henay mifdai*.

An Amhara rural singer from Shoa named Wondu Areso published the following verse in the Amharic *Reporter* newspaper.

> Awaken!
> Prepare [for combat]!!
> March!!!
> Even if the rainy season is heavy and torrential,
> Even if it comes to you [the Ethiopian army] with its thunderous clouds,
> Even if it comes to you in its lightning fire;
> Confront and challenge him! You too march on towards him.
> Flow like a flood over him and impress him – the son of my country!
> Arm yourself! And march! March![18]

The song, encouraging the Ethiopian people to mobilise and prepare themselves to confront the adversary who has destroyed something that was theirs, indicates revenge and retaliation, as found in the concept of *henay mifdai*. Retaliation was a common theme in most of the songs and couplets about the Badme battle.

An important factor inspiring retaliation is the feeling of betrayal. Since the Eritrean and Tigrayan peoples fought the Derg regime jointly, and the two governments of EPLF and EPRDF cooperated in development after 1991, the Eritrean invasion was seen by many as the ultimate betrayal. 'We accepted Eritrean independence in 1993, and helped them financially to rebuild their country, and all we got in return was armed aggression,' was a point often made in Ethiopia in the summer of 1998. The topic of betrayal was thus a theme touched upon in many of the songs.

> *Wayen* the tiger, how did you treat them at Badme?
> You poured on them a catastrophe on Tuesday morning,
> On the 4th day you made them abide by law and order
> And made them wear metal handcuffs.
> How did you tackle *Shabiya*?
> Those liars who swore by the sun and were treacherous!
> You forced them to renounce their betrayal.
> Some of them had their bones broken and some were killed!
> Now tighten your grip and make them not repeat [their mistake] again.
> How did you deal with the traitors and cowards?
> You drove them like a herd of goats.

You mutilated them like *chibutto!* [19]
How did you deal with the foolish and arrogant?
You beat and beat them like a war drum
A long-lived person can see many things,
and also hear many things.

The issue of courage and the military bravery of the Ethiopian army, as found in the concept of *habbo*, was also often praised.

The next song is composed by a veteran TPLF fighter from Axum, popularly known as Tertaraw (his original name is Gebremedhin Sebu). During the Eritrean war he was a member of the popular Ministry of Defence band, a music band visiting the front lines to inspire and instigate the fighting spirit and morale of the Ethiopian army. His song has made him a national figure in Ethiopia, as explained by a young man: 'It is almost a daily routine that all Ethiopians, irrespective of their ethnicity and language, listen to it as their favourite song. There is, indeed a saying that "even birds tend to shake their body by way of dancing when they hear his song".' The song was composed immediately after the battle of Badme and was played daily on national radio and television.

*Gud! Gud!* [20] What a topsy-turvy talk is this! We could not speak of it!
As if they [*Shabiya*] haven't faced defeat at Bure and Zalambessa,
and been crushed at Badme and Shiraro.
As if they are not touched and impressed at Matewo's trench,[21]
As if they are not trapped and defeated!
They continue bragging while lying on stretchers,
What a time it is! They are people who swore an oath by the sun!
March! March! [22]
Dislodge them; let them evaporate like dust!
Melt and rust like iron!
And let all your people, all your admirers shower in victories.
Let them fear and tremble under our air force!
The cannon to increase shelling!
The tank to speed up!
The infantry to penetrate deep and the trench to be dislodged;
Victory to be heralded!
Annals to be recorded in volumes!

Throughout history, the Ethiopian kings have had royal scribes to note down all significant events in which the king participated. In particular, the annals of wars and battles are important, and as such this song indicates a continuity of tradition with imperial Ethiopia.

The third constituent element needed in considering 'Operation Sunset' as a metaphor of *hinay mifdai*, is an idea of unity and determination by the group seeking retaliation, a spirit of *weyen*. The following song written by a Muslim from Addis Ababa, Assa Ali Fessueh, depicts such a spirit. The title of the song is 'Our army is faithful to its words'.

> Have you ever marched during a sunset?
> Have you walked on the plains and climbed the hills?
> When the invader is uprooted like a decayed acacia tree,
> The world was surprised and had nothing to say;
> We were right from the outset about your success,
> Let them now cry to Europe and America [for mediation].
> The Issaiasians have now become *garawayna*; [23]
> Until now they have only received a spoon taste,
> Much more and more suffering is yet to come;
> A catastrophe will come to break their ribs,
> Till they surrender and evacuate.
> *Wayen* is a tiger and a man of his words,
> He will never return easily once he has taken out his shields.
> Resurrection of his unity;
> Resurrection of his freedom and the heroism of Adwa,
> Here it has been renewed on the valleys of Mereb river.
> You wicked fellow and liar, what are you to say now?
> Let your tongue be silent for you will not be crucified
> and your sin be cleaned,
> There is no mountain cliff that our army and we can't climb.[24]

Again, we see the emphasis on the past in order to make sense of the current context. Contemporary sacrifices and wars are linked to past events to give them historical depth and legitimacy and to align them with the master narrative of Ethiopian nationalism: 'Ethiopia standing alone against foreign aggression'.

The last constitutive element needed to consider Operation Sunset as *henay mifdai* is a reference to land and belonging – the 'blood and soil' connection. The primacy of land, and thus *risti* rights, in Ethiopian history is profound and well documented (for an authoritative overview, see Crummey 2000). The land factor is a theme in songs and couplets about the war and the Badme battle. The quasi-official Amhara Development Band had great success in the aftermath of 'Operation Sunset' with the following song:

> Unthinkable it is to ditch an inch of ground from Ethiopia;
> It is impossible, it is truly impossible and a nightmare.
> Fight them thus as vanguards and in the rear.
> They [the Ethiopian army] went onto them [*Shabiya*] like an avalanche;
> and their hearts melted like wax.

The professional composer and singer, Alemayuoh Fanta, toured the front lines with his popular band to inspire the troops. He emphasised the Ethiopian right to land and the farmers' right to till the soil, in several songs, for example:

Let *Shabiya* be demolished and driven out of the hills of my country,
Show him your spirit and turn him to dust for his anti-peace [attitude],
restless and vagabond [as he is],
Show him your muscle, my country's hero;
While we put down our arms and resort to tilling the soil.
They thought we have abandoned everything [fighting abilities] and
become lazy;
It is surprising, indeed, to learn that they have invaded us.

Other compositions focused on the seasons and the agricultural cycle,
with peace and prosperity succeeding the misery of the invasion and
occupation of the land.

Listen to the sound of the footsteps of the rain.
When the enemy is driven out, the masses will rejoice.
Listen to the sound of the footsteps of the rain.
Let alone the victims, also the hungry animals are satiated.
In its own time, the period of invasion has passed;
Now the season of plenty has come.
Behold! The plants have blossomed and produced fruit forthwith.[25]

After retaliation come peace and justice. After Operation Sunset,
Ethiopia once again controlled Badme village and Ethiopian civil authority
was restored as the former villagers of Ethiopian origin returned to their
devastated homesteads. This outcome of *henay mifdai* was also portrayed in
poems, as this verse written by a villager from western Tigray shows.

The sun has risen from the dead
With great power and authority;
Christ has put Satan in chains;
He has sent *hayet* [i.e.TPLF] as a marauding force
Peace! Henceforth, let there be peace.
And he brought a herald of joy.

Carrying out *henay mifdai* successfully depends also upon the will of
God. Any outcome of such an initiative, whether loss or victory, is
sanctioned by divine powers.

When I discussed the concept of *henay mifdai* with Tigrayan informants in the aftermath of the war with Eritrea, an elderly peasant from
Mekelle told me that the Ethiopian Operation Sunset was indeed to be
understood as *henay mifdai*.

The Eritreans had fortified their positions on our land for a long time,
but we destroyed it in just four days. This is *henay mifdai* at its best! The
barracks were destroyed, their armaments were also destroyed. Compared with our casualities at the Ayder school, many, many more Eritreans
died, vehicles were burnt down and there was a loss of property.
(Personal communication)

Aregawi Berhe, the former military leader of the TPLF and current chairman of the exiled Tigrayan opposition party Tigrayan Alliance for National Democracy (TAND), had a similar perception of the event. He explained the feeling of betrayal on the part of the Tigrayan population, having helped the Eritreans to their freedom:

> They felt betrayed and the bombing of Mekelle – killing children and destroying schools – acted as a very important emotional turning point. So from that point onwards, Tigrayans wanted revenge, they wanted to assert who they are. They have been doing good not because they were weak, but because they were strong. They wanted to show it. They pushed for revenge, so the war was in fact instigated by the people, rather than by Gebru, Seye or other politicians. (Personal communication)

Not only had the former TPLF leader held such a view, but also the current one. When I asked Prime Minister Meles Zenawi to comment on the concepts of *habbo* and *henay mifdai* in relation to the Eritrean-Ethiopian war, he immediately acknowledged the cultural-political relevance of the concepts.

> Many of the peasants in Tigray, and in the rest of the country too, felt that the war was an arrogant and unprovoked aggression by Eritrea. And it is an insult. And we don't accept insults, so the concept of *habbo* is relevant, and also *henay mifdai*. They [Eritrea] can't and shouldn't get away with insults. Many people felt that they had sacrificed a lot in favour of Eritrea to obtain peace. Some had had misgivings about Eritrean independence [in 1991], particularly outside of Tigray. But they thought it was necessary for the sake of peace. Others had supported the struggle for independence in Eritrea. Both factions felt betrayed by the invasion. Those who have not been particularly enthusiastic about Eritrean independence said, 'We have accepted Eritrean independence for the sake of peace. Now we don't have peace. So what was the point? What was the point of accepting Eritrean independence?' Those who have supported Eritrean independence felt 'Is this how they pay us for our support?' So the insult and feeling of betrayal was there and people wanted to make sure that Eritrea does not get away with murder. (Personal communication)

Operation Sunset can thus be interpreted within a customary Tigrayan framework of handling land disputes, as an action of *henay mifdai* – to obtain revenge.

Operation Sunset was an event celebrated by Ethiopians from all walks of life, in all corners of the country. It will be remembered as the 'Second Adwa', a battle of epic proportions in which individual histories of courage and sacrifice will feed into the myth of Ethiopian warring superiority and help to sustain the master narrative of Ethiopian nationalism – that 'Ethiopia means anti-invasion'. As such, the battle and the cultural production surrounding it – songs and proverbs, couplets and slogans – may be viewed as a popular, demotic expression of nationalist ideology, or 'informal nationalism' in Eriksen's terminology (1993b). I now turn my focus on the political elites, to see how they conceptualised the dichotomy between 'us' and 'them,' and the manifestation of 'who is the enemy'. As the reader will discover, the demotic manifestations of nationalism and the expressions of the political elite were at times contradictory and competing.

# 'Us' & 'Them':
## reflections on the national political discourse

The reversion to old symbols of 'Greater Ethiopia' nationalism during the war with Eritrea created an awkward situation for key EPRDF cadres and central government officials; it was precisely the manifestation of this symbolism they had fought against for 17 years during the Tigrayan revolution. In the immediate aftermath of the Eritrean invasion, key TPLF and EPRDF officials appeared to have forgotten all about their old rhetoric and ideology, so significant to the EPRDF's hegemonic identity discourse. For instance, the Regional President of Tigray, Gebru Assrat, articulated the need to repulse the Eritrean invasion in a public speech in Mekelle on the occasion of the seventh anniversary of the downfall of the Derg regime, 28 May 1998 (only two weeks after the invasion):

> This is because *Ethiopia means 'anti-invasion'. Ethiopian means one who dies for his honour and fights for freedom and independence.* You have seen this week how all Ethiopians from Moyale [southernmost point of Ethiopia on the Kenya border], to people in Gode and Wardier [Ethiopian Somalis] have felt sad and have condemned the act of aggression. ... They [the Eritrean leadership] might have wrongly felt that the confrontation is only with the people of Tigray, whom they undermine most. That is not the case. They have made a wrong evaluation. They should know that they now have to face the entire Ethiopia![26]

TPLF administrators at the grassroots also conveyed similar sentiments. The *tabia* chairman of the village of Negash projected the following interpretation of war and the Ethiopian response to it in June 1999: 'We have to see the war in a broader context than as a pure Tigrayan issue. It is not the Tigrayan or Amhara or Oromo spirit fighting on the battlefields. Rather, it is a collective Ethiopian identity and feeling of nationhood that has stopped the Eritreans. We are fighting as one Ethiopia.' He then linked the current expression of unity in war with parallel historical events.

History tells us that Ethiopia has been challenged by a series of external aggressors: Turkish, Madhist and Italian. At that time, we were fighting with traditional and primitive weapons and spears and using pack animals for transportation. All Ethiopians as one, no matter their region or nationality, defeated these successive enemies and left the present Ethiopia for us. Now today, we have a better leadership, better technologies like aeroplanes, and we are repeating the history of our forefathers. Therefore, the present unity and harmony being displayed by Ethiopians in this war is not something new. It is what we have inherited. Indeed, it is a cultural spirit virtually flowing in our blood! (Personal communication)

To express such sentiments in Tigray and to provide such an explanation of Ethiopian unity and history by a TPLF cadre would have been unthinkable prior to the outbreak of the Eritrean-Ethiopian war. Prior to 1998, the EPRDF's ideologies rejected the basis for Ethiopia forming a 'natural unity'; the EPRDF leadership even stated explicitly that Ethiopia – as a national entity and concept – did not exist!

## THE VIEW OF THE EPRDF GOVERNMENT

In order to make sense of the sudden emergence of formal Ethiopian nationalism and the rhetoric of unity, the top EPRDF leadership tried to reinterpret the unity within their own political framework. Sebhat Nega, the founding chairman of the TPLF and the gray eminence within the Front, was cautious about capitalising on the national spirit in the war with Eritrea. In an interview conducted some months after the outbreak of hostilities in 1998, he framed the situation in the following way:

We don't believe that the unity of Ethiopia should be based on confronting a foreign invader, or any other force. The unity of Ethiopia can come fundamentally from adhering to the implementation of the constitution, human rights questions, economic development, and government services in all aspects, in health, in education, etc, etc. These are the bases. For example, if we have to fight against the EPLF, we will not feel that it will serve as enhancing Ethiopian nationalism. No, no, no, no! It will warm up for a short period of time, but in the final analysis, it is economic rights, it is political rights – basically, it is the political, social and economic development of the country that can enhance Ethiopian nationalism and Ethiopian identity. And we don't want to exploit the war to warm up Ethiopian nationalism. It won't last. It may last for three or four months, but finally the people need to count on the advantages they get from their government, in health, in education, in justice and economic benefits. Therefore, this war will bring no change; it will only stimulate the Ethiopians for a short period of time. It is not sustainable. And we shall not capitalise on it. (Personal communication).

A similar attitude was also conveyed by Hassan Shifa, the Tigray security chief and TPLF central committee member. In an interview with him in the spring of 1999, after Operation Sunset and the repeated offensives on the Tsorona front, he explained that the true reason for a united Ethiopia and a seemingly strong Ethiopian nationalism was not based on the heightened spirit a war creates, but on the political groundwork done by the EPRDF:

There are two or three basic reasons why we see a strong unity now. One important issue is the history of Ethiopians in general. Diversity and unity have always been an issue in the Ethiopian context. Throughout Ethiopian history, when war comes, internal differences are put aside and everybody tries to fight the aggressors. Always. The Italians, the Somali. Always. But the unity then and the unity now are very clearly different. At that time people were united just because the enemy threatened them all. That was the essence of the unity. If somebody came and wanted to invade Ethiopia, we had to be united. Religion was the main uniting factor, since most of the Ethiopians were Orthodox Christians, and those who were attacking were against this religion. So Orthodox Christianity was the umbrella that united Ethiopia into one force to drive out the enemies. If you take the current situation, it is essentially different from what was happening in the past. What is the difference? In the first place, it is the economic development Ethiopia has undergone in the last eight years. I can't give you the figures, but if you look at Ethiopia, you see new schools in every *kebele*, you see new clinics, water construction, etc. This has gone beyond the expectations of the people and they try to grasp this. Every village has a sense of it. Secondly, economic development has also influenced the agriculture and has helped every peasant household. Peasants are free to sell their production at market prices. There is no force or coercion used. So, economically there is some resource added to every household in Ethiopia. In the last five years jobs have also been created in the cities, due to liberalisation of the investment code and the boom in construction. Nobody would have expected such changes in such a short time. Plus, there has been peace in the country. There is no *shifta* [banditry]. Crime has decreased. Politically, diversity in unity has been implemented, the regionalisation, the equal distribution of the wealth of the country. In fact, additional wealth is given to poor nationalities, and equal distribution of power. This had never happened before in the history of Ethiopia. We have democracy and a democratic Constitution. So Ethiopians do not want to lose these economic and political advantages. That is why we have united. (Personal communication)

After the war and after the Border Commission had passed their decision in 2002, I had the opportunity to ask Prime Minister Meles Zenawi to reflect on the war and the political processes it had created within Ethiopia. He had the same view of the apparently collective Ethiopian resistance to the Eritrean invasion as Sebhat Nega and Hassan Shifa had expressed during the war. The Ethiopian people did not defend their country because of nationalistic feeling alone, the Prime

Minister claimed, but they defended it on the basis of the political progress and liberties achieved during EPRDF rule. He exemplified this point with reference to the Ethiopian Somalis' participation in the war:

> For the first time in the history of Ethiopia, thousands of Somali youths volunteered to fight, without knowing concretely what the war was about. They didn't care about Badme as such. But they cared about the fact that some one who ought to be grateful was challenging the new dispensation of federalism – and that our peace was being threatened together with the new federal dispensation. They might have misgivings here and there about specific issues, but the totality of the constitution package, the basic principles, was acceptable to them – and they wanted to defend that. (Personal communication)

## THE VIEW OF THE POLITICAL OPPOSITION

Not all political actors shared EPRDF officials' view that popular support for the war was primarily based on the success of their development policies and political liberalisation, downplaying the importance of the use of nationalistic symbols and rituals of war. Merera Gudina, chairman of the opposition party Oromo National Congress (ONC) and an academic scholar of political science, commented on the EPRDF's politics of nationalism:

> The ruling party is trying to reconcile itself with what we call standard Ethiopian nationalism. The symbols of Ethiopian Empire builders are now coming back and the national flag is now being used as a symbol of mobilisation. The 'defence-of-the-motherland' language is coming back, some of which used to be employed by the Derg. The defence of the national integrity of the country is coming back. The old warriors who fought at Adwa, the Ethiopian patriots who carried out the resistance struggle during the Italian occupation; their names are now being used by the government for the propaganda of war. Menelik, the great empire builder, his name was for the last seven years relegated to the museum, now it is coming back into active politics. ... The EPRDF is the same as former Ethiopian rulers – the emperors and leaders of the military regime. They all use the same Ethiopian symbols of defence of the mother land, the national integrity of the country, the history of Ethiopia that fought all kinds of aggression from outside, the challenges of the Egyptians and so on. For the last seven years those who have been trying to advance this type of Ethiopian nationalism used to be accused of being chauvinist by the EPRDF. Now it is no more the case. The EPRDF is using the very same symbols, the same history, and the same personalities as those who built the empire. In fact, Prime Minister Meles used to say that the national flag was simply a piece of cloth. Now, he is using the national flag as one of the most important symbols of mobilisation. To die for the motherland, the national flag, and so on is being used as a

means of mobilisation. So all symbols of Ethiopian nationalism since the days of the Emperor are now being used for defence of the motherland against the Eritrean aggression. (Personal communication)

In Merera Gudina's view, much of the support for the war could be found in other reasons than the so-called economic development and political liberalisation, reasons playing on the notion of retaliation (*henay mifdai*):

In fact many Ethiopians did not want Eritrea's separation, but once it was separated, the Ethiopians wanted it to be complete. But the Eritreans wanted to use Ethiopia, to have their cake as well as eat it. So that is why many people have supported the TPLF [in this war]; not out of love for TPLF policies, or the belief that the TPLF is a good government, or a good party. But to settle that historical wound with Eritrea, that Eritrea is found to be the source of the problem. So I think that is what the TPLF has benefited from; in fact many people are encouraging the TPLF to take even stronger measures against the Eritreans. (Personal communication)

Admassou Gebeyihu, the chairman of the Ethiopian Democratic Party (EDP), the most prominent multi-ethnic opposition party in Ethiopia at that time, had a similar interpretation to that of Merera Gudina of the reasons behind the popular support of the war.

Before the two groups of the TPLF and the EPLF were working together to suppress and oppress the entire country and to get the fringe benefit from every corner of the country and carry it to either Tigray or Eritrea. People from all walks of life were very much terrified by the joint forces of these two groups. So when they quarrelled and started to fight many people were happy. If they did not join in the war themselves, they supported those who did, or they supported the government which wanted to fight the war. But the end result is that the people are hoping that when these two groups fight each other, they will weaken themselves and their grip on power will be more relaxed and people will feel less repression and control. This was the hope of the people and to some extent it was achieved. (Personal communication)

All Ethiopian political parties and fronts, both within Ethiopia and in exile, issued proclamations and statements propounding their view of the war. For some, simple retaliation was important for their support of the war, like the All Amhara People's Organisation (AAPO): 'Since Eritrea is an integral part of Ethiopia, the so-called border dispute between Ethiopia and Eritrea ought to be viewed in this context,'[27] suggesting full support for a war with the objective of re-conquering Eritrea in order to re-annex it as Ethiopia's 14th province. Others had a more complex approach to the issue. A joint statement issued by six political fronts,[28] some within the country and others in exile, was careful to distinguish support for the war-stricken Ethiopian peoples at the border from support for the EPRDF regime. They explained that 'the policies of the TPLF and the EPLF are exposing our country to further division', reassured that 'we give our full support to the people of Tigray and Afar who are bearing the brunt of the EPLF's hostility and aggression', and concluded that 'we call on all the armed forces of the political organisations fighting out in the bush for unity, equality and democracy in Ethiopia, to demonstrate their worth by concentrating their efforts on cooperating with the people of Afar and Tigray who are resisting the EPLF'.[29] Other exiled groups with links to the former Ethiopian regimes were quick to utilise the war to denounce the EPRDF:

> The fact that Meles is half Eritrean can hardly justify his regime's lack of loyalty and integrity to a people of whom he is supposed to be the Prime Minister. His betrayal has been not only of the nation that gave him a country of birth, an identity and the high prestige and dignity as Head of State of one of the oldest free nations in the world, but also of his own Tigre ethnic group. His sudden espousal of the defence of Ethiopia – whose nationhood he has been striving systematically to destroy for the past seven years – sounds hollow and self-serving.[30]

The rhetoric of the Prime Minister's Eritrean descent in particular undermined the EPRDF government's legitimacy in the war and its politics of identity, a point I shall return to below. The exiled-based, pan-Ethiopian opposition party EPRP followed in the same vein and declared:

> We denounce the political regime currently in power in Ethiopia. The Ethiopian people are not new to the national task of defending their borders. Nothing is of greater concern to them than the territorial integrity of their motherland. We are ready to stand by all sides committed to advance the democratisation process in Ethiopia. However, it is strange for the incumbent Ethiopian government to have 'given away the elephant and plunged itself into a full-scale war over its tail'.[31]

The political discourse in Ethiopia during the Eritrean-Ethiopian war did not display a coherent and focused agenda. Several different objectives of and perspectives on the war were promoted by the various political actors, creating a partly fragmented, and contradictory political discourse. Moreover, the discourse among the political elite differed in content from that projected by the 'masses', as represented at the Adwa/Badme celebrations. The political actors expressed divergent goals, inspired and set in motion by the war. Thus, the conventional understanding that when a people is at war its objectives will become uniaxial is challenged by the Ethiopian material.

## STEREOTYPING 'ONESELF' AND THE 'ENEMY'

After the first heated sentiments of the war had calmed down, it was important for the Ethiopian leadership to create a distinction with Eritrea, based not on a primordial nationalist ideology – as projected by some of the Ethiopian opposition groups – but on modern principles of governance, as stressed by the EPRDF leadership. Ethiopia had apparently undergone political liberalisation and democratisation after the EPRDF came to power in 1991. The new Constitution enshrined full human rights protection for Ethiopian citizens, and several so-called democratic elections had been conducted during its tenure. The EPRDF was thus trying to establish legitimacy through an international human rights discourse, and not relying solely on an Ethiopian nationalist discourse.

Strong evidence for such a policy came in a statement issued by the Ethiopian government press spokesperson in the summer of 1999, in connection with the OAU peace negotiations and after several months of repeated Ethiopian offensives along the Badme, Tsorona and Zalambessa front lines. The title of the statement was 'Ethiopia, Eritrea: Approaches to Peace Process Reflect Divergent Systems of Governance.'[32] In the preamble the Ethiopian government criticised the Eritrean President's individualistic and insincere engagement in the peace process, as opposed to 'the Ethiopian government's commitment to democratic procedures and consensus building within the decision-making process'. The statement emphasised that 'The varying approaches of the governments of Ethiopia and Eritrea in regard to implementation of the OAU Framework Agreement should come as no surprise, given that the two governments are diametrically opposed in various ways.' A list of a number of stereotypical characteristics of both themselves and the Eritrean government was provided, stressing the democratic, human rights-oriented values and practises of the Ethiopian government, contrasted with the authoritarian, human rights-abusing values and practices of the Eritrean government:

- *Federal Democratic Republic of Ethiopia*
Ethiopia's democratically elected Constituent Assembly ratified the Constitution in 1994, forming a Federal Democratic Republic with a multiparty system of governance. There are currently 60 registered political parties throughout the country.
- *One-Party State of Eritrea*
Eritrea is a one-party state that forbids the existence of opposition political parties.

- *Federal Democratic Republic of Ethiopia*
Ethiopia will hold its second national elections in May 2000 to elect the Councils of the Federal States and Parliamentarians for the House of Peoples' Representatives.

155

• *One-Party State of Eritrea*
Eritrea has never held any Presidential or Parliamentary elections.

• *Federal Democratic Republic of Ethiopia*
The Ethiopian government is led by the Ethiopian Peoples' Revolutionary Democratic Front (EPRDF), a coalition party comprising other political movements.
• *One-Party State of Eritrea*
Eritrea is ruled autocratically by President Issaias and a small cohort of elites.

• *Federal Democratic Republic of Ethiopia*
Ethiopia's Constitution recognises the rights of all nations and nationalities, including the right to representation at the federal level regardless of a nation's size.
• *One-Party State of Eritrea*
Eritrea does not support cultural diversity or recognise the rights of diverse nations.

• *Federal Democratic Republic of Ethiopia*
Freedom of the press is constitutionally guaranteed and there are 69 privately-owned newspapers in addition to five government papers, nine newspapers owned by religious organisations and six papers run by political organisations.
• *One-Party State of Eritrea*
There is no private press in Eritrea.

• *Federal Democratic Republic of Ethiopia*
Ethiopia has consistently permitted the International Committee of the Red Cross access to prisoners of war and other detainees.
• *One-Party State of Eritrea*
Eritrea has continuously denied the International Committee of the Red Cross access to prisoners of war and other detainees.

• *Federal Democratic Republic of Ethiopia*
Ethiopia respects international law and the sovereignty of its neighbours.
• *One-Party State of Eritrea*
Eritrea has made a habit of aggressive behaviour against its neighbours, including Yemen, Djibouti, Sudan and Ethiopia.

• *Federal Democratic Republic of Ethiopia*
The Ethiopian defence forces consist of volunteers, aside from a small professional army that includes all nations and nationalities, as mandated by the Constitution.
• *One-Party State of Eritrea*
All Eritreans must fulfil a military service requirement and the government has been forcefully conscripting its citizens, including 14-year-old children.

• *Federal Democratic Republic of Ethiopia*
Ethiopia is a signatory to the Geneva Conventions regarding the binding customary rules of warfare, the Ottawa Accord banning the manufacture and use of landmines, as well as various other international conventions.
• *One-Party State of Eritrea*
Eritrea has failed to sign any international conventions and is one of the few countries in the world that has not ratified the Geneva Conventions.

Political elites encourage the construction of stereotypes, of insiders and significant others. To list stereotypes as binaries, as is done here by the Ethiopian press spokesperson, is a common principle of ranking political inequality (Herzfeld 1997: 15). The EPRDF worked hard in both the domestic and the international arenas to present itself as a democratic and human-rights-respecting government. Since the political situation in Eritrea was more oppressive than in Ethiopia, many actors in the international community accepted the democratic legitimacy of the EPRDF (and implicitly the undemocratic practice of the EPLF). However, Ethiopians from various backgrounds did not so easily accept the self-proclaimed classification of the EPRDF as democratic. Party chairman Merera Gudina of the ONC emphasised that the war had not changed the repressive policies of the EPRDF.

> There is no substantive political change at all. In the areas of democratisation, of sharing of power, of accommodating the opposition – nothing has changed. You know those areas still remain the same. What they are trying to do is to mobilise the people in the name of Ethiopian nationalism without making the necessary adjustments or making political accommodation for the opposition. (Personal communication)

The study of the creation of stereotypes has often formed the basis of the analysis of nationalism and national identities. What is often overlooked within this perspective, however, is that official stereotyping – whether of the national self or of some despised 'other' – offers a basis on which power relations can be contested and reproduced at the local level (Herzfeld 1997: 160). I shall pursue this argument as I now turn my focus on the discourse on national identity as it unfolded in the multi-ethnic state of Southern Nation, Nationalities and Peoples Region. Ultimately, one should, of course, have included many different case studies from several regions of Ethiopia, in order to illustrate the variety of perceptions of the Ethiopian polity, and the many competing nationalisms which were projected. However, this is impossible to include in one monograph, so the Hadiya people in Southern Ethiopia are deliberately selected as a case study in order to illustrate this diversity. Who did the Hadiya people consider to be their primary enemy?

157

# Peripheral voices – national discourse

From the point of view of the Abyssinian state and its political culture, the non-Shoan Amhara groups, and southerners in particular, were looked down upon as backward and savage; they became objects of scorn and ridicule, both literally and symbolically. The members of the dominant Shoan Amhara elite, while considering themselves dignified and politically astute, had a stereotypical view of nearly all the ethnic groups, including even the Amhara of the northern provinces. However, none of their views was as demeaning and degrading as their attitude toward the non-Abyssinians, comments Gebru Tareke, who illustrates this with an old Amhara proverb:

> The Gurage is thief, the Gojjame treacherous,
> The Tigrayan is flighty, the Gondare proud.
> The Galla [Oromo] is an animal,
> The Wellamo [Wolaita] slothful and lazy,
> Make sure that power always resides in us. (Tareke 1996: 71–2)

The official discrimination against the southerners came to an end with the fall of the imperial regime in 1974, when the Derg made certain concessions to the southerners. However, it was not until the new ethnic federal system was introduced by the EPRDF in 1991 (formally sanctioned by the new Constitution in 1995), that the southern groups became elevated – at least officially – to an equal status with the highland (*habesha*) groups.

## THE RESISTANCE OF THE HADIYA

The reconfiguration of Ethiopia into an ethnic federation entailed radical changes in the periphery. The Hadiya, as well as other southern groups, were designated as a separate administrative zone.[33] The Hadiya zone is the constituency for the Hadiya National Democratic Organisation (HNDO), one of the best organised and longest running opposition political parties in Ethiopia. The HNDO is a member of the coalition, the Southern Ethiopian Peoples' Democratic Coalition (SEPDC), which again is part of the more recent coalition, the United Ethiopian Democratic Forces (UEDF). The chairman of both the HNDO and the SEPDC is Dr Beyene Petros, a prominent politician and academic scholar.

I had the opportunity to travel in Hadiya for some weeks during the regional and federal elections of May 2000, in order to carry out a study of the election process. This was during the final phase of the war with Eritrea, and two days before election day Ethiopia launched its last big offensive on the Zalambessa-Tsorona front line which finally crushed the

Eritrean military capability to sustain the war. I expected an election campaign inspired by national sentiments created by the war and in support of the EPRDF in their efforts to 'defend the sovereignty' of Ethiopia. What met me in Hadiya, however, was a totally different story. The Ethiopian government's claim that it was a democracy and respected human rights contradicted its practices on the ground, where wide-scale election rigging and human rights abuses occurred (on the 2000 elections in general, see Pausewang and Tronvoll 2000; Pausewang et al. 2002; on the Hadiya elections, see Tronvoll 2001). The abusive human rights context on the ground in Hadiya certainly influenced the discourse on national identity in the periphery and the marking of boundaries of identity.

## CONFRONTING ENEMIES FROM WITHIN AND WITHOUT
Before leaving for Hadiya, I had several discussions with the opposition leader Dr Beyene Petros in Addis Ababa in order to learn his point of view about the conditions in his constituency. Dr Beyene Petros was rather pessimistic, already several months prior to the elections:

> There is a military presence in all four *woreda* (districts) in Hadiya zone. These are external military [federal troops] brought in from the north. They are not neutral security forces, but interfere and take action. They go from house to house, demanding that the peasants produce land taxation receipts. If they can not produce the document, they are beaten and arrested.[34] Then the peasants are asked whether they have registered for voting and whom they intend to vote for. If they say they want to vote for Beyene's party, they are beaten up. There was no reason for starting this kind of activity. There was no prior unrest in the area. The place was absolutely stable, but the peasants are voicing their political preferences. (Personal communication)

Beyene Petros was depressed, due to grave incidents of violence in southern Ethiopia, where supporters of his coalition in certain areas were injured and even killed by government troops and police (EHRCO 2000). However, since these events took place in rural Ethiopia, out of sight of the international community, they could be sustained without much criticism being levelled against the government. The harassment of peasants in Hadiya and elsewhere in the southern region was therefore continuing during the run-up to the elections, but the people were still determined to vote for change. A teacher I met in a small town outside the regional capital Hossana, told me:

> From the point of view of the local population, I can say that 95 per cent will vote for Dr Beyene's party if they are allowed. But there are so many mechanisms used to suppress people. Cadres are going from house to house to persuade the people, they give some grain and money, and

even threaten them. I am a teacher myself and some of us who are government employees are threatened with being transferred to Gambella [considered to be the most peripheral region of the country] if we do not vote 'right'. Yesterday, about 200 federal troops arrived from Awassa and Addis to suppress us. We know the local police and militia, but these are mostly Tigrayans. They do not know our culture and language. These strange people are placed in every *kebele*. We are afraid that the election will be carried out by force and cheating. 'If you don't elect this person, you will not be safe here', is the order given to many peasants. But we will rather die than accept this! Our blood will bring us our freedom! This is the last time we would sacrifice our blood for our freedom!'. (Personal communication)

All over Hadiya, there were similar expressions of resistance and protest against the EPRDF party and government interference (see Tronvoll 2001 for elaboration). The majority of the voters had marked the EPRDF as the enemy – both in a military, political and cultural sense. Many used the metaphor of occupation to describe how they perceived the political situation in Hadiya, with the presence of federal troops in the area observing and suppressing the local population, in addition to a local administration perceived to be under the control of the *Weyane*. Two elderly men I was chatting to in a *bunnabet* (coffee-shop) described the run-up to the election in the following way:

We know that we have the right to choose in a democracy and that no force should be applied to us. We appreciate the EPRDF bringing us democratic practice, but before we get a chance to practise the democratic agenda, they are also introducing force and suppressing us. As the beginning was best, so must the end be too. They cannot let us only smell democracy, now they have to allow us to eat it too! Election is personal and personally one must vote as one desires. Up to now, many military men have arrived to threaten us and make us feel fearful. These men are not our people; they don't know our culture and they cannot understand the physiological pressure we live under. They don't care about us, and we are afraid that they will open fire on us and kill us. (Personal communication)

The same view was endorsed by a middle-aged man who noted our interest in talking about the current political situation. 'We live as if under occupation – Tigrayan troops are all over our land. We are not even safe in our homes,' he claimed. Non-Hadiya people in the area also acknowledged the suppression of the Hadiya. An Amhara civil servant in the local administration explained:

I am not a member of any party. I am originally from Amhara but have been living here in Hadiya for five years working for the government. During this time I have observed the situation closely. The EPRDF is publicly suppressing the Hadiya people ... If people were free to choose, they would surely vote for Beyene's party. But everybody suspects that the election will be manipulated and that the EPRDF will win. This is because the people feel threatened. The federal government has brought in military troops to the area, and they have taken up positions throughout Hadiya zone. If they start fighting, the Hadiya people will bring their ancient weapons out of their huts – swords and spears – and fight back … They are a very brave people who do not want war, but I think they have reached a limit now. (Personal communication)

## NATIONALISM AGAINST ETHNICITY

Although many families had sent their sons to the war-front in the north, they still regarded the government as the main enemy. This was not only based on resistance to the wide-scale political repression in the area. The enemy image of the EPRDF was also based on a more policy-oriented factor. Despite their multi-ethnic character and partly peripheral status, the peoples of the southern region of Ethiopia have in modern times generally supported the integrity and sovereignty of the Ethiopian state. They generally consider themselves as 'good Ethiopians', as one informant explained. They were fiercely against the Eritrean invasion, and accused the EPRDF of mismanagement, of not being prepared for the conflict. Also in this regard Beyene Petros and his family stand out as prominent nationalists. Beyene's brother, Colonel Beshaby Petros, is the best known Ethiopian prisoner of war in Eritrea. Beshaby is a veteran fighter-jet pilot, serving in the air force both during the Derg regime and under the EPRDF. He was shot down and captured by the EPLF in the 1980s, while bombing EPLF positions in northern Eritrea. During several years of captivity, he was 're-ideologised' and transferred into the custody of the TPLF. When the new war erupted in 1998, Beshaby was once again called to action – and once again shot down and captured by the EPLF, this time over Asmara. Thus, the personal courage exhibited by Beyene Petros' family fighting for Ethiopia was well known and often referred to as an example for others to follow.

An important element of the Hadiya resistance to the central government was hence based on a nationalist ideology, rejecting the ethnic policies of the EPRDF. Both Hadiya intellectuals and peasants took a critical stand against the EPRDF ethnic policies, which, it was argued, undermined the brotherhood and integrity of the Ethiopian state. A popular song heard during the election campaign, called 'The voice of the people of Hadiya', conveyed these concerns: 'Disunity – we do not wish for. Let the wise unify and lead us together. We should forsake ethnic warfare.'

Travelling throughout Hadiya during the time of war and elections in May 2000, I was struck by the contradictory concern for Ethiopia's integrity and peace, and accusations against the divisive policies of the EPRDF government, the very same government that portrayed itself as the defender of Ethiopia's sovereignty. In the midst of a bilateral war against an enemy state, the government party was losing the grassroots constituency since, as it was argued, they were against Ethiopian unity! It is a paradox that the people of Hadiya would accuse the EPRDF of being 'anti-Ethiopian unity' at a time when EPRDF politicians and military commanders were trying to capitalise politically on the war with Eritrea. A middle-aged peasant in Sorro district in Hadiya explained his political preferences in the midst of this political turmoil.

> I am a supporter of Beyene's party since the EPRDF is looking down on us as slaves. They have openly stated that 'we came to power by 17 years of struggle. Now, when we bring democracy to you, you want to bring our regime to an end. If a hand does not vote for the EPRDF, he can get one of two things: a bullet or torture to death.' ... Beyene we like because of his political programme. He strives for unity. He does not separate Amhara from Hadiya, Gurage from Hadiya, or Kambata. ... But the EPRDF has another agenda – its agenda is the division and separation of nationalities, creating quarrels among the population. Because of this, we love Beyene for his words and programme, and reject the EPRDF. ... We have seen since 1992 and onwards that EPRDF simply cheats [to make] people vote for its leadership. The people have never elected their own leaders voluntarily, but the EPRDF is doing it by manipulation. An Ethiopian is not left alone to freely live his life, because the EPRDF interferes in every political and economic aspect of life of the individual. (Personal communication)

The sentiment of political resistance to EPRDF repression and divisive politics, and the praise and glorification of the wisdom of Beyene Petros, was the topic of many songs heard at rallies and opposition meetings. One of these songs was simply called 'Dr Beyene':

> By unifying the people
> Enabling them to join their hands together
> Vanquishing those who want to disintegrate the society
> And those who want to destroy brotherhood
> And who try to estrange the people from each other.
> Those who want to disturb the peace of the people,
> By extinguishing cooperation and harmony.
> Those who creates chaos,
> Who sow distrust among the nations.
> Defeat them all –
> and re-establish harmony and love among the people.
> Lead the people into brotherhood and cooperation.
> The people say let us raise our hands and vote for such a man!

Many of the songs highlighted the extraordinary qualities of the opposition leader Beyene Petros, in contrast to the weak performance of the EPRDF party representatives. Beyene Petros was a 'man of the pen', as it was phrased – highly educated and a professor of biology at Addis Ababa University. The EPRDF cadres were often ridiculed as being uneducated peasants or school drop-outs who did not have the skills and knowledge necessary to run the country; they were only trained in guerrilla warfare. Moreover, Beyene and his party, it was stressed, were the legitimate representatives of all ethnic groups, not only the Hadiya, contrary to the EPRDF which was seen as a Tigrayan-dominated party. The popular song 'What are the people saying, in which direction is the wind blowing?' conveyed such points.

> He is always in the company of wise men,
> He went to all places searching for and accumulating immense knowledge,
> He brought it to his people and used it for the welfare of his nation.
> In his commitment to the well being and development of his people,
> He labours day and night.
> He is a man of knowledge
> He has worked both for his own people and for others,
> The son of Badawacho [his birth district] – Hadiya people
> The pioneer of development
>
> So let us elect this man – Beyene!
> Say the people;
> For the Hadiya and the Kambata,
> The Oromo and all Ethiopians
> He serves all without discrimination.
> Beyene is better than anybody in leading Ethiopians the right way,
> So let us elect in unison this man – Beyene who can really serve us.
>
> The Ethiopian peoples pray to God,
> So that his creatures can live in peace.
> But the devil sowed discord among us,
> and brought about ethnic strife.
> But we cling to our unity.
> So, let all hands be raised as one.
> To elect that man of vast knowledge.
> To elect Beyene who is concerned about us all.
> The man with immense wisdom and who thinks broadly,
> Let us all elect him – this man Beyene!

Beyene Petros' party, the HNDO, did win an overwhelming victory within their constituency in the regional and federal elections, despite massive and wide-scale government intimidation and election fraud (Tronvoll 2001). However, the political situation at the grassroots did not change, since the opposition delegates in the regional and federal assemblies are a small minority, and thus do not have any influence on shaping the policies of the EPRDF government (Pausewang et al. 2002).

## THE 'IRRELEVANCE' OF THE PERIPHERY

After the elections in mid-May 2000, the political discourse in Addis Ababa focused mainly on the final military offensive against Eritrea, and the conduct and outcome of the elections were secondary. Immediately after my return to Addis Ababa from Hadiya, I went to the Ethiopian Foreign Ministry to interview Yemane 'Jamaica' Kidane, *chef de cabinet* and senior TPLF cadre, about the situation. He was elated by the successful offensive, and did not want to talk about the problems of elections.

> The entire [Eritrean] front collapsed in one day! We out-flanked them and they were retreating desperately. We therefore followed after them. We learned after Badme that they will not give up. At that time we stopped at the border, which gave them time to regroup and to continue the war. This time we will not stop until they are defeated militarily. We will push and settle this by force, once and for all. They will no longer pose a threat to us. No matter if there are sanctions from the UN or others. The United States can impose 10,000 sanctions on us, but the war will continue until the defeat of *Shabiya*. (Personal communication)

Yemane Kidane and the EPRDF elite in Addis Ababa appeared not to be aware of, or did not care about, the deep and sincere anti-EPRDF sentiments at the grassroots in the south. The fact that, from a Hadiya viewpoint, the EPRDF meant 'anti-Ethiopia' and that they were considered to be the primary enemy of Ethiopian unity and integrity, seemingly fell on deaf ears in Addis Ababa. The following day I visited Beyene Petros, who expressed strong disappointment with the election rigging. He was particularly upset at the use of the war to rally support for the government, in order to eclipse the election rigging on the ground.

> The EPRDF is desperate and wanted public support. They had been saying that they could not campaign because they were preoccupied with fighting the war with Eritrea. They were appealing for mass support since they were seriously engaged in the war. Another thing is that this was useful to divert international attention away from the elections. The embassies cancelled almost all observer missions due to the offensive, which hurt our candidates badly. In diverting attention to the war, the EPRDF could continue their dirty game on the ground. (Personal communication)

Many national and international observers believed that it was no coincidence that the offensive began only two days prior to election day. This enabled the government to 'kill two birds with one stone', as it was phrased. First, it was able to capitalise on popular, nationalistic sentiments in the election. Secondly, international attention was diverted from the elections, allowing wide-scale election fraud. The problematic issue of launching the military offensive just before election day, was partly acknowledged by Dawit Yohannes, Speaker of the Parliament and senior EPRDF spokesperson, when I challenged him on this point after the election.

There are three major issues confronting Ethiopia now: the war, drought and elections. A crucial time for Ethiopia, and despite the invasion and drought, we would not hesitate to carry out the elections and the constitutional process. ... Despite some tragic events in the south, the struggle over politics is positive. In such a manner it symbolises that people are getting on their feet to struggle for local politics. It is the first time that such a political struggle has been able to be carried out in Ethiopia. (Personal communication)

Dawit Yohannes did also acknowledge that opposition politics is difficult in Ethiopia, due to the rural composition of the electorate, as he explained it:

It is a question of political culture to accept that opposition is part of national politics. This is a new situation in Ethiopia. But the rural population is very rigid and it will take a very long time to change. This is why the opposition parties have such problem to gain a stronghold in rural areas. (Personal communication)

Due to the wide-scale election rigging and intimidation of voters, the National Electoral Board ordered fresh elections in several constituencies in southern Ethiopia, among others in Hadiya. The second round of elections was, according to international observers, conducted in a more satisfactory manner (Pausewang et al. 2002).

## THE EPRDF 'DISEMIA'

As shown above, the political discourse on national identity and enemy images was formulated and projected differently within the social fields of the Ethiopian masses during the victory celebrations, within a political elite segment in Addis Ababa, and among an ethnic minority in the Ethiopian periphery. What follows from the analysis of these three discursive fields is an understanding of the competing and contradictory views of defining the national among both the masses and elites, in the centre and at the periphery. Moreover, a host of relevant others/ enemies, with which the national was contrasted, can be identified. The EPRDF nationalist rhetoric of war and the Hadiya discourse of Ethiopian identity show that the EPRDF government is caught up in what Herzfeld terms *disemia*: 'the formal or coded tension between official self-presentation and what goes on in the privacy of collective introspection' (1997: 14). The EPRDF was at first reluctant to officially endorse the 'Greater Ethiopia' nationalism, since it was the antithesis of its ethnic-based ideology, but on several occasions it did so anyway. It accepted and facilitated, however, a popular, demotic expression of symbols conveying the notion of a 'Greater Ethiopia'.

Furthermore, the official EPRDF discourse made a binary distinction between Ethiopia and Eritrea based on respect for and implementation of international human rights and democratic liberties, with Eritrea portrayed as a dictatorial regime in contrast to a democratic Ethiopia. The EPRDF government, however, continued to violate human rights and democratic liberties and subdued domestic criticism, since this would undermine its self-presentation within the war discourse on national identity. Within this context of parallel discourses, several over-lapping and contradictory enemy-images were produced and endorsed. Eritrea was generally portrayed as a main enemy, but the EPRDF was also classified by many as an enemy. For the outside observer, this may seem like an untenable situation. Ethiopians, however, managed to participate in, switch between, and comprehend these discourses simul-taneously without much difficulty.

# Re-establishing Ethiopianness in Tigray

The war reshaped identities all over Ethiopia, as sentiments of Ethiopianness were interpreted and negotiated differently by variously situated actors. Before concluding this chapter, let us re-visit Tigray, in order to see how Ethiopian nationalism was re-established in this heartland of TPLF ethnic ideology. I revisited the field area in Wuqro in Tigray after the final Ethiopian offensive had led to the *de facto* Eritrean capitulation in May 2000. Although the situation was still tense and emotions were running high, the impressions conveyed to me were more or less uniform. For instance, the *tabia* chairman in Negash explained:

> In the old times, in all periods up to the start of the war, there were separate feelings of identity within Ethiopia. Let alone between the different nationalities, there were also parochial identities within Tigray itself [*awrajanet*]. But the war has killed these identities, and an all-embracing Ethiopian identity has emerged. (Personal communication)

A similar view was also argued by Miriam, the local WAT leader of Wuqro. Her fighter husband rejoined the TPLF army immediately after the Eritrean invasion, and one son was mobilised and sent to the war-front in 1999. Both of them were injured in combat, but luckily they survived. Miriam was quite definite in her opinion about the new relations created by the war:

> The war has created a permanent closure between Eritrea and Tigray; we will never again be like brothers. ... However, sometimes it is even

possible to say that Issaias did well in invading us. We are only a short drive from Eritrea here. He could have occupied all Tigray. But thanks to the heroic people of Amhara, they came and saved us. They are now our brothers. The war was as such a good testing ground for us to identify our real brothers, the people of Ethiopia. (Personal communication)

The identity boundary between Tigrinya-speaking Eritreans and Tigrayans, from being a boundary that used to establish a cross-boundary identity, was re-conceptualised by the war as a boundary of separation and dichotomisation. Simultaneously, the opposite effect could be observed with respect to the boundary between Tigrayans and Amhara, which was played down in order to create a feeling of brotherhood between the two formerly distinct groups. A similar reconceptualisation of boundaries took place between other groups, too. For instance, another of Miriam's sons had just managed to return from Eritrea where he had been for three years doing wage labour when I visited the household in July 2000. He made the following observations on the changing perceptions of enemies and friends, based on his experiences from Eritrea:

The situation created by the war is indeed surprising and strange. For instance, we never used to consider the Kunama and the Tigre as human beings.[35] We felt that the *Kebessa* [highlanders] were our brothers – they were similar to us in language, religion and culture. But those we were considering to be our brothers became our invaders. And those who we did not even consider to be human, they were our true brothers and supporters. Yes, it is indeed strange. (Personal communication)

In the aftermath of the war, Tigrayans were relieved that they had received support from the other ethnic groups in Ethiopia, despite the alleged fragmenting effect of the ethnic federal system. The claim made by the Eritrean President Issaias Afwerki at the start of the war in 1998, that the ethnic federation had destroyed an Ethiopian feeling of nation-hood and the capacity for unity, was put to shame. Teame Medhin, an elder Tigrayan farmer, offered the following explanation:

Take my home. I have ten children. During the day they quarrel and fight each other, but during the night everybody sleeps peacefully under the same roof. Then they have one language [snoring]. Is it for a joke that we elected an Oromo as President? No, we know that he is our brother and we are Ethiopians. Being a Tigrayan, Amhara or Oromo does not matter; such feelings of separate identities have gone. They will not take us anywhere. The Eritrean invasion and war might have dealt a final blow to the existence of separate identities in Ethiopia. (Personal communication)

Being in a state of war, the sentiments of unity and nationalism as created by the war were, of course, exaggerated by most Tigrayans. However, one of the few individuals who did not attribute the re-emergent feeling of Ethiopianness to the effect of the war was Wode Goshu, the deputy *woreda* administrator in Wuqro. Being a battle-hardened and loyal political cadre, he tried to present the spirit of nationhood as a natural feeling for Ethiopians, forgetting that by such a claim he was undermining the core 'ethnic' ideology of the TPLF (as emphasised prior to the war).

> This feeling of Ethiopianness is not something the war has brought. Basically it is not created by the war. It was there before. Not merely an Ethiopian identity, it has been an African identity not to be ruled and colonised by others. This feeling has been flowing in our blood and veins. At least we have felt like this since the battle of Adwa [in 1896]. This feeling was further consolidated and enlivened during the 17-years-of-struggle. And, finally, after the overthrow of the Derg, EPRDF politics have consolidated an Ethiopian identity. (Personal communication)

When I confronted him with the pre-war TPLF/EPRDF stated ideology of 'anti-Ethiopianness', and Meles Zenawi's pre-war expressions that the 'Ethiopian flag was just a piece of cloth', and that the 'Ethiopian nation was just a territory hosting so-and-so many national-ities', Wode Goshu fell silent. After a while he rejected my question by saying that those statements had to be explained by the people making them. However, a more experienced and diplomatically trained TPLF cadre, Yemane 'Jamaica' Kidane, at the Ethiopian Foreign Ministry, managed to capitalise both on Ethiopia's proud history of nationalism and defence of the country, whilst simultaneously remaining loyal to the TPLF/ERPDF ideology of ethnic federalism. When I interviewed him after the fighting had ceased in the summer of 2000, he acknowledged that the war had had a formative impact on Ethiopian identities.

> The war has brought the people together. As is traditional in Ethiopia, an outside threat brings us together. Historically Ethiopia has always been federated. We had princes, kings, and a king of kings. So, historically we can say that Ethiopia was a federation. Haile Selassie and Mengistu tried to centralise, but they failed. The survival of Ethiopia is not as a centralised state, but a federal one. Before, you had to negate your ethnicity to be Ethiopians. A Somali is a Somali; an Oromo is an Oromo, an Afar an Afar, and so on. But they are also proud to be an Ethiopian. You cannot negate your ethnic background to be an Ethiopian. I am both a Tigrayan and Ethiopian. These identities are complementary. The cohesiveness created during the war was not there in 1995 [when the ethnic federal system was established]. The emphasis has shifted a bit. Before the war, the form was 'first the ethnic group, then Ethiopia'. Now it has first been Ethiopia, then the ethnic identity. Due to the circumstances of war, this shift happened. From now onwards, however, we will go back to the ethno-regional

emphasis, since the national focus is no longer needed to that degree. (Personal communication)

Jamaica demonstrated an instrumentalist understanding of war, i.e. its mobilising capacity and effect on Ethiopian nationalism. He viewed the many ethnic identities in Ethiopia as nested within an Ethiopian national identity, in which the primary repository for identification shifts according to the perceived external threat to Ethiopia. As such, Yemane 'Jamaica' Kidane advocated a cohesion-theory approach to the understanding of the formation of identities in war. However, such an approach, I believe, is too simplistic. For instance, the cohesion theory does not manage to explain the subaltern discourses of identity which also take place during war. Furthermore, such a theoretical paradigm does not shed enough explanatory light on the constant shifts of identity and alliances, both individual and collective, which also unfold during war. In other words, it does not properly reflect the fact that a boundary of identity can simultaneously work both as a distinction in separating identities and as a connection in establishing cross-boundary identities.

In this regard, some of the peasants of Tigray exhibited a more sophisticated understanding of the mechanisms of boundary creation during the war. Let me cite three such explanations given by my Tigrayan informants in the aftermath of the war. Miriam elaborated on her explanation of the change in relations cited above, in which she emphasised the growing distinctions between the Tigrinya-speaking Eritreans and Ethiopians created by the war. Subsequently, she focused on the connections created across the boundary to the Amhara:

In the old days we were closer to the Eritreans, because we had the same language and culture. But now our brothers have turned out to be our foes. Even when it comes to the Amhara, yes, we have different languages. The only barrier we had was the language and we did not have any kinship links. But because of the war, they sided with us. Hence we proved that the language was not a real dividing line. And from now onwards, the relationship with the Amhara will be strengthened. (Personal communication)

Miriam's son also emphasises this shift in cross-boundary connections: 'Certainly, the war has, at least temporarily, closed the chapter of the historical relationship with the *Kebessa*. But it has narrowed the gap and created a new chapter of relationship and brotherhood with the Amhara.' Teame, the elderly peasant quoted above, was more specific in his analysis of the emergence of a Tigray-Amhara identity, stressing the importance of language as an identity-maker:

Even if our children [Tigrayans] are learning in Tigrinya and hence developing the Tigrinya language, this is not at the expense of Amharic.

169

We know that Amharic is the national language and learning Tigrinya has its boundaries. We know that Amharic is a bridge that helps us connect and communicate with our Ethiopian brothers. (Personal communication)

The Eritrean-Ethiopian war created a new political context in which former cultural brothers and political allies became enemies, and vice versa. The above reflections made by the Tigrayans themselves on these shifts of identity clearly indicate that the concept of boundaries, if understood as something that both distinguishes and connects, is also a notion that they can subscribe to. This also confirms Barth's (1969) contention that the substance of ethnicity responds to the nature of the boundary, as the Tigrayans redefined their cultural content to align it more closely with the Amhara (*Habesha*) sphere, thereby distancing themselves from the *Kebessa* Eritreans.

## Ethiopianness: a Janus-faced nationalism?

National identity is made up of a set of ideas and notions manifested, created and sustained through symbols, myths, rituals and actions. Symbolic expressions of nationalism may, from an outside macro-oriented perspective, seem to contain a homogenous and consolidated interpretation of the great national narrative of the state, generally subscribed to and endorsed by both government and citizenry. However, the intrinsic quality of symbols and rituals is ambiguity and multi-vocality, in combination with their potential for great emotional impact and the capacity to mobilise people. Symbols have different meanings for different actors in the same context, and different meanings for the same actor in different contexts. Moreover, the same symbol may even have diverse and conflicting meanings for the same individual in the same context (Kertzer 1988: 69). Herein lies the power of symbols: that a symbol may convey meaning and understanding to a great variety of people in the same setting. As such, symbols enable people to experience and express their affiliation to a group or state without compromising their own individuality. Indeed, the members of a group may not even recognise the idiosyncratic understandings which others have of their shared symbols, so that they are unaware of alternative interpretations (Cohen 1994b: 17–19).

This fact helps to explain the massive support for the EPRDF government's war against Eritrea as, *inter alia*, displayed during the 1999 Adwa celebrations. The symbols of nationalism as exhibited during the celebrations were perceived differently by the people participating in the event: some understood it as support for the EPRDF, others as a manifestation of 'Greater Ethiopia' nationalism – a notion antithetical to the EPRDF.

The nationalist idea is to create homogeneity out of the realities of heterogeneity that characterise all states, by creating national myths of cultural commonness and symbols of uniqueness that distinguish the people of the state. The effect of nationalism is that it 'reifies culture in the sense that it enables people to talk about their culture as though it were a constant' (Eriksen 1993a: 103). As shown in this chapter, however, the popular image of Ethiopia is not singular. There exist several parallel and competing notions of Ethiopian nationalism. No doubt the Eritrean-Ethiopian war did re-ignite Ethiopian nationalism, but in plural forms.

National identity is a double-edged relationship, defined both from within and from without. From within, the Ethiopian myth of origin and its sacred territory in principle unites all Ethiopian citizens, and forms the foundation upon which their national identity is established. However, the EPRDF's hegemonic identity discourse prior to the Eritrean–Ethiopian war challenged the existence of an Ethiopian nation, claiming that the Ethiopian territory was just a territory without any national identity attached to it. With the outbreak of the war, on the other hand, an immediate re-emergence and consolidation of the boundaries of the nation occurred, inspired by both government and demotic initiatives. But a myth, some symbols and a territory are not enough to create an identity; an understanding of identity is always constituted in interaction with others. Triandafyllidou writes that 'the history of each nation is marked by the presence of significant others that have influenced the development of its identity by means of their "threatening" presence' (Triandafyllidou 1998: 600). The Derg-Ethiopia had the Eritrean and Tigrayan resistance forces as the contrasting other. However, when the EPRDF toppled the Derg in 1991 and established friendly relations with the new independent state of Eritrea, Ethiopia simultaneously lost its contrasting other. For the new EPRDF government, with its stress on ethnic equality and autonomy, this was no loss since in its view the Ethiopian nation no longer existed. During the pre-Eritrean war period (1991–97), Ethiopia passed through a period of gradual nation-withering, in which its citizens' allegiances to the imagined nation waned and the loyalty to their respective ethnic groups increased. It was the eruption of the Eritrean-Ethiopian war in 1998 that transformed internal diversity into a notion of distinctness with the advent of the new significant other – Eritrea (cf. Bringa 1995; Conversi 1995; 1999).

However, even though Eritrea came to represent the new overall enemy for many Ethiopians, other enemy images were also maintained and constructed. In other words, the boundary of the nation was interpreted differently by the many groups caught within it. For many, the EPRDF government was still an enemy that had captured the state, although it was a secondary enemy in comparison with Eritrea. Although the Eritrean-Ethiopian war did create an idea of a master-enemy for a brief period of time (in particular during the main military offensives), several other enemy-images were also created and sustained simultaneously, thus blurring the categorical distinction between the in-group – the nation – and the out-group – the enemy.

There were two groups of people on Ethiopian territory, however, who were, from the point of view of the authorities, marked out as clear 'inner' enemies of the state, namely, Ethiopians of Eritrean origin and the Oromo political opposition. As the war developed, the Ethiopian government's policies on who belonged within the Ethiopian nation and who were considered alien were sharpened, resulting in the identification of the nation's malcontents, a process discussed in the next chapter.

# Notes

1   The current national holidays of Ethiopia are: Ethiopian New Year (Sep. 1 EC/Sep. 11 GC), Meskel festival (Sep17/Sep27), Id aifater/Ramadan (Dec.18/Dec.27), Ethiopian Christmas (Dec.29/Jan.7), Ethiopian Epiphany (Jan.11/Jan.19), Establishment of TPLF/Commencement of the Tigrayan revolution (Feb.11/Feb.18), Victory of Adwa (Feb.23/March2), Id al Adaha/Arafa (Feb.27/March6), International Women's Day (Feb.29/March8), Ethiopian Good Friday (April5/April13), Ethiopian Easter Day (April7/April15), International Labour Day/May Day (April23/May1), Patriots' victory day (April27/May5), Downfall of the Derg (May20/May28), Birthday of the Prophet Mohammed (May27/June4), and Martyrs' day (June15/June22).
2   19 February is still commemorated, but not marked as an official holiday.
3   The first events described refer to incidents which happened soon after the TPLF takeover in 1991. During 1991–2, in certain areas of Ethiopia the EPRDF did not manage to establish full political/military control. Local groups thus capitalised on the lack of state presence in order to settle old grievances, resulting in, *inter alia*, the 'ethnic cleansing' of Amhara settlers (*neftenya*) from Oromo areas. The latter incident, the Awassa massacre, took place in May 2002, when a group of peasants were marching into Awassa city to demonstrate against the decision to make Awassa a 'Chartered city' (i.e. 'de-ethnify the city's status as the Sidama capital). The riot police opened fire on the demonstrators just outside the city centre, killing some 30–40 people.
4   *Dagim Wonchif*, 28 May 2002; reproduced and translated by *Press Digest*, 30 May 2002, p.8.
5   Interview with Eritrean television 8 July 1998, written transcripts published under the title 'No solution can be attained through force,' *Eritrea Profile*, July 1998.
6   *Wayen* 25 Tiqemt 1991/5 November 1998, No. 318, vol. 23.
7   Hayelom Araya was killed in Addis Ababa during a bar-fight in 1995. A man of Eritrean origin, Jamil Yasin Mohamed, was sentenced to death for the killing. At the time of the killing, there were a number of conspiracy theories concerning the 'actual' reason for the event, i.e. as a deliberate act perpetrated by Issaias Afwerki to get rid of a competent Ethiopian general and the threat to Eritrea's interest in the region. Others speculated that the killing was ordered by Meles Zenawi, in order to get rid of a strong competitor for the post of party chairman. Jamil Yasin Mohamed appealed against his death sentence, but nothing was heard of the case until 4 June 1998 when he became the first person to be executed under EPRDF rule. The timing of the execution was obviously linked to the Eritrean invasion, and it is plausible to believe that the Ethiopian government used the case of Jamil Yasin Mohamed to herald its new 'anti-Eritrean' policies.
8   *Gumaya* is an exclamatory term used in southern Tigray to inspire people to go to

war/to fight. It can be translated both as a hero and a murderer.

9  *Wayen* 6 Meskerem 1991/ 16 September 1998, No. 311, vol. 23.

10  Number given by Yemane 'Jamaica' Kidane, at that time Chief of Cabinet in the Ministry of Foeirgn Affairs, to me in an interview on 2 March 1999. According to the Ethiopian government spokesperson, the Eritrean forces defending Badme were composed of 40,000 troops, hundreds of heavy artillery and 70 tanks (statement 'Total Victory for Operation Sunset', 28 February 1999). In order to counter this, the Ethiopian forces must have been at least on a par with the Eritrean forces.

11  Eritrean presidential adviser Yemane Gebremeskel told the international press that Ethiopia had faced losses of 9,000 dead and 12,000 wounded (Reuters and AFP, 28 February 1998), whereas the Ethiopian press spokesperson reported that the Ethiopian defence forces had 'captured, killed and wounded tens of thousands of enemy army personnel' (statement of 28 February 1998). None of the numbers have been verified by independent sources.

12  See 'Ethiopians celebrate victory over Italians, Eritreans', Associated Press, 2 March 1999.

13  See also 'Ethiopia celebrates success over Eritrea', Reuters, 2 March 1999.

14  'Statement by H.E. Ambassador Duri Mohammed, Permanent Representative of the Federal Democratic Republic of Ethiopia to the United Nations Before the Adoption of the Draft Resolution on the Situation between Ethiopia and Eritrea,' 11 February 1999, UN Security Council, New York.

15  'The people of Ethiopia who have maintained their independence for thousands of years, on their own and against all odds, had once the misfortune of placing full confidence in collective security. The frustration and the disappointment they faced in this regard is highlighted by the infamy the League of Nations is known for. The imposition of an arms embargo by the League of Nations on Italy, the colonial aggressor, and on Ethiopia, the victim of colonial aggression, is still fresh in the memories of the Ethiopian people. The League of Nations felt the steps were necessary for peace and because equity demanded that the League be even-handed. This looks farcical now because subsequent events have made most wiser and able to see the injustice behind the decision and the double standard for which the League of Nations is remembered. But double standards hardly seem to have died with the League of Nations. It is Ethiopia's fate again as a victim to be treated in the same way as the aggressor.' Statement by the Foreign Ministry: 'Ethiopia's response to the Latest Security Council Resolution', 15 February 1999, Ministry of Foreign Affairs, Addis Ababa.

16  See, for instance, statement by Gebru Asrat, the regional president of Tigray, during the TPLF anniversary celebrations in Mekelle, 'Ethiopia determined to fight for respect of sovereignty: Gebru Asrat', *Ethiopian Herald*, 19 February 1999.

17  See Resolution 01/1999 of the House of People's Representatives of the Federal Democratic Republic of Ethiopia: 'On the war of aggression by Eritrea against Ethiopia and on the resolution of the United Nations Security Council No. 1227/1999', 1 March 1999, The Federal Parliament of Ethiopia, Addis Ababa.

18  *The Reporter* (in Amharic), 18 September 1999.

19  *Chibutto* is an Ethiopian variety of thin, flat bread that easily breaks into small pieces when crushed.

20  '*Gud*' is a Tigrinya exclamatory word denoting surprise at what has happened and expressing determination to resist it.

21  The main trench-line which Ethiopian troops confronted at the Badme front was called Matewo (i.e. Matthew).

22  The term *wefer* is here translated as 'march'. However, the verb from which it derives also signifies the encouragement to take up arms, to be ready for a fight, to be vigilant, etc.

23  *Garawayna* is a big barrel which is used to prepare *tej* (mead) and *tella* (beer).

24  *Wayen*, 30 Megabit 1991/ 8 March 1999, No. 340, vol. 24.

25  *Wayen*, 30 Megabit 1991 EC, No 340 (8 March 1999, GC).

26 Translated from transcripts published in *Wayen*, 27 Genbot 1990/4 June 1998, No. 297, Vol. 23 (my emphasis).

27 See *Addis Tribune*, 'Political Parties' Declarations on the Ethio-Eritrean War', 19 June 1998. AAPO has later been re-named the All Ethiopian People's Organisation (AEPO).

28 Afar Revolutionary Democratic Unity Front, Coalition of Ethiopian Democratic Forces, Gambella National Democratic Alliance, Moa Anbessa, Southern Ethiopian People's Democratic Coalition, and Tigray Alliance for National Democracy.

29 'Joint Statement of Ethiopian Opposition', 12 June 1998.

30 International Ethiopian Action Committee: 'Ethio-Eritrean Border Conflict', 26 May 1998.

31 See *Addis Tribune*, 19 June 1998. See also EPRP statement 'Meles must not be allowed to hijack the anti-EPLF campaign', 26 May 1998.

32 Issued by the FDRE Office of the Government Spokesperson on 25 August 1999, Addis Ababa.

33 The Hadiya are approximately one million people (according to the 1994 census) of the Cushitic language family with mixed religion, living in southern Ethiopia. They are predominantly hoe cultivators and they harvest *ensete*, in addition to several types of cereals. Coffee is the main cash crop. Historically the Hadiya was organised as an independent kingdom, at least from the fourteenth century (Markakis 1974). The Hadiya king was periodically forced to pay tribute to the Ethiopian emperor, before the Oromo migration cut off Abyssinian influence in the area in the seventeenth century. The Hadiya fought fiercely against Menelik's expansion of the Ethiopian state in the late nineteenth century, but in 1888 their resistance struggle was crushed and they were subdued by the central government (Zewde 1991).

34 A common method employed by the government in intimidating peasants' support of the opposition was to demand payment for land taxation and fertiliser loans before they were normally due. There is usually a grace period up to June for these payments due to the marketing of the harvest.

35 Two minority ethnic groups straddling the border area between Eritrea and Tigray, and Sudan, Ethiopia and Eritrea respectively. The relationship between these groups and the Christian highlanders has historically been hostile.

# Seven

## Ethiopia & its Malcontents
### Purifying the Nation

Socially created identities refer not only to a relevant other, but are also linked to space and territory – whether individuals belonging to the family farm, the ethnic group's identification with a homeland, or the nation's claim to a specific territory of the state. As such, land is not only a territory considered as an exclusive domain of an individual or group, it is also subject to cultural and social organisation and becomes part of individuals' or groups' symbolic representation of the world (Malkki 1992). 'Human societies', writes Mach, 'have physical and conceptual relations between themselves and their land' (1993: 172), relationships which are in a continuous process of creation, maintenance and negotiation.

During certain historical periods the forging of such links between people and their land, as part of a nationalist expression, is much more pertinent and needed. In particular during conflicts and wars, a government needs to produce national symbols in order to legitimate the resources used and the sacrifices offered to protect the 'homeland', as examples in this study show. What is important to keep in mind is that when a nationalist ideology is claiming territorial rights for a specific group of people – and cements this relationship by political, social and cultural means – it not only involves the right of that specific group to inhabit a particular territory; it also implies that other groups of people are not allowed those prerogatives. This may result in an explicit process of identifying 'foreigners', 'aliens' and 'others' in their midst and construing them as enemies. This draws attention to the processes of purifying the nation of its malcontents, processes aimed at creating distinctions where there previously were none (or few). The construction of national boundaries of identity not only influences relationships with and perceptions of people in other countries than your own; it also has a direct impact on relationships and perceptions among the country's own citizenry, as I will show in this chapter.

Since the Eritrean-Ethiopian war was a conflict fought between two countries previously joined together, it inspired a questioning of who was eligible to be a rightful Ethiopian citizen. From that question followed two parallel processes. First, as we have seen, symbols and rituals of national consciousness and territorial sovereignty were promoted by state organs, in order to defend and sustain the notion that not a single inch of land belonging to the Ethiopian nation could be taken away, no matter the cost. Secondly, when the notion of relevant other(s) is linked to territory in times of war, questions of who belong to the in-group and have legitimate claims to the land will be raised. The direct consequence of such a process is the attempted political alignment of 'national identity' with 'national territory' (cf. Gellner 1983); consequently a process of identification of the nation's malcontents – those who do not have any legitimate right to reside on the nation's territory, namely the 'enemies' – began. In the Ethiopian discourse during the war with Eritrea, two groups of people were singled out and stigmatised in this regard: Ethiopians of 'Eritrean descent and origin',[1] and, to a certain degree, politically conscious Oromos supporting the autonomy of Oromia. This chapter will address the discourse surrounding these two cases.

# Purifying the nation: deportations of Eritreans

Throughout the centuries, the rulers of the Ethiopian polity had not distinguished its citizenry according to criteria of ethnicity or descent. Individuals living within the territory of the political realm were by definition subjects of the Ethiopian crown. The effective assimilation policies of the central government also made it possible for individuals of non-*Habesha* origin to aspire to posts at the top level within government or the royal house, as long as they conformed to Amharic language and tradition, and adhered to the Orthodox Christian faith (Clapham 1988: 195). Not even during the thirty years of warfare against Eritrean liberation movements from the early 1960s, did the Imperial government or the Derg regime stigmatise Eritreans – on the basis of ethnic origin or descent only – as a collective enemy of the state. Throughout the war against the Eritrean liberation movements, people of Eritrean origin and descent served in top-level government and military posts. This century-old tradition changed abruptly with the outbreak of the Eritrean-Ethiopian war, in which 'Eritreans' and 'Ethiopians of Eritrean origin or descent' suddenly became stigmatised as the inner enemy and the multi-ethnic nation's malcontents. This resulted in a process of ethnic purging of tens of thousands of Eritreans and Ethiopians of Eritrean origin from Ethiopian territory (75,000 to be exact (HRW 2003a)). It is beyond the scope of this book to go into the full political and juridical context and outcome of these deportations. The focus here

176

is rather on how the policy of deportations influenced the discourse on enemy-images within Ethiopia, following this study's guiding metaphor on 'who is the enemy?'

## THE PROCESS OF 'OTHERING'

At a press conference with the national media on 26 May 1998, only two weeks after the outbreak of war, Prime Minister Meles Zenawi replied as follows to a question as to whether the Ethiopian government had changed its position towards the treatment of Eritreans residing in Ethiopia:

> The EPRDF is of the opinion that it is a grave crime to label grossly any people as enemy. We should try to treat separately government and people. ... This being the case, our attitude toward Eritreans will not change at any rate. If there are individuals who would like to harm the interest of our country, they will bear the consequences individually. The EPRDF can never take any 'anti-people' stand.[2]

The same perception was later advocated by Gebru Assrat, the Regional President of Tigray, on the occasion of the anniversary of the fall of the Derg regime on 28 May 1998, when he explained: 'We have to like and respect the Eritrean people. We should not develop hatred of people as a result of worthless propaganda [of the *Shabiya*]. ... Especially you Eritreans who are in Ethiopia! You are our brothers and the Ethiopian people are your brothers.'[3]

In the immediate aftermath of the outbreak of war, top politicians reassured both the Ethiopian public and Eritreans in Ethiopia that 'Eritreans' still belonged within the Ethiopian nation, and that they had legitimate rights in the Ethiopian state. The Eritreans were 'brothers', as Gebru Assrat described it, brothers in both a cultural and a political sense. However, only a couple of weeks after the statements by Meles Zenawi and Gebru Assrat were made, Eritreans were being rounded up in Addis Ababa and elsewhere. First the Federal Police and Prisons Bureau gave an order that all arms possessed by Eritreans residing in Ethiopia should be handed over to the police before 17 June 1998. Subsequently, a new statement was released ordering 'all Eritrean military personnel, Eritreans who have completed their national service and those who had been to the Sawa Training Centre[4] and are now residing in Ethiopia, to report to their respective or nearest *woreda* police office on June 18.'[5] These first calls to Eritreans residing in Ethiopia were targeting Eritrean citizens with a political and/or military back-ground, a move which by many national and international observers was seen as legitimate for a country at war.

Subsequently, however, other groups of 'Eritreans' were targeted: civil servants of 'Eritrean' origin were put on forced leave, 'Eritrean' merchants and gas-station owners were forced to close down their businesses, etc.[6] On 1 July 1998, the UN High Commissioner for Human Rights issued a statement in which she expressed her deep concern over 'the violation of human rights of Eritrean nationals being expelled from Ethiopia.'[7] The shaming of Ethiopia by the High Commissioner was embarrassing for the EPRDF, which immediately rejected her claims. In an interview on national radio on 9 July 1999, Prime Minister Meles Zenawi made the infamous statement that foreign nationals living in Ethiopia do so based on the goodwill of the Ethiopian government. Thus, Meles explained, 'if we say "go, because we do not like the colour of your eyes," they have to leave' (quoted from Legesse 1999: 55).

Soon, however, it became clear that not only were Eritrean citizens being expelled, but the group of 'Eritrean' malcontents expanded to include people with Ethiopian citizenry too, but of 'Eritrean origin or descent', as it was termed. Several reports were issued by both Eritrean organisations and independent groups describing the uprooting of people in all walks of life: individuals living in Ethiopia all their lives, but who happened to have a parent or grandparent who came from the former Ethiopian province of Eritrea, were detained; children were parted from their parents; and elderly and sick were placed on buses and shipped north to the border where they had to cross on foot to the Eritrean side (AI 1999; Calhoun 1999; HRW 2003b; 1998; 1999; 2000). Also included in the list of potential deportees were all Ethiopians of Eritrean origin who had registered and voted in the Eritrean referendum of 1993. At the time of the referendum, Ethiopians of Eritrean origin were encouraged by the EPRDF to register and vote and no information was given on possible later consequences of such action. After the war broke out, the Ethiopian government interpreted registration in the referendum electoral rolls as an active expression of one's nationality, thus their Ethiopian citizenship was revoked. As of mid-August 1998, 20,000 Eritreans had been deported, and according to some sources, this continued at a rate of 7,000 deportees per month, reaching a total of approximately 75,000 by the end of the war (HRW 2003b). The politics of deportations had an extent and impact on the Ethiopian society at large that cannot be explained by safety precautions only; the politics of deportation became a matter of the EPRDF's identity politics.

It is plausible to argue that the policy of deportations was an attempt by the Ethiopian government to purify the nation; that it was intended to start a process of boundary creation that was so rigid and targeted that it managed to create distinctions where there were hardly any, i.e. between the Tigrinya-speaking Eritreans and Tigrayans residing in Ethiopia for generations. This distinction was vital for the TPLF/ EPRDF government in order to legitimise the different treatment of Tigrinya-speakers originating from the northern shores of the Mereb river from those from the southern shores. To recast the *Kebessa* Tigrinya-speakers as a separate ethnic group was to construe them as aliens to

Ethiopia. Let me now present some of the consequences of such a policy of purity.

## WHERE IS THE ENEMY?

Depending on context and personal life histories, civilian Ethiopians reacted differently to the deportations, and sometimes also in contradictory ways. At Addis Ababa University, all Eritrean exchange students were rounded up and put in a detention camp outside Addis Ababa. Faculty at departments where the students had been affiliated were quiescent about the action of the authorities. In private, however, they vented their opinions, some supportive – others reluctant. One lecturer of social sciences explained to me:

> You must understand that we cannot any longer trust these students, since they are Eritreans. When Issaias states that he has the potential to hit the middle of Addis, all Eritreans are under suspicion of being capable of carrying out some kind of armed attack. We are at war, they are our enemies, so they have to be taken care of. (Personal communication)

The next day, the very same lecturer complained about the 'outrageous' deportations, and referred to an incident in which his neighbour had been taken away to the police station for registration for future deportation – a neighbour he had known for over 25 years:

> It is stupid to think that he [the neighbour] would do us any harm. He is as good an Ethiopian as any. During the revolution [the Derg era], he even served in the army to fight the *Shabiya*. Moreover, when I had trouble and was arrested by the Derg, he helped my family to survive. (Personal communication)

In the first phase of the war, people were confused about the new enemy image. After the nine-month-long build-up to the second phase of armed clashes as a precursor to 'Operation Sunset', many had accepted the enemy image of Eritrea, and expressed clear support for the war and the deportations. A lecturer at the university in his mid-thirties said:

> You foreigners have difficulties in understanding that for us, war is a normal situation. All my life I have experienced war. My brother was killed in Eritrea by the EPLF, and my father was killed by the TPLF when they entered our hometown. It is the seven years of peace between 1991 and '98 that is an abnormality for me. Now, we are back to normal, and we will crush Eritrea once and for all. I hope we will go all the way to Asmara to recapture the whole country. For me all Eritreans are enemies. (Personal communication)

But who exactly were these domestic Eritrean enemies? During the two former regimes of Haile Selassie and the Derg, the Tigrinya-speaking population of northern Ethiopia had been treated as more or less one ethnic group, generally termed either 'Eritreans' or 'Tigrayans' according to the context. Thus, the category 'Eritreans'/'Tigrayans' traditionally connoted Tigrinya-speakers, and not individuals from the geographical entity of either Eritrea (which also incorporates eight other ethnic groups) or Tigray. For non-Tigrinya Ethiopians, it has always been difficult to distinguish between a Tigrinya-speaker from the north side of river Mereb (Eritrea), and those from the southern side (Tigray/Ethiopia). This led to several puzzling incidents, where Tigrayans were accused of being Eritreans, and Eritreans were not deported since they passed as Tigrayans. A good example of this ambiguity was a rumour circulating in Addis Ababa in the early autumn of 1998, about the handling of the Eritrean deportations in the Southern Regional State of the country. The story was that when the political leadership in the southern region was ordered to round up all Eritreans for deportation, they detained all known Tigrinya-speakers. Thereafter, they sent a message to Addis Ababa requesting assistance to distinguish between who were 'Eritreans' and who were legitimate 'Ethiopians' (i.e. Tigrayans), since, as was quoted in the private press, the regional president had said 'to us they all look the same'.[8]

## WHO IS WHO?

It is difficult for many Tigrayans also to distinguish between the two groups of Tigrinya-speakers. A long-time Tigrayan friend shared with me the following story in order to explain the problem of trying to separate the Tigrinya-speakers of Tigray and of Eritrea.

You remember after the EPRDF takeover in 1991, and the subsequent development of ethnic policies, which led to trouble concerning where various people lived. Suddenly you heard that the Oromos and Somalis were claiming that their regions were their land, and Amharas and others who lived there had to move away from their homes. A friend of mine told me about this old Amhara who lived in Wollega [eastern Oromia]. He was married to an Oromo woman, and they had several children together. Then one day he received visitors who demanded that he should go back to Amhara and hand his land over to them, the Oromos. The old man asked why he had to do this, and the Oromos claimed that he was alien to the area, he did not belong there. The old man inquired whether they could do him a favour, before he left his farm. Could they possibly get him a quintal [100 kg] of teff, of white teff?[9] The Oromos went and gathered the white teff, and after some days they were back at the old man's farm and gave it to him. Then he asked if they could possibly get him one quintal of teff, red teff this time. The people thought, 'well, he probably wants this for his travel back home', so they accepted that they should provide him with one quintal of red teff too. When the old man had both sacks of teff in his house, he asked his evictors to pour the teff out on the floor in two separate piles. They did so, and the old man took his stick and mixed the red and white teff into one pile, making it impossible to distinguish the red from the white teff. Then he asked the Oromos if they could separate the red teff from the white, and put the teff back into the two sacks again? The Oromos protested and said 'No, that's impossible. As soon as red and white teff is mixed, it is impossible to separate them again,' they claimed. 'Well', said the old man, 'as the red teff is mixed with the white, so is my Amhara blood mixed with my wife's Oromo blood. Who can separate our children and us? This is where we belong.' (Personal communication)

My friend then concluded his story: 'This is the situation between the Tigrayans and the Eritreans. No one can separate them from each other. Only some few politicians are pushing for that.' Such a view was also endorsed by representatives of the political opposition in the country. The chairman of the pan-Ethiopian party EDP, Admassou Gebeyihu, offered this comment on the deportations to me after the war was over:

Before, the TPLF and the EPLF were working together to suppress the entire country and to get benefit from any corner of the country and carry it off either to Tigray or Eritrea. People from all walks of life were very terrified by the joint forces of these two groups. So when they started to quarrel many people were happy and supported the war on that basis. ... The end result the people were hoping for is that when these two fight then they weaken themselves and the people will suffer less repression and can relax. This was the hope and to some extent it was achieved. ... However, the government has been trying its best – using the media, its cadre system, and everything – to make us hate the Eritreans. But that did not happen because people, as people, have to be respected. So had it been up to the propaganda of the government, I think you would not have seen one single Eritrean left in Ethiopia at this time. It was very difficult; they were claiming that the Eritreans are evil, that they are all spies and everything. But the common people hate all the Tigrayans, [and do not distinguish between] this Tigray or that Tigray. It can be Eritrea, it can be Meles' group, it can be Issaias' group – it is all just [like] one pocket. (Personal communication)

For Admassou and his supporters, all Tigrinya-speakers are the same, and their political representatives work against Ethiopian interests, be that the EPLF or the TPLF. The boundary of identification in this context encompassed all Tigrinya-speakers. To separate the two groups would be to create an artificial distinction where there is none. As such, both groups should be treated on an equal footing, a view similar to that of the Hadiya peasants as presented in the previous chapter. On the other hand, Merera Gudina, the chairman of the Oromo opposition party ONC and a political scientist, drew a parallel between Ethiopia and Idi Amin's Uganda, in order to explain the reactions to the Eritrean deportations.

At the people's level, at the mass level, the deportations are very popular. Because Eritreans were exploiting everything, you know, key businesses, transport, etc. The deportations are a very popular measure, but it is like stupid Idi Amin chasing the Asians out. Many people did not like Idi Amin, but what he did to the arrogant, affluent Asians many Ugandans supported. So many Ethiopians are happy that these people [Eritreans] who held key government positions, key business ventures, occupying a lot of areas, are chased out. (Personal communication)

A senior Ethiopian intellectual of Amhara descent substantiated Merera's interpretation in a confidential talk we had at the height of the deportations. In particular he stressed the tragic effect of the stigmatisation of Eritreans:

Most Ethiopians live in destitution and poverty, with nothing to offer their children. When they now find the comparatively rich Eritreans being targeted and blamed for their problems, they cheer the deportations. When the government says that the Eritreans have been extracting money and goods from Ethiopia, the poor people think they are the cause of their miseries. In addition, we Ethiopians are born to be sceptical and hostile towards outsiders. When the authorities are targeting one group as despised, it gives legitimacy for everyone to fall in line. No one questions the rationale of the government, as long as the politics do not affect him or her. It is just like the old Amhara saying: 'When your father's property is looted, join in the looting'. (Personal communication)

This interpretation is also supported by the findings in a report of Human Rights Watch (2003a). But what did the TPLF representatives actually think about construing people of Eritrean descent as internal enemies?

## THE TPLF: ITS OWN WORST ENEMY?
During the resistance war against the Derg regime, the inherent ambiguity of the Tigrinya-speaking identity was an advantage for the political entrepreneurs of the resistance movements straddling the river Mereb (notably the EPLF and TPLF). The founders of the TPLF were Tigrinya-speakers who traced their origin to both sides of the river, and in the leadership of the EPLF you also find individuals who have their origin in Tigray. 'The individual didn't matter', explained the former military leader of the TPLF, Aregawi Berhe: 'You could have Eritrean blood or Tigrayan, as long as you subscribed to the ideas of the revolution'. That was the case in the past, but when the deportations of Eritreans took off, the issue of 'Eritrean blood' among the TPLF leadership returned with a vengeance, and senior TPLF/EPRDF cadres with an Eritrean background were considered by many Ethiopians to be spies for Issaias and Eritrea. And at the centre of people's attention in this regard, was the family origin of Prime Minister Meles Zenawi himself.

182

The discourse on the identity of Meles Zenawi during the war can to a certain extent be compared with processes taking place under the Derg regime. Donald Donham writes in his book on the Derg revolution that the ambivalence of ethnic and national identities can be summarised in the personal history of Mengistu Hailemariam himself, details of which have never been clearly established (1999: 129). Donham quotes Lefort on how the myths that grew up around Mengistu assumed their own reality:

> What does it matter if Mengistu's past remains unknown? The stories about him are much richer in symbols that speak to the crowds than the little nothings that he could have dragged up and embellished ... What do the precise facts matter, the ones reported by the radio, the television, the newspapers? There they only reach a handful.... Far more powerful and more effective is rumour, which runs from one street to the next, from village to hamlet, so big and exaggerated that it becomes the truth. (Donham 1999: 129)

Mengistu's origin was important – coming from a poor background in southern Ethiopia, but with a probable kinship link to an Amhara lord – since it mirrored the idea of the ancient Ethiopian nation. Your social or ethnic background does not matter as long as you drape yourself in the language, customs and religion of the Abyssinian state. Against this background, the former revolutionary insider Dawit Wolde Giorgis gave the following characterisation of Mengistu:

> The fact that he [Mengistu] was not an Amhara, but seemed an outsider, was in his favour. But Mengistu, trained in an Amharised Ethiopian military tradition, is not really an outsider at all: he plays the feudal intrigue dressed up as Ethiopian nationalism. (Cited in Donham 1999: 130)

As the rumours of Mengistu's background took on their own life, so also did the rumours about the background of the top TPLF cadres, and in particular Prime Minister Meles Zenawi himself. As the myth of Mengistu mirrored the master narrative of Ethiopian nationalism, the myth of Meles reflected the ideology of ethnicity and 'anti-Ethiopianism'. Meles was brought up in Adwa, a town close to the Eritrean border. His father was part of the lower nobility (*dejazmatch*), and it is said that, already at a young age, Meles criticised him for owning too much land compared with the poor peasants in the neighbourhood. Meles' mother is of Eritrean origin, and she enthusiastically voted 'yes' to independence in the Eritrean referendum in 1993. As noted, Meles is considered to be the ideological architect behind the dissolution of the unitary Ethiopian state into an ethnic federation. After coming to power in 1991 he has repeatedly criticised and ridiculed Ethiopian nationalism and the myth of Greater Ethiopia. Thus, when the war broke out in

1998, Meles had very little public legitimacy to encourage the population to rally behind the Ethiopian flag – the same flag he had some years earlier called 'just a simple piece of cloth' – to protect the unity and territorial sovereignty of Ethiopia. Most Ethiopians did support the war against Eritrea, not because of Meles or the EPRDF's efforts, but despite them. An Amhara intellectual expressed a commonly shared opinion in this regard:

> I support the war against Eritrea and I think we should go all the way to Asmara. The Eritreans have with the help of the EPRDF for a long time taken advantage of Ethiopia, both economically and politically. It is about time that this should end. Why should the Eritreans hold important positions within our bureaucracy or businesses? No, throw them out, so that real Ethiopians can fill these posts! The only problem is that the government itself should be deported. They gave away Eritrea without any fight or argument in 1993; they have worked for seven years to break up Ethiopia and pitch one ethnic group against the other; in addition to that, several of the top political cadres in the EPRDF are Eritreans! Meles himself is half Eritrean – how can we possibly trust him? This war is entirely their fault to start with. (Personal communication)

Questioning the identity and the true nationality of political leaders by opposing political forces in Africa has almost become a continental habit, in order to delegitimise their political authority. Merera Gudina, the chairman of the ONC, reflected on the distinction of identities within the 'Tigrinya-realm':

> This is the tragedy of the separation of Eritrea from Ethiopia. You can in no way differentiate many Eritreans from Ethiopians, especially the Tigrayans. They speak the same language, the mother can be from this or that side of the river, even someone like Issaias Afeworki is probably more Ethiopian than Meles. ... I could never differentiate between the two, who is born on that side of the river and who is born on this side. And the other thing is that during the last seven years they have been close, as it were hand-in-hand, in elections, in controlling the press and business – they [the TPLF and EPLF] were together. Probably the two groups themselves know each other's identity but for the rest of Ethiopia, we never knew who's who among them. (Personal communication)

The fact that the deportations of Eritreans after a while took on a more random form was also a concern for many: 'How come the mother of Meles is not expelled? She voted in the referendum too!' The authorities acknowledged, to a limited degree, that there were mistakes made in the deportations, as confirmed by Yemane 'Jamaica' Kidane, at the Ethiopian Foreign Ministry. He himself embodied the Tigrayan/ Ethiopian identity ambivalence and became a victim of the politics of identity. He is of 'mixed origin' (his father being Eritrean and mother

Tigrayan) and most of his relatives live in Eritrea. Yemane first joined the EPLF in 1973, but later in 1975 he and another EPLF cadre joined the TPLF as the first recruits with military training, in order to assist the new movement with military expertise. He disclosed to me that he had nine nephews and nieces fighting on the Eritrean side of the war, and three of them were on the Badme front line during 'Operation Sunset'. In November 1998 I asked him to comment on the deportations of his Eritrean 'sisters and brothers'.

If you want to ask me if some injustice has been done, I say yes. Yes, some things were hastily done. Yes, I believe that. But not all. Because, if we hadn't done that, I don't think Addis and Ethiopia would have been safe today. Because you could read it in the way Issaias put it in May, 'we could create instability at the heart of Ethiopia', or something like that. It was a scary position. That really roused us from our deep sleep. So, usually, when you do these kinds of things, you always have some problems. You do some wrongs. There were some people who were hastily kicked out. We know that he's capable of doing anything, Issaias and EPLF as an organisation. We know, because there have been a lot of killings here of [Eritrean] opposition forces. Inside Ethiopia itself! So in this kind of organisation, there are a lot of personnel who have been in the military, they were in the EPLF, they were in the training course, they have these businesses which are in the front line for EPLF companies. So it was very difficult for us to live with, so it had to be done quickly. It was not pre-planned, or anything like that. Because after the bombings of civilian targets in Mekelle, the bombing of civilian targets in Adigrat, we didn't want to take any risks. We can't take any risks. So we did it. We did it, but we have always tried to correct mistakes. But some wrongs have been done, some injustices. Some people who have never been involved [politically or militarily] have been deported. (Personal communication)

Despite the war and the deportations, some still believed that, owing to the strong bonds across the Mereb, a Tigrinya cross-boundary identity would prevail. Yemane Kidane showed some optimism in this regard in the early days of the war:

There might be some anger from the people who have been deported, but then again there will be some anger from our people who have been mistreated in Eritrea. But, in the whole process, whether we like it or not, we are one and the same people. *The Eritreans might think that they are different, but we are, I believe, one and the same.* Just because of Italian colonialism, they cannot be different. *They are Tigrayans, we are Tigrayans.* Whether they like it or not. (Personal communication)

The ambiguity of identity – of who is the enemy – is clearly understood by Yemane, but the actions of his party and government were directly trying to eradicate this ambiguity. As we shall see below, the optimism expressed by Yemane in late 1998 was later toned down, both by himself and other EPRDF representatives.

## THE AMBIGUITY OF DEPORTATIONS

Although the EPRDF claimed in certain contexts (in particular, where foreigners were the audience) that the reasons for deporting Eritreans and Ethiopians of Eritrean origin were based purely on military considerations and safety concerns, the Ethiopian public did not perceive them in that manner. Merera Gudina, chairman of the ONC, offered the following points to me:

> I think the TPLF is doing it not so much for security reasons as for political reasons, because in the eyes of the Ethiopian people they want to make sure that Ethiopians believe that they are serious – that they are true Ethiopians. They can drive away those who stood against the interest of Ethiopia or work against the interest of the Ethiopians. So regardless of what kind of people, whether children, or elderly or others, are sent out, I think on the part of the government it is not so much of a military issue, it is a political one. (Personal communication)

Some intellectuals also drew a historical parallel of Tigrayan ambiguity concerning the protection of Ethiopian sovereignty and territory. A lecturer in history at Addis Ababa University made the following comment while we were discussing the war in early 1999:

> You must remember that the Tigrayan nobility has always played a somewhat dubious role when it comes to protecting Ethiopia from foreign aggression. You do of course have strong Tigrayan nationalists, like Emperor Yohannes and Ras Alula, but history has also shown that Tigrayans also cooperated with the Italians. Today, we know of the strong bonds between the TPLF and the EPLF, so it is not the best for Ethiopia that we have Tigrayans in government during this war. (Personal communication).

As discussed earlier, Tigray has often been the geographical location of contact between the outside world and the Ethiopian state, which had its political centre in the heartland of the country south of Tigray. It was through Tigray that visitors had to travel to visit the royal court, and trade routes to the Red Sea coast traversed the rugged mountains of Tigray. The Tigrayan nobility took advantage of this geo-political position in their internal rivalry with the Amhara nobility, to seek control over the Ethiopian sphere. In this regard, all means possible were used to gain, or remain, in political control. Even betraying one's country, Ethiopia, to the Italians, as the historian Haggai Erlich has discovered (1986: 130), was done in order for the nobility to position themselves within the socio-political hierarchy.

It is plausible to say that the ambiguity of the 'Tigrinya' identity, both historical and contemporary, did have an impact on how the EPRDF government conducted and communicated the war with Eritrea. In the aftermath of the war, we also witnessed the split of the TPLF leadership, with several top cadres expelled from the Central Committee and the party (see Tadesse and Young 2003; Vaughan and Tronvoll 2003). The origin of this dispute lies in an internal critique within the Front on how to handle the Eritrea issue, in which the dissenters would have liked to see a much harder line against Eritrea, both politically prior to the war and militarily after the war had begun. Meles and his supporters, on the other hand, emphasised the common history of the two people and fronts, and sought to reconcile differences and disputes by negotiation, rather than by force. For this reason, Meles was accused by the dissenters within his own party of being too Eritrea-friendly because of his Eritrean ancestry. The accusations against Meles Zenawi and several of his top politicians of being Eritrean spies and traitors to the Ethiopian cause were not something stressed by non-Tigrayans alone; the same criticism was also raised from within the TPLF. Meles Zenawi was, of course, aware of the difficulties of balancing his 'Tigrinya-identity' with an Ethiopian one. He told me that what the Eritrean-Ethiopian war unfortunately did, in this respect, was to make new distinctions where there used to be ambiguity. In his own words:

After the end of the war [of resistance against the Derg] the relations were so close [between EPLF-TPLF and the Eritrean-Tigrayan peoples] that the lines of demarcation became fuzzy again – the demarcation line between Eritrea and Ethiopia. And one sort of stepping-stone in making these fuzzy lines between Eritrea and Ethiopia was Tigray – linguistically, culturally, and so forth. You have a river, and if you have a stone in the middle of it, it becomes easy to cross, and the lines become fuzzy. If you do not have a stepping stone in the middle, the lines are more clearly demarcated. By diminishing – not eliminating – the significance of this stepping-stone in the middle of the river, the lines between Eritrea and Ethiopia become much clearer. Secondly, by creating solidarity amongst the various groups in Ethiopia, not around the mythical ideology of Abyssinia or Ethiopia, but around the new dispensation of decentralisation, it also clarified identities on this side. I don't necessarily believe this is all for the good, but I think it is an unfortunate fact that this is the case. (Personal communication)

Prominent Eritreans share Meles Zenawi's view on this matter, and argue that the wounds from the war itself may heal, but the effect of the deportations has left a permanent scar on the Eritrean-Ethiopian relationship and the perception of identity among the Tigrinya-speakers. Although tens of thousands of Ethiopians of Eritrean origin still reside within Ethiopia, the deportations have symbolically purified the Ethiopian territory of some of its malcontents. Eritreans have been removed from the public scene and ousted from positions of importance within political, bureaucratic and economic spheres.

## BEING ETHIOPIAN OR NOT?

The Ethiopian historian Gebru Tareke claims that 'Ethiopian leaders have been far less successful in nation-building than in state creation and consolidation' (1996: 29). Due to the considerable expansion of the territory under the control of Addis Ababa at the turn of the nineteenth century, without sufficient strategies of including the new citizens in the identity-sphere of Ethiopia, the loyalty of the citizens to the nation-state was wanting. As a consequence of the lack of nation-building processes, a host of regional and ethnic resistance movements emerged in response to the twin crises in authority and identity that followed in the wake of the Derg socialist revolution in the 1970s. 'Based on their different perceptions or interpretations of Ethiopian society and history,' concludes Gebru Tareke, 'members of the new social classes, more specifically the intelligentsia, have attempted to construct their own communities by violent means' (Tareke 1996: 29). This interpretation is also appropriate to describe some of the effects of the Eritrean-Ethiopian war. I have shown how the politics of war and identity recast the perceptions of belonging for Ethiopians of Eritrean origin, and thus altered the relationship between the Ethiopian state and a somehow marginal segment of its citizenry. However, the Eritrean-Ethiopian war altered other relationships within the Ethiopian state and between the state and segments of its citizenry too. Participation in the war was used by the state as a test of groups' and people's 'Ethiopianness': who was willing to fight for the territorial integrity of the country?

Almost all Ethiopian opposition parties and fronts were sceptical of the EPRDF regime, but still gave their full support to defending the territorial integrity of Ethiopia. However, some parties were not willing to support the war at all. The most important event in this regard was the call for non-engagement in the war from the Oromo Liberation Front (OLF) to the Oromo people of Ethiopia, the largest population group in the country. The OLF is one of the oldest political fronts in the country and has also the greatest potential to challenge Ethiopian statehood in Oromia. Consequently their position towards the war was important for the Ethiopian government. Just a couple of weeks after the Eritrean invasion the OLF made their position clear:

The TPLF/EPRDF propaganda regarding this conflict is reminiscent of the late days of the Derg regime that was hoodwinking the people to echo their war-mongering slogans. The motive is to divert the attention of the Oromo and the international community away from the day-to-day atrocities being committed against the Oromo people in Oromia and to channel the meagre resources available to build its war machinery to perpetuate its grip on the peoples in the Ethiopian Empire. It is also trying to take advantage of this conflict to muster public support by mobilising elements which have always opposed the principle of self-determination and are eager to reverse the political gains of the subjugated people. ... Therefore the Oromo National Council would like to remind the Oromo and other peoples in the Empire State of Ethiopia to alienate themselves from this conflict which does not bring any positive economic or political change in their way of living.[10]

The OLF statement denouncing the EPRDF and calling for Oromos not to participate in the defence of the 'Ethiopian Empire State' suddenly reclassified the politically conscious Oromos who supported the OLF and Oromos at large (who by ethnic descent were by default classified as potential OLF members by the EPRDF), as possible 'enemies of the state' threatening the territorial integrity of Ethiopia, rather than as somewhat 'ambiguous Ethiopians'.

# The ambiguity of Oromoness: being Ethiopian or not?

When the Ethiopian state is under pressure or threatened by foreign aggression, issues of allegiances and belonging always arise. These issues are often more acute for people either belonging to peripheral groups on the edge of the Ethiopian political realm, or affiliated to the largest and most amorphous of Ethiopian ethnic groups, the Oromo (see also Clapham 1988: 196). The Oromo constitute some 24-30 million people, spread across western, central and south-eastern Ethiopia. There are Oromos who are adherents of Orthodox Christianity and Lutheranism and of Islam and indigenous beliefs (*Waqefachaa*); they are settled agriculturists, urban dwellers or pastoralists. Traditionally, major parts of the Oromo population belonged to several independent kingdoms, but with the expansion of the Ethiopian state at the end of the nineteenth century they were forcibly subdued by the Ethiopian crown. Ethiopian history, as interpreted from a segment of the political Oromo movement, claims that Ethiopia was not a given historical polity, but came into existence through the colonisation of the Horn of Africa (Holcomb and Ibssa 1990; Sorensen 1993). Thus, the Oromo Liberation Front (OLF) – as the main representative political movement within Oromia – claims that the modern history of Ethiopia is the history of colonisation of the Oromo people, a people still yearning for their freedom from the *Habesha* colonisers:

Ethiopia is an empire state. It consist of the core Abyssinian state, which was first founded by the Tigrayans and then consolidated over centuries by the two ethnic groups of Abyssinia – Amhara and Tigrayans.

Emperor Menelik II (1871–89) of the Amhara ethnic group is the creator of present-day Ethiopia. ... Menelik conquered the Oromo and other non-Abyssinian peoples during the era of the 'scramble for Africa'.[11]

It thus follows naturally for the OLF to conclude:

The current struggle of the Oromo people has its roots in its opposition to political domination, economic exploitation, and cultural repression by successive Abyssinian regimes. The fundamental objective of the Oromo liberation struggle, led by the OLF, is to exercise the Oromo people's inalienable right to national self-determination.

In an interview in the aftermath of the war, Lencho Bati, the OLF foreign spokesperson, eloquently elaborated on the Oromos' view of the Ethiopian state:

For a nation to exist or to flourish it needs to produce citizenship. People need to identify themselves with the state; people need to identify themselves with the leaders of the state; people need to identify themselves with the history of the state. When it comes to the Oromo, we do not identify ourselves with the state, because the state marginalised us. We do not identify ourselves with the leaders of the state, because most of the leaders belong to the North and serve the interest of the North. We do not identify ourselves with the history of the state, because most Ethiopian history is written in such a way as to serve the rulers and the makers of the Ethiopian state, who are the Amhara and the Tigray. So this is how the Oromos view the Ethiopian state. (Personal communication)

I shall not delve into the accumulated academic literature on Oromo identity and discourse (see, in particular, Baxter 1994; Baxter et al. 1996; Jalata 1998b; Sorensen 1992; Sorensen 1993). Suffice it to say that the politicised Oromo identity discourse is adopting a similar strategy to the former hegemonic Ethiopianist discourse. John Sorensen explains from the point of view of the Oromo that:

Ethiopian writers have presented the northern highland cultures of Abyssinia, especially that of the Amhara, as a unified, constant subject and the motivating force of national history. These narratives of history and identity have constructed the Oromo as Ethiopia's Other: uncivilised barbarians, lacking any original or creative cultural tradition. (Sorensen 1998: 229)

Today, the Oromo nationalists claim the opposite: the existence of a homogenous, democratic, all-embracing Oromo 'national' identity contrasted with the authoritarian, human-rights-violating and power-abusing 'other' – the *Habesha*. The existence of a unified Oromo history and perception of identity centres, *inter alia*, on the traditional Oromo system of governance called *gada* – an age-set administrative system which,

190

according to the anthropologist turned Oromo activist Holcomb, 'organised the Oromo people in an all-encompassing democratic republic' (cited in Jalata 1998a: 38). By emphasising the egalitarian and democratic character of the Oromo culture, the nationalist movement has reconstructed an Oromo past which is required to be the opposite of, and therefore morally superior to, the *Habesha*, the incessant enemy of the Oromo people (see also Baxter 1994: 177). The sociologist Asafa Jalata is one of the most prominent representatives of the new Oromo national discourse essentialising the Oromo culture. He describes the content of Oromoness (*Oromumma*) in the following terms:

> Oromoness is built on Oromo heritage and cultural markers; it also emanates from the common humiliation and oppression that the Oromo people have experienced under Ethiopian colonialism and international imperialism. Therefore, Oromoness is marked by both pride and victimisation. ... Oromoness is above the individual, regional and religious identities; it is the foundation of Oromo survival, and hence without it, Oromos cannot practice their culture and religions freely or promote their interest as a nation and as individuals. Oromoness, communality of oppression, and humiliation facilitated the emergence of Oromo nationalism. (Jalata 1998a: 39–40)

Based on such a perspective, an Oromo identity is antithetical to Ethiopian nationalism.

## A 'NON-OROMO' WAR

When the Eritrean-Ethiopian war started in 1998, the armed Oromo nationalist struggle had been ongoing for 24 years, since the establishment of the OLF in 1974 (with a brief interlude of one year after the fall of the Derg in 1991–92 when the OLF was part of the transitional government run by the EPRDF). After their first statement on the war, quoted above, the OLF received massive criticism from several quarters, including other opposition movements and Oromos, since the lack of defence of the Ethiopian state and territory was interpreted as active support for Eritrea in the war. Thus, the OLF was forced to elaborate on its stand of 'non-engagement':

> There have been fabrications by some people that the OLF has taken sides in the Ethio-Eritrean conflict. We want to make it clear that the Oromo people do not owe any loyalty to the Ethiopian state and its government whose authority is not founded on the consent of the people. ... The present conflict between the two states ... will cause huge human and material losses. Because of demographic and other economic realities, the Oromo people will be more affected. This is further aggravated by the political reality that determines who should shoulder the burden of the war. That is why we warn our people and others to refrain from participating in this war.[12]

The chairman of the OLF, Dauwd Ibsa, later commented to me that in Oromia during the war they were actively putting forward three reasons for not joining the Ethiopian army to fight the Eritreans. First, Eritrea received its independence in 1993 with the consent of the EPRDF and nothing substantial had happened since then to legitimate a new war against Eritrea. Since Meles was in power both in 1993 and in 1998, the reasons for the war had to be politically grounded within the EPLF-TPLF relationship, and not in any territorial issues. Secondly, why should the Oromos join the EPRDF army to protect Abyssinian interests, when the same army waged a war against the Oromo people in Oromia? And thirdly, argued Dauwd Ibsa, to waste tens of thousands of lives over a border that was not demarcated in the first place, was not going to help either the Ethiopian or the Oromo people. Dauwd Ibsa saw the re-emergence of Ethiopian nationalism in the wake of the war as a clear politically engineered process:

> Even today Meles is not an Ethiopian nationalist – he never has been. All this rhetoric that he is fighting for Ethiopian unity and sovereignty emerged when the problem with the EPLF and the Eritrean government arose. ... Meles was supposed to play [the role] as a statesman serving the Oromos, the Hadiyas, the Welayetas, and the Ogadens equally with the Tigrayans. He has never served as a true president during the interim government, never served the Oromos and Tigrayans and the other Ethiopian peoples equally. Even today he is not doing that. ... Just because there was a problem between the EPLF and the TPLF the whole country has to burn. (Personal communication)

## COMPETING OROMO DISCOURSES

The political identity discourse advocated by the OLF subscribes to the idea of an independent Oromia state. The notion of an independent Oromia casts the *Habesha* as their principal relevant other (a discourse centring on victimisation, internal colonisation and human rights abuses). However, it is also of vital importance for the OLF and its followers to de-legitimise other Oromo political movements in order to undermine alternative Oromo identity discourses. Merera Gudina, the chairman of the Oromo National Congress (ONC), is one of the prime advocates of an Oromo discourse that champions the natural place of Oromos within the Ethiopian polity. Merera Gudina explained:

> In Ethiopia there is either confusion or selective reading of history. The Oromos for the last four to five hundred years at least, are both Ethiopian ruling class, whatever that means, and part of Ethiopian oppressed people. So the Oromos are both sides of the coin. The Oromos, for example, controlled the imperial seat at Gondar for two generations; for 80 years the Oromos were the ruling class of Wello; for centuries the Oromos were the ruling class of Gojam. Even in the so-called Amhara heartland of Shoa, the Oromos were part of the ruling class. Emperor Haile Selassie

and Emperor Iyasou, these are Amharised Oromos. So the Oromos are not as downgraded or second- class citizens as it appears from outside or is argued by some. Neither are they the beneficiaries of the Ethiopian state, as some Ethiopians want to believe. So the balance is somewhere in between. Oromos are oppressed and most Oromos lost their land, and were exploited economically and politically. Our culture is suppressed and so on and so forth. However, at the same time the Oromos were part of the Ethiopian state which exerted the repression. (Personal communication)

The moderate Oromo discourse, represented by Merera Gudina, argues that Oromos have always participated in the defence of Ethiopian territory and integrity, and as such they are true Ethiopians. This layered notion of Oromo identity – being an Ethiopian on the surface, while underneath lies an Oromo – first emerged after the fall of Haile Selassie. Clapham reports on the situation during the early days of the socialist revolution in the mid-1970s, that some people – Amharic speakers with Amharic names – 'surprised even their closest friends by declaring themselves to be Oromo, or as "having an Oromo side"' (1988: 196). However, when the political cleansing began in the late 1970s, Clapham observed, an ambiguous identity was no longer permissible.

The Oromo party in the EPRDF coalition government, the Oromo People's Democratic Organisation (OPDO), holds, on the surface, quite a similar view of identity interpretation to that of the ONC. Almaz Mako, the former Speaker of the House of Federation, a former senior OPDO cadre and one of the most prominent female politicians in the country, also emphasised Oromos' belonging to Ethiopia in an interview with me during the war.

Without being proud of our ethnic identities, we cannot build a strong Ethiopia. I'm an Oromo and an Ethiopian. I can be that simultaneously. In the past we were forced to deny our first identity and accept the second identity only, but not any more. Even in the current crisis [Eritrean-Ethiopian war] we see that this is a strength. This has become the strength of our unity. A strong sense of Ethiopianness has emerged since the crisis. In my opinion the strong Ethiopianness we see today is a result of our seven years of work. If some one says that this strong Ethiopianness comes from Eritrean aggression only, it is very difficult to accept that. (Personal communication)

Although Almaz Mako gave an impression of endorsing the EPRDF policies and interpretation of identities in Ethiopia during the war with Eritrea, in its aftermath she defected from Ethiopia and issued the following statement on 11 August 2001.

Instead of resolving the Oromo question by democratic means, the EPRDF government has brought untold miseries and sufferings on the

193

Oromo people. Any proud Oromo who has not sold his soul to the TPLF is categorised as an OLF sympathiser and targeted for persecution. OPDO is being prevented from becoming an autonomous organisation representing the Oromo national interest in the government and reduced to a rubber stamp for TPLF rule over Oromia. As a result, thousands of innocent Oromos have disappeared, perished in detention centres from torture and many more forced to flee the country. Today, even that superficial resemblance of independence that OPDO had is gone, and is replaced with direct rule from Prime Minister Meles Zenawi's office. It should be clear to every Oromo that there is neither democracy nor federalism in Ethiopia. The lip-service to democracy is done only to impress Western donor countries. Federalism is propagated only to hoodwink Oromos and other nations and nationalities. In reality, today Oromia has lost her autonomous status and has become an appendage of Tigray. Oromo resources are mobilised and looted to develop Tigray, while Oromos who oppose this are branded as narrow nationalists and persecuted. The ruling party is categorically rejected by the entire Oromo nation and survives only on the backs of its repressive security forces ....

Almaz Mako, like many other high-level OPDO cadres, came to recognise that being a true Oromo implies a strong defence of Oromo values and self-determination, issues which could not be defended under the EPRDF/OPDO umbrella. When the ERPDF underwent an internal process of dissent in the aftermath of the war and several high-ranking OPDO cadres defected, Meles Zenawi reportedly said: 'If you scratch the skin of an OPDO, you will find an OLF underneath'.

The defections of Oromos from the government were embarrassing for Meles Zenawi and the EPRDF – the 'dirty linen' of the EPRDF was put out to everyone to see (cf. Herzfeld 1997). The defections put in focus the tensions between official presentation and what goes on in the privacy of governmental affairs, and so undermined the legitimacy of the government. Nevertheless, the EPRDF continued its anti-OLF politics, waging an open war on the so-called secessionist movement that threatened the territorial integrity of Ethiopia. The ambiguity of Oromoness was thus confined, in the sense that the space for politically conscious Oromos to define themselves as Oromo first and Ethiopian second, was becoming more limited.

# The politics of disclosure

The Eritrean-Ethiopian war, and the politics of identity and the deportations carried out by the Ethiopian government, had a radical effect on the discourse of nationalism and identity in the country. I have shown how government policies changed as a consequence of the war, with previously held ideological principles downplayed or rejected in order to facilitate the re-emergence of the old nationalist discourse of 'Greater Ethiopia'. Furthermore, the government's rhetoric on upholding human rights standards clashed with its practice of human rights abuses on the ground. Similarly, the statements made by several top EPRDF leaders immediately after the outbreak of the war that Eritreans residing in Ethiopia had nothing to fear and should be considered as 'brothers' soon proved to be false. Of course, a government's policies are based on both historical trajectories and current issues. It is obvious that the various political and identity discourses referred to do not exist independently of each other, but are somehow integrated and interdependent, although simultaneously competing and contradicting.

As shown in this chapter, the political elite in Ethiopia tried to initiate a process of boundary creation by changing its politics of identity and implementing ethnic deportations. The EPRDF elite tried to establish by political dictate who was entitled to be a member of the Ethiopian nation and who not. They based their identification of the nation's malcontents partly on 'biological' evidence of descent and partly on expressed support for the war effort. This was in order to draw a sharp distinction between *us* and *them*, between the nation and the enemy. Brackette Williams has explained that 'in constructing boundaries between groups based on categorical identities and their links between these boundaries to cultural systems in nation-states, humans create purity out of impurity' (Williams 1989: 429). It was this process of identifying the nation's malcontents that pushed 'Ethiopians of Eritrean descent and origin' and politically conscious Oromos out of the conceptual space of Ethiopia as conceived by the political elite, and on to the other side of the boundary. However, as shown above, to create distinctions by political dictate in a field of flux, where the symbols of ethnicity and nationalism hold a multivocal capacity, is not that easy.

The EPRDF's ideology and pre-war discourse on the rights of 'nation, nationalities and peoples' were clearly contradictory to their anti-Oromo policies during the war. The EPRDF was claiming the 'national high-ground', and at the same time pursuing ethnic policies. Furthermore, the government's human rights and democracy discourses clashed with the practices of deporting Eritreans and of election-rigging.

The identity discourses created by the Eritrean-Ethiopian war demonstrated that they are dynamically interrelated. For instance, any discourse on Greater Ethiopian nationalism presupposes a notion of ethnicity, since the Greater Ethiopia ideology builds on an Amharaised domination of the state and consequently represents the repression of ethnic minorities in the country. In other words, the reverse side of the coin of the nationalist discourse of Greater Ethiopia is the repression of minority ethnic groups. In the following concluding chapter I shall try to sum up and explain these apparent contradictions.

# Notes

1 The concept of 'Eritrean descent or origin', as it was phrased by the Ethiopian government, is a rather loose and flexible criterion of identification. For instance, since Eritrea was an integral part of Ethiopia from 1962 to 1991, how should people who were born in Eritrea during that time be classified? Moreover, 'Eritrean' is not an ethnic category, like 'Tigrayan' or 'Oromo'. The Eritrean population is made up of at least nine different ethnic groups, many of which inhabit areas on both sides of the Eritrean-Ethiopian border.

2 'The Eritrean government has committed a grave historical blunder', Ethiopian News Agency, 26 May 1998, Addis Ababa.

3 *Wayen,*27 Genbot, 1990 EC No. 297, Vol. 23 (4 June 1998 GC).

4 The Eritrean military 'boot' camp where all individuals serving national service undergo six months of military training.

5 *The Ethiopian Herald*, 17 and 18 June 1998, respectively.

6 See *The Sun*, 25 June 1998, quoted in *Press Digest*, 2 July 1998.

7 Press Release 'High Commissioner for Human Rights expresses deep concern at continuing expulsion of Eritrean nationals from Ethiopia', HR/98/44, 1 July 1998.

8 Later I had the opportunity to run this story by a close contact who was a high-ranking civil servant in Awassa (capital of the southern region) during that time, and asked him to verify it. He laughed and denied this had happened in Awassa, and claimed that the regional leadership in the Southern Region had heard about a similar incident taking place in the Somali region of Ethiopia. So, the story might not be true, but it nonetheless captures one aspect of the popular interpretation of the politics of deportations.

9 *Teff* is a cereal indigenous to Ethiopia, which the stable food *injera* is made of. The *teff* grains are very tiny.

10 OLF, Foreign Affairs Committee, 21 May 1998, Washington, DC.

11 From the pamphlet *Liberating the Oromo people for stability and development in the Horn of Africa*, Foreign Relations Department, Oromo Liberation Front, March 2001, Washington, DC, pp. 21–22.

12 Press release, Oromo Liberation Front, Foreign Affairs Committee, Washington, DC, 1 July 1998.

# Eight

## Conclusion
### Arresting Ethiopian Nationalism

War destroys the cultural web of significance as it existed until the outbreak of violence. However, as this book has illustrated, the outcome is not a cultural vacuum, since war concurrently spins new webs of significance – created by and fitted into the new socio-political environment caused by the war. Furthermore, the new cultural understandings created by war are of no less 'cultural' significance or value than the socio-political dynamics created during peace-time.

The Eritrean-Ethiopian war was ostensibly fought over a sliver of land. But, as perceived by peasants and politicians alike, the war had everything to do with notions of identity: who 'we' were; how 'we' were distinct from 'them'; the connection with and the perception of land; how a 'brother' turned out to be an enemy; and how enemies became allies. At the same time, variously situated actors perceived the overarching metaphor of 'who is the enemy?' differently in relation to a consciousness of boundaries – their own and those of others. The resulting 'sedimentation of stories within stories' has provided the framework for this book (cf. Donham 1999: 177).

The overall narrative in the preceding chapters has tried to be true to the context of war and the metaphor of the enemy. As described, the war unfolded and impacted with various degrees of intensity on different localities throughout Ethiopia.[1] The outcome of this might appear as fragments of war narratives – variously related and disjointed, incomplete, fluid and contradictory. If such is the case, this study has managed to convey accurately the experience of war on the ground, as explained by Nordstrom: 'People's lives are lived amid bits and pieces of information and misinformation, and their survival depends on trying to gather these into some pattern of meaning' (Nordstrom 1997: 109). It seems clear that war and violence are not socio-culturally fragmented phenomena that occur 'outside' the arena of everyday life for those who are affected (Broch-Due 2005; Nordstrom and Martin 1992; Richards

2005). War becomes part and parcel of life for the people living within the 'war-scape'. Thus if we are to understand war and conflict – and consequently also their opposite, peace – it is to the people themselves, to the social dynamics and cultural phenomena that inform them, that we must turn our attention. This view stands at odds with traditional studies of socio-political violence that have long focused on the formal institutions credited with defining, waging and resolving aggression: political, military, security, and legal (Nordstrom and Martin 1992: 14). Such a formalistic approach has also influenced the development of theories of nationalism and the formation of collective identities in war. Failure to consider the crucial elements of flux and chaos at the grass-roots – the field reality – has thus been an obstacle to the development of more complex arguments on the formation of identities in war.

In this concluding chapter I shall concentrate on drawing together the strands of the overall argument. The enigma of Ethiopian national-ism will be deciphered, and some thoughts on how we ought to under-stand the formation of Ethiopian identities in war will be offered.

## Conflicting narratives of Ethiopian nationalism

The Ethiopian discourse on identity during the war was not simply a hegemonic vision of a Greater Ethiopia anchored in primordialists' notions. Rather, it incorporated a number of pre-existing and dynamically interrelated discursive fragments, such as images of foreign aggression, the battle of Adwa, Ethiopia's invincibility, and an ancient unified state; as well as impressions of an Amhara-dominated oppressive central government, an authoritarian Tigrayan minority regime and human rights abuses, and even representations of Ethiopia within modernity as democratic, developed and enjoying ethnic autonomy and plurality. One discourse presupposed the image of another, weaving the perceptions of identities into an overall narrative which thus contained contradictory and contesting elements.

Ethiopian history has in itself an historical ambiguity which was exploited in creating nationalistic narratives during the war. Within competing discourses, Tigray and Ethiopia, as separate polities, shifted to be the entity of narration: Tigrayan wars vs. Ethiopian wars; Tigrayan warriors and heroes vs. Ethiopian warriors and heroes. This ambiguity is, of course, not necessarily limited to the dichotomy between Ethiopian and Tigrayan wars and narratives, but might be expanded to include all ethnic/ethno-national discursive fields, like Oromo vs. Ethiopian narratives; Somali, Afar, etc. In contexts of war national myths will constitute a reservoir of meanings which might be recycled to be used in other contexts. Or, as Connerton explains: 'The mythical material contains a range of potential meanings significantly in excess of their use and function in any particular arrangement' (1989: 56-7). This explains why people seemingly accepted the contradictory discourses of identity.

## THE CONTRADICTION AND INCONSISTENCY OF ETHIOPIAN IDENTITIES AND THE EPRDF'S IDENTITY POLITICS

Conceptual inconsistency and contradictory elements are considered to be a central aspect of the knowledge system of the Tigrayan and Amhara peoples (cf. Aspen 2001; Bauer 1989). In relation to religious practice, for instance, it has been noted that the highlanders have access to and act within several 'worlds' of incompatible sets of knowledge systems. However, people seemingly have no difficulty in managing these different ontological realities simultaneously (Aspen 2001: 231). What is important to note is that, although the knowledge system, or in our case the perceptions of identity, are confused, perpetually changing, and internally contradictory, they should be analysed and explained, without denying these qualities; as a matter of fact, it is precisely these qualities which are the constituent features of identity in Ethiopia. And it is precisely these qualities which are so appropriate to use and manipulate through identity politics in the name of a 'sacred cause' (cf. Triulzi 2002).

For the TPLF, and later the EPRDF, the ambiguity of identities in Ethiopia has been utilised to its maximum to legitimise political objectives and gain popular support. I would even go so far as to claim that Ethiopia's complex and contradictory history and patterns of identities form the core of the TPLF's *raison d'être*, and the base for its access to and control of state power in Ethiopia today – a paradox in itself, since its core ethnic constituency (Tigrayans) only constitutes about 4 per cent of the total population. Let me go back a bit in history to substantiate this assertion. First, during the 17-years-of-struggle (1975–91) the TPLF redefined Tigrayanness in contrast to a suppressive Amhara-dominated state. During the formative years of the struggle they thus needed to strengthen the boundary which divided the Tigrayan and Amhara people (the *Habesha* realm), in order to sustain an enemy image of the dominating Amhara. Consider in this regard the pragmatic approach outlined by Sebhat Nega, a founding member of the Front, as he explains the identity politics of the TPLF during this period:

> Tigrayan independence was a last option, and when we were teaching the popular masses, we gave them the impression that we were fighting for independence. There was indeed a tendency towards secession among fighters. In 1985, a self-criticism was made among TPLF forces and narrow nationalist tendencies were denounced ... We had to wait for ten years to tackle the problem of narrow nationalism because the TPLF works in priorities. ... After 1985, more than just passing remarks, we

199

were teaching more emphatically that we were fighting for Ethiopia's unity based on equality ... Before 1985, 'Maybe' used to be the answer to the question 'Could the Amhara-oppressed masses be our allies?' 'Would they struggle for emancipation?' Again the answer was 'They may.' So there used to be a lot of suspicion of the Amhara. That was why we stressed Tigrayan nationalism – language, culture, etc. (Quote taken from Abbay 1998: 198)

When the TPLF considered themselves to be strong and mature enough both militarily and politically, their old policies and promises of a liberated Tigray were overturned in order to define the liberation of all the suppressed peoples of Ethiopia as their objective. Since the Tigrayan question was not clearly defined, this gave them the opportunity and flexibility needed to exert the appropriate identity politics in each context in order to give legitimacy to their shifting objectives (Abbay 1998).

Later, when they assumed state power in 1991, Ethiopia was deconstructed into ethnic component parts and a host of new boundaries of ambiguity were officially sanctioned, boundaries which could be endowed with symbolic markers of connection (establishing cross-boundary identities between the ethnic groups in southern Ethiopia, for instance), or distinction (as, for instance, between Oromos and Somalis in the Borana-Garre conflict). At the centre of this vast theatre of overlapping, contradictory, and conflicting identities were the ideological constructors of the regime, luring other actors in the political opposition to play the same game and thereby accentuating and accelerating the fragmenting effect of ethnic politics. Identity politics in the hands of the TPLF/EPRDF thus became the *Realpolitik* of divide and rule until the new war erupted in 1998.

With the outbreak of hostilities the TPLF/EPRDF again redesigned its identity politics the moment it realised that: a) the Eritrean invasion was too great a military challenge for them tackle alone as Tigrayans, so they needed to tap into the reservoir of Ethiopian troops to be sent to the battlefields; and b) since the attack on Tigray would be interpreted as an attack on Ethiopia by large and important constituencies of other Ethiopian groups (in particular Amhara and southern groups and the politically influential diaspora communities), the TPLF/EPRDF needed to harness this perception to a practical end – namely, recruitment to the national army – so that the masses would not project their anger against the TPLF/EPRDF itself. Overnight, the internal boundaries dividing the Ethiopian population were subdued in order to facilitate cross-boundary connections between the various groups, thus fostering the sentiments of nationhood. The opposite strategy was used to make enemies out of the Tigrinya-speaking Eritreans, a group which had until the outbreak of war been the strongest and most reliable backers of TPLF/EPRDF rule in Ethiopia.

For the people at the grassroots, the sudden change of the government's identity politics created different reactions, and inspired assorted perceptions of the boundaries being re-negotiated. For instance, the TPLF ideology would appear as overlapping or similar to a Tigrayan ethnic identity, but from a local point of view the TPLF political identity was distinguished from a cultural Tigrayan identity. Individuals could shift between a political TPLF identity at war with the Eritreans, and a cultural Tigrayan identity aligned with Eritrea and thus more ambiguous. The boundaries of identity thus had the capacity to distinguish and connect on the basis of political identity. Similar processes were also observed among the Hadiya and Oromo, and most probably among all the ethnic groups in the country. What, then, can we say constituted the dynamics of the upsurge of an Ethiopian nationalism during the war?

# The dynamics of Ethiopian nationalism

The EPRDF's identity politics alone does not fully explain the rapid mobilisation and support for military action to counter the Eritrean invasion, interpreted as an expression of Ethiopian nationalism by many observers. How should we then understand the formation of nationalism in Ethiopia? Can we identify certain cultural and political features which help to explain the support of the war, on the one hand, yet also explain the political resistance against the EPRDF regime, on the other? And lastly, can this support be understood as an expression of nationalism?

To conclude these questions, let me return to the ethnography of the initially disputed territories of the Badme plains. The Badme plains were originally inhabited by the Kunama people, a small group of mixed agriculturalists and hunter-gatherers. The Christian Tigrinya highlanders of both Eritrea and Tigray had always looked down on the Kunama as 'uncivilised,' 'backward' and 'pagan'. History reveals several massacres and the attempted genocide of the Kunama population by the Christian highlanders (Lussier 1997). In the 1940s and 1950s, Tigrinya-speaking agriculturalists from the overcrowded Eritrean and Tigrayan highlands settled in the so-called vacant Badme plains, displacing the Kunamas. Some of the new settlements were inhabited by Eritreans only, others by Tigrayans, whereas Badme village and some other villages were composed of Tigrinya-speakers from both Eritrea and Tigray. After over 50 years of settlement, both the Eritreans and the Tigrayans felt they had acquired inalienable land rights (*risti*) to the area. Thus, when the Eritrean army occupied Badme and its environs in May 1998, it was not only a violation of international borders; from the point of view of the Tigrayan population it was an encroachment on locally defined *risti* rights. This sparked a chain reaction in Tigray: the call of unity (*weyen*), to stand up and fight for their rights (*habbo*), and to seek retaliation (*henay mifdai*). But how can this process help to explain a general Ethiopian support of the war beyond Tigray? In order to tackle this issue, let me draw on a comparative historical case.

During historical times, the Amhara-dominated imperial government suppressed Tigrayan cultural and political expressions and manipulated the Tigrayan nobility, which led to divisions and in-fighting (*awrajanet*). But, by an expression of collective revenge (*henay mifdai*), the Tigrayans mobilised against the centralised state in unity (*weyane*) in order to retake what they saw as theirs, both land and dignity. The first *weyane* failed, but the second *weyane* arose on the same basis, as 'fire from the ashes'. In 1991 Ethiopia was split in two parts, as the EPLF liberated the former Ethiopian province of Eritrea and claimed independence. This created resentment among broad sections of the Ethiopian peoples, and many expressed sadness and anger, as if 'one of my limbs has been amputated', as an Amhara intellectual expressed it. Furthermore, the accentuated ethnification of Ethiopian society after the introduction of the ethnic federal system led to divisions and in-fighting between regions and groups as they struggled to control material and political resources, an *awrajanet* phenomenon writ large. In addition, non-Tigrayans generally perceived the EPRDF regime as a minority government, controlled by Tigrayans from within *and* without. The fact that the EPLF, and Eritreans residing in Ethiopia, were the strongest supporters and backers of the EPRDF government, led many to believe that the EPLF was still controlling internal Ethiopian affairs post-1991. The close link between the TPLF and EPLF leaderships, at least as it was understood from the outside, led to the belief among the Ethiopian peoples, and particularly the Amhara, that they were ruled by outsiders. In this context, the ethnic federal system was perceived as a deliberate plot to divide and rule the Ethiopian peoples and political elite, imposed by the TPLF and assisted by the EPLF.

## NATIONALISM FROM ABOVE: HABESHA POWER-PLAY

The subsequent Eritrean invasion of Ethiopian territory thus had two connotations. On the one hand, it made people recall the protracted war against the 'northern rebels' (both EPLF and TPLF) during the 1970s and '80s and the loss of Eritrea. On the other hand, it created outrage, based on the idea that Eritrea had been helped and subsidised by the TPLF regime in Ethiopia and their way of showing gratitude was by invading. The memory of the loss of the Eritrean territory and the subsequent humiliation of being indirectly controlled by Eritrea through their ethnic and political brothers, the TPLF, led to massive support for the war in order to retaliate not only for the invasion of Badme, but for the previous eight years of humiliation and the loss of Eritrea itself. As such, a similar process of unity – to fight for the land and for retaliation – to what was taking place in Tigray was also unfolding on the Ethiopian scene, driven by the nationalistic rhetoric of the political opposition. Ethiopians from all walks of life wanted to take back the land which they felt was rightfully theirs, and to restore the dignity they felt was lost in 1993 when Eritrea gained independence. Simultaneously with crushing the EPLF, they also felt that the TPLF was humiliated, since these had been comrades-in-arms. Prime Minister Meles Zenawi concurred partly in such an explanation, when I discussed it with him in the aftermath of the war and asked him whether one could compare the Ethiopian reaction to the Eritrean invasion with the Tigrayan protest against Amhara rule in the *Weyane* revolts (emphasising the issues of resistance, *habbo*, and retaliation, *henay mifdai*):

> Absolutely. It is the same concept ...; not accepting injustice and insult, and resisting it by all necessary means whatever the sacrifice. That was the motivating factor not only within Tigray but also in the rest of the country – particularly among the peasant masses. When you come to the intelligentsia in the cities you have a mixed image. There were some who felt this was a blessing in disguise. A blessing in disguise in that now Eritreans have provoked us and we will fight them and crush them and reoccupy the whole or parts of Eritrea .... There was also a feeling that this would weaken both parties [EPLF and TPLF/EPRDF], and create opportunities for others to exploit. (Personal communication)

The more or less unanimous backing for the EPRDF's war effort by the people and the political opposition in Ethiopia (with the notable exception of the OLF), should be explained by historical conceptions of state and power in Ethiopia, and not because of primordial identities (neither ethnicity nor nationalism) (cf. Erlich 1986; Taddia 1994). The political elite in the country used the war both as an occasion to try to regain lost territories – both Badme and Eritrea – and to position themselves in the internal power-play within Ethiopia. The rhetoric of war, as described in the earlier chapters, was in substance antithetical to the EPRDF ideology. Consequently, the war did not boost the EPRDF's popularity, as one might have expected, but quite the contrary: it undermined the legitimacy of the EPRDF, for two reasons. First, the origins of the war were generally understood as a Tigrinya affair, implicating the TPLF itself; thus, the Ethiopian government was blamed for the outbreak of war. Secondly, the EPRDF call for war backfired, since they did not achieve the popular objective of the war: to regain lost territories (since the Boundary Commission later granted Badme to Eritrea). On this basis, I believe it is plausible to claim that the Eritrean-Ethiopian war forms the last link in a long chain of conflicts and wars fought by the Abyssinian elites as part of their constant internal power struggle. It was, however, both a modern nation-building war fought over a piece of land and backed by arguments grounded in international law, and also a pre-modern war in its political rationale, conceived as feuding between different feudal princes within the imperial realm of Abyssinia.

## NATIONALISM FROM BELOW:
## INDIVIDUAL STRATEGIES OF SURVIVAL

The Ethiopian history of power struggle may well explain why the majority of the political elite in the country supported the war, but is this enough to explain individual recruitment? In the previous section, Prime Minister Meles Zenawi touched upon a distinction between the rural masses and the urban intellectuals in the way they perceived the issues, emphasising that the peasants were closer to the land and thus more bound by the tradition of retaliation, than by modern hatred. According to my own understanding, after talking to a number of recruits and dozens of other informants, one can identify three reasons for individual recruitment to the war, one more important than the other two. Let me start with the less important ones.

Every time in history the Ethiopian central government has mobilised the peasantry for military campaigns (*zamacha* and *gesgassa*), an element of coercion has been applied. If the peasants did not join, they would be punished by the confiscation of harvest or land. In modern times, the Derg regime gave orders to the regions to supply a certain number of recruits to an offensive. Districts (*woreda*) and neighbourhoods (*kebelle*) received a quota of soldiers they had to fill. The same system was also applied during the Eritrean-Ethiopian war; local administrators throughout Ethiopia were given quotas. If the quotas were not met by volunteers, the local administrators were inclined to recruit the remaining individuals by force, threatening to cut services from the *kebelle* (deny fertiliser credit, access to land, permits of various kinds, etc.) if the community did not provide the young men needed.

A second motivating factor for recruitment was poverty and payment. In the extremely poverty-stricken rural areas of Ethiopia, there is a general surplus of labour due to a lack of agricultural land. When the central government called for a general mobilisation, and offered payment to the recruits and compensation to the families left behind, many young men were sent to the recruitment camps by their families. To take up arms for the central authorities has throughout history been regarded as a noble occupation in Ethiopia. To send a family member to the war today means that the household has one mouth less to feed at the same time as receiving compensation, both in money and kind (grain) from the authorities. This leads to the last, and possibly the most important, motivating factor for recruitment to the war, namely, a cultural tradition of warring.

As an anthropologist, I avoid the simplistic argument that certain people are more culturally inclined to go to war than others. However, a number of studies have emphasised that 'Ethiopians', and in particular the highland people, do have a long and strong tradition of warring (cf. Ayele 1984; Donham 1986; Hoben 1970; Levine 1965a; Lewis 1998; Messing 1985 (1957); Molvaer 1995). As mentioned earlier, a social

204

norm in Ethiopia stipulates that if you are offended or your land is taken, you are expected to retaliate and fight. Molvaer explains that 'Cowardice and fear of fighting in times of war are despised and denigrated, and physical and open expression of contempt for one's enemy and a readiness to die for a national (or more personal) cause are extolled and highly admired' (1995: 147). Such a view still finds resonance in Ethiopia today, as expressed by Admassou Gebeyihu, chairman of the opposition party EDP: 'War has always been part of Ethiopian history. No matter where the war was fought, in Adwa, in Jimma or elsewhere, people from all groups participated to fight for Ethiopia' (personal communication).

The tradition of warring can most easily be explained with regard to gender roles and the importance of displaying male characteristics such as courage, determination, fighting skills, etc. However, more important than a tradition of warring as such to explain individual recruitment are two related culturally accepted notions: obedience and social mobility. In the strictly hierarchical *Habesha* society, authoritarian relationships are considered legitimate and necessary to sustain social order. An 'order from above' is thus supposed to be carried out without any questioning or doubt, which also applied to the call for recruitment to the Eritrean-Ethiopian war. Moreover, a particular feature of the hierarchical order in Ethiopia is its somewhat open character, allowing everyone, in principle, to rise from 'peasant to lord' by means of individual achievements. Upward social mobility was most easily achieved by participating and showing bravery in war campaigns, as referred to by Donham:

> It is, indeed, impossible to sum up in terms that are too strong the attraction of the military life for the Ethiopians ... The humblest villager once he was armed and mounted on his sorry nag, with even one ragged squire trotting at his side, had become a real man on the road to fortune and adventure. (Donham 1986: 7)

To sum up, let me take the EDP chairman Admassou Gebeyihu's words as my own: 'Ethiopianness is a process!' As shown above, the dynamics of Ethiopianness (*Ethiopiawinet*) involves interrelated and inter-dependent notions of: land and belongingness; elite alliances and power play; hierarchy and obedience; and maleness and bravery. The interplay between these notions helps to explain the massive backing for the war, at the same time as many also expressed a criticism of the central government itself.

## TRAJECTORIES OF ETHIOPIAN NATIONALISM

As shown in this book, collective expressions of identity (be that ethnicity or nationalism) are constantly changing and adapting to current affairs. Let me try to sum up and include the idea and development of Ethiopian nationalism in a conceptual framework, a framework which identifies the different expressions of nationalism during the shifting ideological regimes in the country.

Nationalism is basically an ideological expression of identity commonly shared by a certain group of people, an identity which is linked to a territory and may, *inter alia*, contain notions of common descent, a shared history, joint political interests, mutually understandable symbols, etc. From the perspective of the state (and its rulers) the nationalist identity is supposed to embrace – or to be superimposed on – a number of sub-identities (be they ethnic, regional or religiously defined) located within the political realm of the state. During the imperial reign, Ethiopian nationalism was a dominant ethnie-based nationalism, in which the state was draped in expressions of Amhara culture, symbols and religion. Thus, subaltern identities were subjugated to a dominant national identity

The Marxist-military regime of the Derg, coming to power in 1974, aimed to change the culturally dominant nationalist expression of the Ethiopian state, by draining the cultural content out of the nationalist idea. Thus, Ethiopian nationalism during the Derg regime (1974–91) was ideologically anchored as a territorially based political nationalism. Ideally, this nationalism was supposed to be free of any connotations of culture or ethnicity, and commonness should be anchored in political symbols and territorial expressions.

However, the legacies of the Imperial reign and the Amharaised expressions of the Ethiopian state lingered on, and many minority groups still experienced the nationalism projected by the Derg regime as culturally dominant and subjugating in character. Thus, the ethno-nationalist and ethnic-based resistance wars against the central government continued during the 1970s and '80s, leading to the collapse of the Derg regime in 1991, and the takeover of power in Addis Ababa by the EPRDF. As described earlier, the EPRDF came to power with a non-nationalist vision of Ethiopia, i.e. in its view the Ethiopian nation did not exist. For the EPRDF, Ethiopia was only a territory, hosting a number of different ethnic groups. Based on this perspective, the unitary Ethiopian state was reconfigured into an ethnic federation, which constitutionally put all ethnic groups in the country on an equal footing; they were all 'nations' by themselves. Thus, federal nationalist expressions and symbols were more or less non-existent in official state politics.

As we have seen in this study, however, with the outbreak of war in 1998 Ethiopia experienced a resurrection of nationalism, but in the plural. Since the EPRDF did not have the political legitimacy to define an overarching and hegemonic nationalist discourse and ideology capable of embracing the various Ethiopian communities, new expressions of nationalism took on a variety of forms, embedded in ethno-nationalist, nationalist and ideological discourses. The officially sanctioned nationalism designed and expressed by the EPRDF government was not powerful enough to neutralise other competing nationalist discourses, creating a complex and sometimes contradictory context of nationalist expressions. Ethiopian nationalism today, thus, comes in the plural.

# Note

1   One location or field of discourse not touched upon in this book where the war did have a massive impact is among the Eritrean/Ethiopian diaspora communities (particularly in the US and Europe). Immediately after the outbreak of hostilities, a number of new websites discussing and advocating the war from various political stand-points were established. Since 'long-distance' nationalism and diaspora studies are partly research fields of their own, I have deliberately not included a section on it in this book. For relevant studies so far on the Eritrean-Ethiopian 'cyber-war', see Sorensen and Matsuoka (2001); for an overview of different pieces posted on various internet sites, see the collection by Walta Information Centre (2000); and for an insight into the most active 'Eritrean diaspora cyber activist' see the compiled stories by Tekie Fesschatzion (2002).

# *Postscript*

## *After War, New Enemies*

The cycle of war in the Horn of Africa seems to be incessant. Instead of peace and stability, it is more likely that conflict appears after war. As this postscript is being written, eight years after the signing of the Algiers peace agreement between Eritrea and Ethiopia on 12 December 2000, the two countries are yet again closer to war than ever before. The Algiers agreement has collapsed and the UN peace-keeping mission to Eritrea and Ethiopia (UNMEE) terminated its operations during the summer of 2008 and pulled out all troops and military observers from the two countries.[1] The failure of the UN to pressure Ethiopia to accept the Boundary Commission's decision on the ground, in combination with Eritrea's obstructions to UNMEE's operational mandate, effectively eradicated the peace-keeping mission which UN diplomats eight years earlier had characterised as 'doomed to succeed'. The end result? The border is yet to be demarcated on the ground; Eritrea and Ethiopia are in disagreement on where the physical border markers should be erected; both countries have mobilised a huge number of troops along the border; and the parties continue their proxy war and hostile rhetoric against each other.

In this postscript I shall briefly revisit Ethiopia and present some of the changes that have taken place in the aftermath of the war which are of relevance to the argument of the book: the emergence of new enemies from within and without.

## Tigray: the nexus of conflict

Revisiting Tigray in the aftermath of the Eritrean-Ethiopian war reconfirmed the impression of the people's ambiguous perception of Eritrea: as an enemy in one context, and a friend and brother, in another. For

208

instance, the deputy chairman of Wuqro *woreda*, Wode Goshu, was pessimistic and claimed during the summer of 2000 that: 'We have brought peace by force and we will sustain the peace by force. If there is any provocation by Eritrea we will not hesitate to give them the final blow.' One year later, Thedros Adhanom, the head of the Bureau ('Ministry') of Health in Tigray, explained to me that 'People in Tigray do not want reconciliation yet, the feelings are too heated. They say "it is better to make friends with the devil, than to be reconciled with Eritrea".' However, such categorical remarks did not reflect the continued ambiguous and shifting perceptions of the image of Eritrea among many Tigrayans. Miriam, one of my main informants in Wuqro, was frustrated by the situation in July 2001, a year after the end of the war. She explained:

> Still there is no peace. I do not understand why people say this is peace. Our government is just sleeping, saying it is peace. But our people on the border are still being killed and harassed by Eritrean soldiers. We need peace. People on both sides are dying, and we are brothers in faith. But Issaias is still there and he doesn't want peace. The Eritrean soldiers are forced to enlist and they are thrown into the fire by Issaias. They are just poor peasants like us.

The frustrations with the TPLF/EPRDF government for not putting a firm end to the war, the hatred of the Eritrean leadership, and the commonality felt with Eritrean rank-and-file soldiers and civilians, were common emotions in Tigray in the aftermath of the war. However, the persistent hostile rhetoric and 'war of words' between the two governments, and their reluctance to enter into a normalisation of relations, continue to produce – eight years after the active hostilities ceased – officially sanctioned enemy images which prohibit any reconciliation on the ground between the 'brothers in faith'.

Compounding the frustrations and confusion in Tigray was the internal dissent movement within the TPLF/EPRDF which emerged in the wake of the war. One *shoabet* lady stated in anger: 'We have not even taken off our black dresses before our leaders start quarrelling.' What I had heard rumoured during the war about an internal disagreement between the upper echelons of the party and the military, came to the surface after the war was over. The internal dissent movement was close to achieving what Eritrea's President Issaias Afwerki had failed to do: to oust Meles Zenawi from power.

### NEW ENEMIES FROM WITHIN:
### THE POST-WAR TPLF/EPRDF CRISIS

The internal dissent within the TPLF/EPRDF became apparent during the Eritrean-Ethiopia war, although its full magnitude did not surface until 2001.[2] It is of interest here to comment briefly on how the dissent process reflected notions of identity and fighting.

The key initial factor creating the schism within the TPLF and its Central Committee was a disagreement over the handling of relations with the Eritrean government. The dissenters asserted that they had argued for a tougher stand against Eritrea prior to the outbreak of hostilities (i.e., that Ethiopia should not 'sponsor' Eritrean development), and after the outbreak they pressed for a more radical military strategy to beat back the invasion and to eliminate the political and military capacity of the Eritrean regime. *Inter alia*, it is claimed that the dissenters wanted to continue the final Ethiopian military offensive of June 2000 all the way to Asmara in order to topple – or at least paralyse permanently – the Issaias regime; a strategy Meles Zenawi blocked personally. Meles stood firm – at that time – on the principle that the offensive should stop once the disputed territories had been reclaimed. Thus, it is widely believed that Meles Zenawi was keener to engage in negotiations than in military options to settle the war, as he seemingly did not subscribe to the hegemonic enemy-image of Eritrea as projected by the dissenters. The reason for this 'weakness', people argued, was his partly Eritrean 'bloodline'.

The Eritrean issue clearly exacerbated the internal TPLF dispute,[3] but one should be careful to interpret it as only its primary cause. As argued elsewhere (Vaughan and Tronvoll 2003), it is plausible to suggest that another important source for the split was a general breakdown of trust, and consequent power struggle, between the leaders of two groups whose day-to-day interaction was no longer close enough to sanction and overcome divergence.[4] Yemane 'Jamaica' Kidane, a former key TPLF official at the Ministry of Foreign Affairs, accepted that the crisis was linked to the war, but its deeper roots he considered to be puzzling. However, he also stressed the issue of identity and enemy images as a pretext used by the dissenters: "The Eritrean issue is very emotional. They [dissenters] wanted to present it as if they were the only defenders of Ethiopian unity. But this is a falsification!"

Later, when the party's internal discussions moved to an overall evaluation of the conduct of government during the previous decade, the debate centred on ideological differences and divergence of opinion on the optimal development strategies for Ethiopia. The original group of dissenters, composed of twelve senior TPLF cadres in central positions within the party and regional government,[5] challenged the legitimacy of the views put forward by Meles Zenawi, accusing him of betraying core party principles and giving in to imperialism (i.e., 'accepting' priorities and demands imposed by the World Bank, the IMF and other donors in relation to development aid). The TPLF dissenters rallied support for their move against the chairman both internally within the TPLF and from the other EPRDF partners. In the initial phase, the chairmen of the TPLF coalition partners OPDO and the SEPDF supported the dissent against Meles, whilst the ANDM leadership maintained a neutral stand, or came out in support of Meles.[6] In the intense power struggle that followed, the key dissenters made the mistake of withdrawing from the CC meetings, and were subsequently discharged and later expelled from the organisation. Following the expulsions, the whole political and military apparatus underwent a process of critique/self-critique (*gemgum*), and thousands of party cadres sympathetic to the dissenters were removed. The OPDO and SEPDF leaderships were changed as a consequence of their support for the dissenters, and the key leaders were arrested on charges of alleged corruption.

Soon after the internal turmoil had settled somewhat, I asked Meles Zenawi to explain from his point of view what the origin of the internal dissent was based on:

> As the war progressed, weaknesses within the whole system of the EPRDF, ... weaknesses of government and of vision, became very visible. So the war was more like a magnifying glass. ... Some of us came to the conclusion that the biggest threat to Ethiopia under EPRDF was not the EPLF, but it was our own internal weaknesses and that we had to set our priorities correctly. We therefore felt that we should cut the war short and focus on revitalisation of the EPRDF. ... It was very clear that there was a lot of confusion, on who we were, what we were for? and so on. So we felt we should stop the war and clean up our own house. ... So the fundamental issue was what we now call the *tehaddaso*, renewal or rejuvenation movement of the EPRDF. ... It was what type of economic system we have, what type of democratic governance we have, what type of international relations we have, what is our vision, what is being carried on by way of baggage from the past, what is new, how do they relate to each other? ... *Then* it began to have an Eritrean dimension to it; the dimension of how do we relate to Eritrea? Is the issue to be understood the way the peasants understand it: one of fighting injustice, correcting injustice and insult? Or is it going to be understood as something going beyond that to revenge and cause pain? And even further beyond that, to a resurrection of imperial policy? The resurrection of imperial policy was too repugnant in the EPRDF for it to have any currency, but causing pain beyond what is required to correct injustice began to manifest itself in some quarters in the EPRDF.[7]

Although the internal dissent was anchored in a complex foundation, Meles Zenawi stressed the image of significant others/enemies and the perceptions of identity boundaries as important in understanding the dissent. Furthermore, his explanation has several layers of references to the core issues debated in this book: the understanding of what constitutes Ethiopia (as an ethnic federation or as a 'Greater Ethiopia' notion?); what Tigray/Tigrayanness represents (Tigray as a component part of the Ethiopian federation, or as a separate 'Greater Tigray' entity?);[8] and the image of Eritrea as an enemy or a friend/brother.

No doubt the 2001 dissent process altered power relations within the TPLF, within the EPRDF coalition, and between the TPLF and its constituencies. More importantly, it created new categories of enemies in

Ethiopia (enemies defined from within); it altered the perception of Tigrayan unity and struggle; and it inspired a shift of alliances within the EPRDF.

The dissent process resulted in the expulsion of a number of senior TPLF cadres and liberation heroes of the 17 years of struggle, stigmatising them as 'narrow-chauvinists', 'expansionists', 'corrupt' and working against the interest of the people. Since many of the dissenters were held in great esteem in Tigray (for their war record during both the struggle against the Derg and the Eritrean war), many Tigrayans and other Ethiopians who supported more active warfare against Eritrea became disillusionised. The expulsion of the dissenters thus resulted in the alienation of large parts of the Tigrayan constituency, although many had also resigned themselves to the situation. Consequently, the TPLF – who were once viewed as sons and daughters of the Tigrayan people – can no longer claim to have the united backing of its home constituency. It seems, for instance, impossible that Tigrayans will continue to speak of 'our organisation' (*wedibna*) and refer to the TPLF fighters/ cadres as our 'cubs' (i.e. closeness/familiarity, *hayet*) in the remarkably uniform way that was prevalent during the war and up to the eruption of the crisis in 2001. As such, the self-perception of Tigrayanness, as a unified people struggling (*weyane/ habbo* metaphor) to achieve common objectives, has changed and been replaced with confusion and divisions (emerging *awrajanet* metaphor).

This impression was confirmed when I revisited Tigray after the turmoil of the dissent process had settled. Contacts in Mekelle were openly critical of the 'new' TPLF and the way the dissenters were treated. A group of Tigrayan intellectuals explained in the spring of 2003 the fear many Tigrayans face in contemporary Ethiopia: 'The TPLF no longer represent us. Due to their ethnic policies, authoritarianism and conflicts, they have turned all other Ethiopian groups against us. We are pushed from all corners and stand with our backs against the wall. Meles is pulling us all down with him.' The rural informants, on the other hand, were more careful and expressed a cautious disengagement with regard to the TPLF dissent process, excusing themselves by the fact that the conflicting issues were discussed at top level 'out of reach' for them, both physically and conceptually.

## DEMOCRACY NO MORE:
### MELES SHOWING HIS TRUE COLOURS?

The Eritrean-Ethiopian war and its unclear outcome, the internal dissent process, and the multiple other development challenges facing the EPRDF government severely undermined its popular base and authority during the post-war period. The political desperation of the leadership became obvious in the language which was used in the so-called 'forums of dialogue' which the government hosted in 2002/3 with the commercial sector, institutions of higher education and opposition parties as part of its 'renewal' (*tadhesso*) campaign – in order to persuade them to follow its development policies. An experienced social scientist at Addis Ababa University sent me the following e-mail of concern after Meles Zenawi himself had spent three weeks deliberating with the University faculty over the future of Ethiopia and the policy of higher education in the summer of 2002:

> The language of the government is alarmist – meaning that the views stated by the government officials, including Meles Zenawi himself, are based on a discourse of danger. It is often stressed that the issue of democracy in Ethiopia is the issue of 'survival' [*hiliwuna*]. Moreover, they emphasised that the issue of Ethiopian unity and the right to self-determination for 'nations, nationalities and peoples' are, at one and the same time, an issue of survival of the Ethiopian state as such. Without endorsing the constitutional principles of self-determination, Ethiopia may face the danger of disintegration and fragmentation [*yemebetaten adega*], it was claimed.

My contact at the university was confused by the government's alarmist rhetoric, and by the way key government officials admitted possible future scenarios of chaos, anarchy and mayhem in Ethiopia, if civil society questioned government policies. At the university meeting, Meles Zenawi went so far as to claim that 'Ethiopia could be worse than Somalia and Rwanda' and that the very survival (*hiliwuna*) and territorial integrity (*yemebetaten adega*) of the country were threatened.

This warning was to be repeated during the 2005 post-election chaos, when opposition leaders were accused of plotting Rwanda-style genocide in Ethiopia. In the aftermath of the dissent process, however, the government still proclaimed its support for democracy as the best system of governance for Ethiopia. In a confidential meeting with the Prime Minister, at which concerns about the TPLF/EPRDF's genuine commitment to democracy were raised, Meles responded with all the right phrases to deflect criticism, seemingly accepting the supremacy of human rights and democracy:

> Democracy is the best system to accommodate diversity, and for us it is a matter of choice. Countries can be democratic and survive. Countries can also be undemocratic and survive. For Ethiopia, however, we have to be democratic to survive. For us there is no choice. Democracy is a question of survival for many reasons. We are a multi-ethnic country. Throughout history we have tried forced assimilation; we have pretended that ethnicity is not relevant; it has all failed. In 1991 we saw a possible collapse of Ethiopia if something was not done: either we accommodate diversity and survive, or we'll start to consume each other. For us it is a matter of survival.[9]

Developments in recent years in Ethiopia – in particular since the 2005 elections – appear as a stark contrast to Meles Zenawi's earlier guarantees of democracy. In the run-up to the 2005 election, however, it seemed that the ruling party was willing to permit more genuine competition between political contenders, at least in urban settings and through the national media (Harbeson 2005; Lyons 2006). However, when the counting began and the government became aware of the huge electoral advance made by the opposition, it immediately suspended the counting and imposed a blanket ban on freedom of assembly in Addis Ababa. The EU observer mission assessed the closing and counting process negatively in almost half of the urban polling stations observed and even more in rural stations (EU-EOM 2005). After a highly dubious process of recounts and re-elections in certain constituencies, the Ethiopian National Election Board proclaimed the EPRDF as the winner. Although the opposition block had gained a dramatic increase in representation in the parliament in comparison with earlier elections, they protested at the announcement. Nation-wide demonstrations were called for, in which close to 200 demonstrators in total were killed in Addis Ababa during protests in June and late November 2005. In order to curb the increasing resistance to the government, a nation-wide clamp-down was ordered. About 20–30,000 opposition members and sympathisers (predominantly belonging to the Coalition for Unity and Democracy, CUD) were detained for shorter and longer periods. The CUD leadership, including the newly elected mayor of Addis Ababa, were arrested on charges of instigating violence, attempting an unconstitutional change of government and even attempting genocide (a charge later dropped by the court). Also civil society organisations and the private media were targeted and closed down. The promising electoral process in 2005 as experienced prior to the election day in May turned into a bloody and failed affair by the end of the year (Abbink 2006).

The 2005 elections were an eye-opener for the EPRDF government, as they suddenly realised that they did not have the latent support of the rural constituencies which they had previously taken for granted. The self-perception of the EPRDF as the 'defenders of Ethiopian integrity and sovereignty' was shattered, as large segments of the electorate accused them of spoiling the victory of the war and jeopardising the country's future by pursuing their ethnic policies. Since then, the government has been closing the political space in the country, step by step, by various means and mechanisms (Aalen and Tronvoll 2009b). Of particular concern is the dramatic increase and broadening of local structures of political administration staffed by EPRDF cadres, in combination with the ratification of a number of new laws – such as the new media law, the political party law and a NGO law – curbing democratic space and undermining human rights in the country. Finally, the conduct of the 2008 local elections – when intimidation, harassment and large-scale obstructionism prevented the opposition parties from registering their candidates – clearly indicated that the EPRDF government is determined to pursue a strategy of political authoritarianism in order to stem opposition gains (Aalen and Tronvoll 2009a).

# New wars on the horizon

It seems clear that the EPRDF government is consistent in its politics of repression and human rights violations – a strategy which has not changed in the aftermath of the war (FIDH 2005; Tronvoll 2008). The continuation of a polarised political landscape within Ethiopia, where the government and the opposition parties are entrenched in a fierce political struggle, also facilitates the emergence of a new discourse on 'enemies', namely, internal enemies of the state, as seen from the point of view of the power-holders. When the EPRDF government tries to convince the Ethiopian public – more by coercion than conviction – that without it in power the country will disintegrate, the government itself has a serious credibility problem. Therefore, 'the people' who perceive themselves as oppressed will thus sustain the demotic image of the government as their enemy. Consequently, images of enemies will be perpetuated in an interrelated and interdependent process of escalating conflict between the government and increasingly larger sections of Ethiopian society. And, as comparative history and politics have shown, the more isolated the government becomes internally, the more authoritarian its strategies must be to maintain it in power.

The Oromos of Ethiopia have for some time been stigmatised as an inner enemy, an image which has been sustained during the post-war period (HRW 2005). Furthermore, with the Ethiopian military intervention in Somalia in December 2007 – so-called heeding a call for support from the Transitional Federal Government of Somalia (TFG) – the position of Ethiopian Somalis became even more vulnerable. The operations of the armed Somali opposition in Ethiopia (most notably the Ogaden National Liberation Front, ONLF) increasingly posed a threat to government positions both in Somalia proper and in Ogaden. A massive military mopping-up operation was undertaken in the Somali region of Ethiopia in 2007, with the two-fold objective of eliminating the military capacities of the ONLF simultaneously with cracking down on growing civil support for the resistance movement. The Ethiopian military operations were conducted in a manner which collectively categorised the Ethiopian Somali people as enemies of the state, resulting *inter alia* in the destruction and burning down of whole villages and ensuing widespread human rights abuses (HRW 2008).

Ethiopia's engagement in Somalia was motivated by several intertwining processes: Eritrea's support for the Union of Islamic Courts (UIC), the Islamist movement which took control of Mogadishu in the summer of 2006; the UIC's expansionist agenda which appeared to threaten Ethiopia's territorial integrity; and finally, as a strategic partner of the US in its war on terror in the Horn. The Ethiopian army's campaign in Somalia is still being sustained as this is being written, although they pulled the military troops out of Mogadishu in early 2009.

Ethiopia's ongoing conflicts with Eritrea in the north and Somalia in the south-west may soon be complemented by a third front against Sudan in the east. Addis-Khartoum relations have deteriorated sharply during 2008, as Asmara-Khartoum relations have correspondingly improved. During the summer of 2008, a border dispute brewing between the two countries became known. Furthermore, as this is being written, the Khartoum government has protested fiercely against Ethiopian-sponsored arm supplies to South Sudan, where the regional government is restocking its military hardware in preparation for the future conflict over the region's independence. With conflicts in the north, south and west, it seems likely that the old Tigrayan proverb will once again come true: 'God fenced the paradise, Ethiopia, with fire!'

Considering the history and current political context of the Horn of Africa, it would be hazardous, if not completely foolhardy, to elevate 'lasting peace' as a practical objective for the region – however cherished a normative principle it might seem (Abbink 2003). The challenge for the Horn of Africa is that state (re)formation is not yet finished: it will continue to produce persistent conflicts on the basis of perceived historical, cultural, material, political and other issues (Clapham 2000). Thus, as noted by Jon Abbink, the most one can hope for in the current conditions of state authoritarianism, ethnic tensions, state interventions, ecological fragility, and political unreliability is a manageable state of 'no armed conflict', and the gradual development of a wider regional conflict-resolution structure.

It is unlikely that an amicable relationship will be re-established between Eritrea and Ethiopia with the current government executives in power. As long as both of them are entertaining the presumption that 'the other party is internally more vulnerable' and 'as long as I hang in there, the other party will eventually collapse', they do not personally hold any real incentive to normalise relations. When I traversed the Ethiopian-Eritrean border from Axum to the Eritrean refugee camp Shimelba on the outskirts of the Badme plains in the Spring of 2008, I passed dozens of military camps and settlements all ready to resume hostilities when ordered to do so. And as long as there is little or no measure of democratic control through, for example, the realisation of civil and political rights, the political leaders can continue to disregard people's interests and economic and social development in their own countries by solving political conflicts with arms.

# Notes

1 UN Security Council Resolution No. 1827, 2008.
2 This section builds partly on what I wrote with Sarah Vaughan in our analysis of contemporary political power and power relations in Ethiopia (Vaughan and Tronvoll 2003).
3 For instance, Gebru Assrat, former President of Tigray regional state and TPLF CC member, at a meeting in London in August 2002 identified the fact that 'Meles Zenawi's group sidelined the nation's sovereignty, independence and territorial integrity' as the basic issue of dissent, while Meles Zenawi's group had advanced 'fighting Bonapartism and corruption' as the primary topic of division (*Press Digest*, Vol. IX, No. 34, 22 August 2002, p. 2).
4 Whilst no hard and fast distinction can be made between those TPLF CC members who supported the dissenters (led by Tewolde Woldemariam and Siyhe Abraha), and those who supported Meles Zenawi, one indicative line of division is perhaps the fact that the former group were largely party officials based predominantly in Tigray (rather than state operatives), dealing primarily with internal party business and through party channels, and having little contact with outsiders or the international community. The latter group, meanwhile, was more closely involved with the development of government and commercial business based predominantly in Addis Ababa, engaging and socialising more closely with social sectors and groups outside the party structure and with the international community, and thus presumably thereby more open to external influence.
5 The original twelve dissenting members were: Tewolde Woldemariam (at that time vice-chairman of TPLF), Abbay Tsehaye, Gebru Assrat, Siye Abraha, Alemseged Gebreamlak, Ms. Aregash Adane, Awalom Woldu, Gebremeskel Hailu, Hassan Shifa, Solomon Tesfai, Abraha Kahsai, and Bitew Belay. Later, Hassan Shifa and Abbay Tsehaye became self-criticised and rejoined Meles' faction and remained in the TPLF.
6 The initial 'division' within the EPRDF was the vote against the adoption of the Technical Arrangements Agreement (in defeat of Meles' view) presented by the OAU/UN negotiating team on the Eritrean-Ethiopian war at the end of 1999. OPDO and ANDM were 100 percent against, and in the SEPDF two voted in favour and the rest against, whilst the TPLF split 17 against and 14 in favour of the agreement. This defeat for Meles probably led the TPLF dissenters to think that they would also have support for a general vote of confidence against him. This move failed, and those who did support the TPLF dissenters from OPDO and the SEPDF seem to have been those with whom the TPLF party liaison people (between TPLF and OPDO and SEPDF respectively) had the best connection. Their failure to garner support within ANDM suggests that this kind of influential liaison relationship did not operate in the same way between the TPLF and ANDM (Vaughan and Tronvoll 2003).
7 Recorded interview, 16 January 2002 Addis Ababa.
8 'Greater Tigray' refers to the idea that the Tigrinya-speaking people of Eritrea and Ethiopia should be united into one polity, an idea that has its historical roots in Italian colonialism and their *politicia tigrinia*. Many believed that the true intention of the TPLF dissenters was to conquer the EPLF in order to establish 'Greater Tigray'.
9 The meeting took place on 9 October 2001 in Addis Ababa; the author and three other persons, in addition to PM Meles Zenawi and his personal assistant, were present.

# List of Official Interviews

In addition to the list of formal interviews below, a number of informal meetings and conversations were carried out during and after the war with party leaders from both opposition and the EPRDF system. Since these conversations have not been quoted in the text, they are not listed below.

Admassou Gebeyihu: Chairman of Ethiopian Democratic Party (EDP). Recorded interview 12 July 2001, Addis Ababa

Almaz Mako: Speaker of House of Federation, senior OPDO/EPRDF cadre. Interview 16 June 1999, Addis Ababa.

Aregawi Berhe: Founding member and former leader of TPLF. Recorded interviewed 23 October 2001, Leiden, The Netherlands

Beyene Petros: Chairman of Southern Ethiopian Peoples' Democratic Coalition (SEPDC). Interviewed 12 February 2000 and 18 May 2000, Addis Ababa.

Dauwd Ibsa: Chairman of Oromo Liberation Front (OLF). Recorded interview summer of 2001, location confidential.

Dawit Yohannes: Speaker of the House of Representatives and ANDM executive committee member. Interviewed 26 April 1995, Addis Ababa; 17 May 2002, Addis Ababa

Ghidey Zeratsion: Founding member and former deputy leader of TPLF. Personal communication, 19 November 2002, Oslo

Hassan Shifa: TPLF Central Committee member and chief of security in Tigray. Recorded interview 7 June 1999, Mekelle.

Iyasou Goshu (nom de guerre 'Wode-Goshu').: TPLF veteran fighter and deputy district administrator in Wuqro. Interviewed 11 June 1999; 27 July 2000. Wukro.

Lencho Bati: Oromo Liberation Front (OLF) foreign spokesperson. Interviewed, July 2001, Washington, DC.

Meles Zenawi: Prime Minister and chairman of TPLF/EPRDF. Interviewed, 9 October 2001 and 16 January 2002, Addis Ababa.

Merera Gudina: Chairman of Oromo National Congress (ONC). Recorded interview, 26 February 1999, Addis Ababa

Sebhat Nega: TPLF/EPRDF executive committee member. Recorded interview, 19 November 1998, Addis Ababa (in addition to several conversations during the war).

Yemane Ghebreab: Head of Political Department, PFDJ/EPLF. Interviewed, 10 October 1998 in Asmara.

Yemane 'Jamaica' Kidane: TPLF/EPRDF senior cadre; MFA senior spokesperson. Recorded interview, 2 March 1999, Addis Ababa; interviews, 19 November 1998, 17 May 2000, Addis Ababa; 10 July 2001, Addis Ababa.

# References

Aalen, Lovise. 2002a. *Ethnic Federalism in a Dominant Party State: The Ethiopian Experience 1991-2000*. Bergen: Chr. Michelsen Institute.

—. 2002b. 'Expressions of Control, Fear and Devotion. The Elections in Mekelle and Wukro, Tigray Region' in *Ethiopia Since the Derg. A Decade of Democratic Pretension and Performance*, edited by Siegfried Pausewang, Kjetil Tronvoll and Lovise Aalen. London: Zed Books.

Aalen, Lovise and Kjetil Tronvoll. 2009a. 'The 2008 Ethiopian Local Elections: The return of electoral authoritarianism.' *African Affairs* 108.

Aalen, Lovise and Kjetil Tronvoll. 2009b. 'The end of democracy? Curtailing political and civil rights in Ethiopia.' *Review of African Political Economy* 36.

Abbay, Alemseged. 1998. *Identity Jilted or Re-imagining Identity? The Divergent Paths of the Eritrean and Tigrayan Nationalistic Struggles*. Lawrenceville, NJ: Red Sea Press.

Abbink, Jon. 1995. 'Breaking and Making the State: The Dynamics of Ethnic Democracy in Ethiopia.' *Journal of Contemporary African Studies* 13: 149–63.

—. 1998. 'Briefing: The Eritrean-Ethiopian Border Dispute.' *African Affairs* 97: 551–65.

—. 2000. 'Violence and the Crisis of Conciliation: Suri, Dizi and the State in South-West Ethiopia.' *Africa* 70: 527–50.

—. 2001. 'Creating borders: exploring the impact of the Ethio-Eritrean war on the local population.' *Africa* (Rome) 56: 447–58.

—. 2003. 'Ethiopia-Eritrea: Proxy Wars and Prospects for Peace in the Horn of Africa.' *Journal of Contemporary African Studies* 21: 407–25.

—. 2006. 'Discomfiture of democracy? The 2005 election crisis in Ethiopia and its aftermath.' *African Affairs* 105: 173–99.

Abir, Mordechai. 1968. *Ethiopia: The Era of the Princes*. London: Longman.

AI. 1999. *Ethiopia and Eritrea: Human rights issues in a year of armed conflict*. London: Amnesty International.

Alonso, Ana María. 1994. 'The Politics of Space, Time and Substance: State Formation, Nationalism, and Ethnicity.' *Annual Review of Anthropology* 23: 379–405.

Alvarez, Robert R. 1995. 'The Mexican-US border: the making of an anthropology of borderlands.' *Annual Review of Anthropology* 24: 447–70.

Anderson, Benedict. 1983. *Imagined Communities. Reflections on the Origin and Spread of*

*Nationalism*. London and New York: Verso.

Appadurai, Arjun. 1991. 'Global Ethnoscapes: Notes and Queries for a Transitional Anthropology.' in *Recapturing Anthropology: Working in the Present*, edited by Richard G. Fox. Santa Fe, NM: School of American Research Press.

Arrowsmith-Brown, J.H. (ed.). 1991. *Prutky's Travels in Ethiopia and Other Countries*. London: Hakluyt Soccity.

Aspen, Harald. 2001. *Amhara Traditions of Knowledge. Spirit Mediums and their Clients*. Wiesbaden: Harrassowitz Verlag.

Ayele, Negussay. 1984. 'A Brief Profile of Wars in the Horn of Africa.' *Northeast African Studies* 6:1–11.

Balsvik, Randi. 1985. *Haile Selassie's Students: Rise of Social and Political Consciousness*. East Lansing, MI: African Studies Centre, Michigan State University.

Barth, Fredrik. 1969. 'Introduction.' in *Ethnic Groups and Boundaries: The Social Organization of Cultural Difference*, edited by Fredrik Barth. Oslo: Universitetsforlaget.

—. 1992. 'Towards greater naturalism in conceptualizing societies.' in *Conceptualizing Society*, edited by Adam Kuper. London: Routledge.

—. 1994. 'Enduring and emerging issues in the analysis of ethnicity.' in *The Anthropology of Ethnicity: Beyond 'Ethnic Groups and Boundaries'*, edited by Hans Vermeulen and Cora Govers. Amsterdam: Het Spinhuis.

—. 2000. 'Boundaries and connections.' in *Signifying Identities. Anthropological perspectives on boundaries and contested values*, edited by Anthony P. Cohen. London and New York: Routledge.

Bauer, Dan F. 1973. 'Land, Leadership and Legitimacy among the Inderta Tigray of Ethiopia.' in *Anthropology*. Rochester, NY: University of Rochester Press.

—. 1989. 'The Sacred and the Secret: Order and Chaos in Tigray Medicine and Politics.' in *Creativity of Power. Cosmology and Action in African Societies*, edited by William Arens and Ivan Karp. Washington, DC and London: Smithsonian Institution Press.

Baxter, P. T. W. 1994. 'The Creation and Constitution of Oromo Nationality.' in *Ethnicity and Conflict in the Horn of Africa*, edited by Katsuyoshi Fukui and John Markakis. London: James Currey and Athens, OH: Ohio University Press.

Baxter, P. T. W., Jan Hultin, and Alessandro Triulzi (eds.). 1996. *Being and Becoming Oromo, Historical and Anthropological Enquiries*. Uppsala: Nordic Africa Institute.

Beckingham, C.F. and G.W.B. Huntingford. 1961. *The Prester John of the Indies*. Cambridge: Cambridge University Press for the Hakluyt Society.

Bekele, Shiferaw. 1990. 'The State in the Zamana Masafent (1786–1853).' in *Kasa and Kasa. Papers on the Lives, Times and Images of Téwodros II and Yohannes IV (1855-1889)*, edited by Taddesse Beyene, Richard Pankhurst, and Shiferaw Bekele. Addis Ababa: Institute of Ethiopian Studies, Addis Ababa University.

Berhane, Mekonnen. 1994. *A Political History of Tigray: Shawan Centralisation versus Tigrean Regionalism (1889–1910)*. Department of History, Addis Ababa: Addis Ababa University.

Berhe, Aregawi. 2004. 'The Origins of the Tigray People's Liberation Front.' *African Affairs* 103:569–92.

Beyene, Taddesse, Richard Pankhurst, and Shiferaw Bekele (eds). 1990. *Kasa and Kasa. Papers on the Lives, Times and Images of Téwodros II and Yohannes IV*

*(1855–1889)*. Addis Ababa: Institute of Ethiopian Studies, Addis Ababa University.

Brietzke, Paul H. 1995. 'Ethiopia's 'Leap in the Dark': Federalism and Self-Determination in the New Constitution.' *Journal of African Law* 39:19–38.

Bringa, Tone. 1995. *Being Muslim the Bosnian Way. Identity and Community in a Central Bosnian Village*. Princeton, NJ: Princeton University Press.

Broch-Due, Vigdis (ed.). 2005. *Violence and Belonging. The quest for identity in post-colonial Africa*. London and New York: Routledge.

Bruce, John W. 1976. 'Land Reform Planning and Indigenous Communal Tenures: A case study of the tenure 'chiguraf-gwoses' in Tigray, Ethiopia,' in *School of Law*. Madison, WI: University of Wisconsin.

Calhoun, Craig. 1999. 'Ethiopia's Ethnic Cleansing'. *Dissent*: 47-50.

Central Statistical Authority. 1998a. *The 1994 Population and Housing Census of Ethiopia. Summary Reports at Country and Regional Levels*. Addis Ababa: Office of Population and Housing Census Commission, Federal Democratic Republic of Ethiopia.

—. 1998b. *The 1994 Population and Housing Census of Ethiopia: Results for Tigray Region, vol. II Analytical Report*. Addis Ababa: Office of Population and Housing Census Commission.

Chiari, Gian Paolo. 1996. *Land and Democracy in Tigray*. Leeds: Centre for Development Studies, University of Leeds.

Clapham, Christopher. 1969. *Haile-Selassie's Government*. London and Harlow: Longman.

—. 1988. *Transformation and Continuity in Revolutionary Ethiopia*. Cambridge: Cambridge University Press.

—. 1996a. *Africa and the International System. The Politics of State Survival*. Cambridge: Cambridge University Press.

—. 1996b. 'Boundary and Territory in the Horn of Africa.' in *African Boundaries: Barriers, Conduits and Opportunities*, edited by Paul Nugent and A. I. Asiwaju. London: Pinter.

—. 2000. 'War and state formation in Ethiopia and Eritrea.' in *The Global Site*. Brighton, UK: University of Sussex.

—. 2001. 'The Price of Land.' *Times Literary Supplement*. London, 23 November.

—. 2002. 'Controlling Space in Ethiopia', in *Remapping Ethiopia. Socialism and After*, edited by Wendy James, Donald L. Donham, Eisei Kurimoto, and Alessandro Triulzi. Oxford: James Currey; Athens, OH: Ohio University Press and Addis Ababa: Addis Ababa University Press.

Clifford, James. 1986. 'Introduction: Partial Truths,' in *Writing Culture. The Poetics and Politics of Ethnography*, edited by James Clifford and George E. Marcus. Berkeley, Los Angeles, London: University of California Press.

Cohen, Anthony P. 1985. *The Symbolic Construction of Community*. London and New York: Routledge.

—. 1994a. 'Boundaries of consciousness, consciousness of boundaries. Critical questions in anthropology,' in *The Anthropology of Ethnicity: Beyond Ethnic Groups and Boundaries*, edited by H. Vermeulen and C. Govers. Amsterdam: Het Spinhuis.

—. 1994b. *Self Consciousness: An Alternative Anthropology of Identity*. London and New York: Routledge.

—. 2000. 'Introduction. Discriminating relations: identity, boundary and authenticity.' in *Signifying Identities*, edited by Anthony P. Cohen. London and

New York: Routledge.

Cohen, John M., and Dov Weintraub. 1975. *Land and Peasants in Imperial Ethiopia. The Social Background to a Revolution.* Assen, Netherlands: Van Gorcum.

Comaroff, John L., and Paul C. Stern. 1995. 'New Perspectives on Nationalism and War,' in *Perspectives on Nationalism and War*, edited by John L. Comaroff and Paul C. Stern. Amsterdam: Gordon and Breach Science Publishers.

Connerton, Paul. 1989. *How Societies Remember.* Cambridge: Cambridge University Press.

Conversi, Daniele. 1995. 'Reassessing Current Theories of Nationalism: Nationalism as Boundary Maintenance and Creation.' *Nationalism and Ethnic Politics* 1:73–85.

—. 1999. 'Nationalism, Boundaries, and Violence.' *Millennium: Journal of International Studies* 28:553–84.

Crummey, Donald. 1986. 'Banditry and resistance: noble and peasant in nineteenth-century Ethiopia,' in *Banditry, Rebellion and Social Protest in Africa*, edited by Donald Crummey. London: James Currey.

—. 2000. *Land and Society in the Christian Kingdom of Ethiopia, from the Thirteenth to the Twentieth Century.* Urbana and Chicago, IL: University of Illinois Press; Oxford: James Currey; Addis Ababa: Addis Ababa University Press.

Daniel, E. Valentine. 1996. *Charred Lullabies: Chapters in an Anthropography of Violence.* Princeton, NJ: Princeton University Press.

Donham, Donald. 1986. 'Old Abyssinia and the New Ethiopian Empire: Themes in Social History.' in *The Southern Marches of Imperial Ethiopia*, edited by Donald Donham and Wendy James. Cambridge: Cambridge University Press.

—. 1999. *Marxist Modern. An Ethnographic History of the Ethiopian Revolution.* Berkeley and Los Angeles: University of California Press; Oxford: James Currey.

—. 2002. 'Introduction.' in *Remapping Ethiopia. Socialism and After*, edited by Wendy James, Donald L. Donham, Eisei Kurimoto, and Alessandro Triulzi. Oxford, James Currey; Athens, OH: Ohio University Press and Addis Ababa: Addis Ababa University Press.

Donham, Donald and Wendy James (eds). 1986. *The Southern Marches of Imperial Ethiopia.* Cambridge: Cambridge University Press.

Donnan, Hastings and Thomas M. Wilson (eds). 1994. *Border Approaches. Anthropological Perspectives on Frontiers.* Lanham, MD: University Press of America.

EHRCO. 2000. *EHRCO's 1st report on the May General Elections: Problems of the registration process.* Addis Ababa: Ethiopian Human Rights Council.

Eriksen, Thomas Hylland. 1991. 'The Cultural Context of Ethnic Differences.' *Man* 26: 127–44.

—. 1993a. *Ethnicity and Nationalism. Anthropological Perspectives.* London: Pluto Press.

—. 1993b. 'Formal and informal nationalism.' *Ethnic and Racial Studies* 16.

Erlich, Haggai. 1981. 'Tigrean Nationalism, British Involvement and Haila-Sellasse's Emerging Absolutism – Northern Ethiopia, 1941–1943.' *Asian and African Studies* (Haifa) 15:191–227.

—. 1986. *Ethiopia and the Challenge of Independence.* Boulder, CO: Lynne Rienner.

—. 1996. *Ras Alula and the Scramble for Africa. A Political Biography: Ethiopia and Eritrea 1875-1897.* Lawrenceville, NJ: Red Sea Press.

EU-EOM. 2005. 'Ethiopia Legislative Elections 2005 Final Report.' Brussels: European Union Election Observer Mission.

Feldman, Allen. 1991. *Formations of Violence. The Narrative of the Body and Political*

## References

*Terror in Northern Ireland.* Chicago and London: University of Chicago Press.

Fernyhough, Timothy. 1986. 'Social mobility and dissident elites in Northern Ethiopia: the role of bandits, 1900-69,' in *Banditry, Rebellion and Social Protest in Africa*, edited by Donald Crummey. London: James Currey.

Fessehatzion, Tekie. 2002. *Shattered Illusion, Broken Promise. Essays on the Eritrea-Ethiopia Conflict (1998-2000)*. Lawrenceville, NJ: Red Sea Press.

FIDH. 2005. 'Ethiopia: Human rights defenders under pressure.' Paris: International Federation for Human Rights.

Firebrace, James and Gayle Smith. 1982. *The Hidden Revolution. An analysis of Social Change in Tigray (Northern Ethiopia) based on eyewitness accounts*. London: War on Want.

Gabre-Selassie, Zewde. 1975. *Yohannes IV of Ethiopia. A Political Biography*. Oxford: Clarendon Press.

Gampel, Yolanda. 2000. 'Reflections on the prevalence of the uncanny in social violence,' in *Cultures under Siege*, edited by Antonius C. G. M Robben and Marcelo M. Suárez-Orozco. Cambridge: Cambridge University Press.

Gelaye, Getie. 2000. *Peasants and the Ethiopian State. Agricultural producers' cooperatives and their reflections in Amharic oral poetry*. Münster, Hamburg, London: Lit Verlag.

Gellner, Ernest. 1983. *Nations and Nationalism*. Oxford: Blackwell.

Gupta, Akhil and James Ferguson. 1997a. 'Beyond 'Culture': Space, Identity, and the Politics of Difference,' in *Culture, Power, Place. Explorations in Critical Anthropology*, edited by Akhil Gupta and James Ferguson. Durham, NC and London: Duke University Press.

— (eds.). 1997b. *Culture, Power, Place. Explorations in Critical Anthropology*. Durham NC and London: Duke University Press.

Gupta, Dipankar. 2000. *Culture, Space and the Nation-state. From Sentiment to Structure*. New Delhi, Thousand Oaks, CA and London: Sage Publications.

Hammond, Jenny. 1990. *Sweeter Than Honey. Ethiopian Women and Revolution: Testimonies of Tigrayan Women*. Trenton, NJ: Red Sea Press.

—. 1999. *Fire From the Ashes. A Chronicle of the Revolution in Tigray, Ethiopia, 1975-1991*. Lawrenceville, NJ.: Red Sea Press.

Harbeson, John W. 2005. 'Ethiopia's Extended Transition.' *Journal of Democracy* 16:144–58.

Hastrup, Kirsten and Karen Fog Olwig. 1997. 'Introduction,' in *Siting Culture. The shifting anthropological object*, edited by Karen Fog Olwig and Kirsten Hastrup. London and New York: Routledge.

Hechter, Michael. 2000. *Containing Nationalism*. Oxford: Oxford University Press.

Herzfeld, Michael. 1997. *Cultural Intimacy, Social Poetics in the Nation-State*. New York and London: Routledge.

Hoben, Allan. 1970. 'Social Stratification in Traditional Amhara Society,' in *Social Stratification in Africa*, edited by Arthur Tuden and Leonard Plotnicov. New York: Free Press.

—. 1973. *Land Tenure among the Amhara of Ethiopia. The Dynamics of Cognatic Descent*. Chicago and London: University of Chicago Press.

Hobsbawm, Eric J. 1983. 'Introduction: Inventing Traditions.' in *The Invention of Tradition*, edited by Eric J. Hobsbawm and Terence Ranger. Cambridge: Cambridge University Press.

Holcomb, Bonnie K. and Sisai Ibssa. 1990. *The Invention of Ethiopia*. Trenton, NJ: Red Sea Press.

# References

Howard, Michael. 1991. 'War and Nations.' in *Nationalism*, edited by John Hutchinson and Anthony D. Smith. Oxford: Oxford University Press.

HRW. 2003a. *Ethiopia. Lessons in Repression: Violations of Academic Freedom in Ethiopia.* Washington, DC: Human Rights Watch.

—. 2003b. *The Horn of Africa War: Mass Expulsions and the Nationality Issue (June 1998 – April 2002).* Washington, DC: Human Rights Watch.

—. 2005. *Suppressing Dissent: Human Rights Abuses and Political Repression in Ethiopia's Oromia Region,* New York: Human Rights Watch.

—. 2008. *Collective Punishment: War Crimes and Crimes against Humanity in the Ogaden area of Ethiopia's Somali Regional State.* Washington DC: Human Rights Watch.

ICG. 2003. 'Ethiopia and Eritrea: War or Peace?' in *Africa Report.* Brussels: International Crisis Group.

Iyob, Ruth. 1995. *The Eritrean Struggle for Independence. Domination, resistance, nationalism 1941-1993.* Cambridge: Cambridge University Press.

Jacuin-Berdal, Dominique and Martin Plaut (eds). 2005. *Unfinished Business. Ethiopia and Eritrea at War.* Lawrenceville, NJ: Red Sea Press.

Jalata, Asafa. 1998a. 'The Cultural Roots of Oromo Nationalism,' in *Oromo Nationalism and the Ethiopian Discourse,* edited by Asafa Jalata. Lawrenceville, NJ: Red Sea Press.

—. (ed.). 1998b. *Oromo Nationalism and the Ethiopian Discourse.* Lawrenceville, NJ: Red Sea Press.

James, Wendy. 1990. 'Kings, Commoners, and the Ethnographic Imagination in Sudan and Ethiopia,' in *Localizing Strategies. Regional Traditions of Ethnographic Writing,* edited by Richard Fardon. Edinburgh: Scottish Academic Press and Washington, DC: Smithsonian Institution Press.

James, Wendy, Donald L. Donham, Eisei Kurimoto, and Alessandro Triulzi (eds). 2002. *Remapping Ethiopia. Socialism and After.* Oxford: James Currey; Athens, OH: Ohio University Press; Addis Ababa: Addis Ababa University Press.

Kertzer, David I. 1988. *Ritual, Politics, and Power.* New Haven, CT and London: Yale University Press.

Koraro, Giday Degefu. 2000. *Traditional Mechanisms of Conflict Resolution in Ethiopia.* Addis Ababa: Ethiopian International Institute for Peace and Development.

Legesse, Asmarom. 1998. *The Uprooted: Case Material on Ethnic Eritrean Deportees from Ethiopia Concerning Human Rights Violations.* Asmara: Citizens for Peace.

—. 1999. *The Uprooted (Part Two): A Scientific Survey of Ethnic Eritrean Deportees from Ethiopia Conducted with regard to Human Rights Violations.* Asmara: Citizens for Peace.

—. 2000. *The Uprooted (Part Three): Studies of Urban Eritreans Expelled from Ethiopia, Villagers Expelled from Tigrai and Communities in Eritrea displaced by Bombardment.* Asmara: Citizens for Peace.

Levine, Donald N. 1965a. 'Ethiopia: Identity, Authority, and Realism,' in *Political Culture and Political Development,* edited by Lucian W. Pye and Sidney Verba. Princeton, NJ: Princeton University Press.

—. 1965b. *Wax and Gold. Tradition and innovation in Ethiopian culture.* Chicago and London: Chicago University Press.

—. 1974. *Greater Ethiopia. The Evolution of a Multiethnic Society.* Chicago and London: Chicago University Press.

Levy, Jack S. 1998. 'The Diversionary Theory of War: A Critique.' in *Handbook of War Studies,* edited by Manus Midlarsky. Ann Arbor, MI: University of Michigan Press.

225

# References

Lewis, Ioan M. 1998. *Peoples of the Horn of Africa: Somali, Afar and Saho*. London: Haan Associates.

Lipsky, Georg A. 1962. *Ethiopia, its people, its society, its culture*. New Haven, CT: Hraf Press.

Longrigg, Stephen H. 1945. *A Short History of Eritrea*. Oxford: Clarendon Press.

Lussier, Dominique. 1997. 'Local Prohibitions, Memory and Political Judgement among the Kunama: an Eritrean Case Study,' in *Ethiopia in Broader Perspective, Papers of the XIIIth International Conference of Ethiopian Studies*, edited by Katsuyoshi Fukui, Eisei Kurimoto and Masayoshi Shigeta. Kyoto: Shokado Book Sellers.

Lyons, Terrence. 2006. 'Ethiopia in 2005: The Beginning of a Transition?' in *CSIS Africa Notes*. Washington, DC: Center for Strategic and International Studies.

Mach, Zdzislaw. 1993. *Symbols, Conflict, and Identity. Essays in Political Anthropology*. Albany, NY: State University of New York Press.

Malkki, Liisa H. 1992. 'National Geographic: Rooting of Peoples and the Territorialization of National Identity among Scholars and Refugees.' *Cultural Anthropology* 7: 24–44.

Marcus, George E. 1995. 'Ethnography in/of the World System: The Emergence of Multi-Sited Ethnography.' *Annual Review of Anthropology* 24: 95–117.

Marcus, Harold G. 1994. *A History of Ethiopia*. Berkeley/Los Angeles/London: University of California Press.

—. 1995a (1983). *The Politics of Empire. Ethiopia, Great Britain and the United States, 1941–1974*. Lawrenceville, NJ: Red Sea Press.

—. 1995b. *Haile Sellassie I, The Formative Years 1892-1936*. Lawrenceville, NJ: Red Sea Press.

—. 1995c. *The Life and Times of Menelik II. Ethiopia 1844-1913*. Lawrenceville, NJ: Red Sea Press.

Markakis, John. 1974. *Ethiopia, Anatomy of a Traditional Polity*. Oxford: Oxford University Press.

—. 1990. *National and Class Conflict in the Horn of Africa*. London: Zed Books.

McCann, James C. 1995. *People of the Plow. An Agricultural History of Ethiopia, 1800-1990*. Madison, WI: University of Wisconsin Press.

Mesghenna, Yemane. 1988. *Italian Colonialism: A Case Study of Eritrea, 1869-1934: Motive, Praxis and Result*. Lund: Department of History, University of Lund.

Messing, Simon D. 1985 (1957). *Highland Plateau Amhara of Ethiopia*. New Haven, CT: Human Relations Area Files.

Milkias, Paulos. 2001. 'Ethiopia, TPLF and Roots of the 2001 Political Tremor.' in *The International Conference on Contemporary Development Issues in Ethiopia*. Kalamazoo, MI: Western Michigan University Press.

Molvaer, Reidulf K. 1995. *Socialization and Social Control in Ethiopia*. Wiesbaden: Harrassowitz Verlag.

Moore, Henrietta L. 1994. *A Passion for Difference*. Oxford: Polity.

Nadel, Siegfried F. 1946. 'Land Tenure on the Eritrean Plateau.' *Africa* 16: 1–22; 99–109.

Negash, Tekeste. 1986. *No Medicine for the Bite of a White Snake. Notes on Nationalism and Resistance in Eritrea, 1890–1940*. Uppsala: University of Uppsala.

—. 1987. *Italian Colonialism in Eritrea, 1882–1941. Policies, Praxis and Impact*. Uppsala: Department of History, Uppsala University.

# References

—. 1997. *Eritrea and Ethiopia. The Federal Experience.* Uppsala: Nordic Africa Institute.

Negash, Tekeste and Kjetil Tronvoll. 2000. *Brothers at War: Making Sense of the Eritrean-Ethiopian War.* Oxford: James Currey and Athens, OH: Ohio University Press.

Nielsen, Søren Walter. 2002. 'Reintegration of Ex-Fighters in Highland Eritrea: A Window to the Historical Process of State Formation and its Lines of Social Stratification'. PhD thesis, Department of International Development Studies, Roskilde: Roskilde University.

Nordstrom, Carolyn. 1995a. 'Contested Identities/Essentially Contested Powers.' in *Conflict Transformation*, edited by Kumar Rupesinghe. New York: St. Martin's Press.

—. 1995b. 'War on the Front Lines.' in *Fieldwork Under Fire: Contemporary Studies of Violence and Survival*, edited by C. Nordstrom and A.C.G.M. Robben. Berkeley, Los Angeles and London: University of California Presss.

—. 1997. *A Different Kind of War Story.* Philadadelphia: University of Pennsylvania Press.

—. 2002. 'Terror Warfare and the Medicine of Peace.' in *Violence. A Reader*, edited by Catherine Besteman. New York: Palgrave Macmillan.

Nordstrom, Carolyn and JoAnn Martin. 1992. 'The Culture of Conflict: Field Reality and Theory.' in *The Paths to Domination, Resistance, and Terror*, edited by Carolyn Nordstrom and JoAnn Martin. Berkeley, Los Angeles and London: University of California Press.

Nordstrom, Carolyn and Antonius C. G. M Robben (eds.). 1995. *Fieldwork Under Fire. Contemporary Studies of Violence and Survival.* Berkeley, Los Angeles, London: University of California Press.

Nystuen, Gro and Kjetil Tronvoll. 2008. 'The Eritrean-Ethiopian Peace Agreement: Exploring the Limits of Law.' *Nordic Journal of Human Rights* 26.

Olujic, Maria B. 1995. 'The Croatian War Experience,' in *Fieldwork Under Fire*, edited by Carolyn Nordstrom and Antonius C. G. M. Robben. Berkeley, Los Angeles and London: University of California Press.

Pankhurst, Richard. 1990. *A Social History of Ethiopia.* Addis Ababa: Institute of Ethiopian Studies, Addis Ababa University.

Parkyns, Mansfield. 1966. *Life in Abyssinia.* London: Frank Cass.

Pausewang, Siegfried. 1983. *Peasants, Land and Society. A Social History of Land Reform in Ethiopia.* München, Köln and London: Weltforum Verlag.

Pausewang, Siegfried and Kjetil Tronvoll (eds). 2000. *The Ethiopian 2000 Elections. Democracy Advanced or Restricted?* Oslo: Unipub Forlag/University of Oslo.

Pausewang, Siegfried, Kjetil Tronvoll and Lovise Aalen (eds). 2002. *Ethiopia since the Derg: A decade of democratic pretension and performance.* London: Zed Books.

Peberdy, Max. 1985. *Tigray: Ethiopia's Untold Story.* London: Relief Society of Tigray UK Support Committee.

Plaut, Martin and Patrick Gilkes. 1999. *Conflict in the Horn: Why Eritrea and Ethiopia are at War.* London: Royal Institute of International Affairs.

Poluha, Eva. 2004. *The Power of Continuity. Ethiopia through the eyes of its children.* Uppsala: The Nordic Africa Institute.

Pool, David. 2001. *From Guerrillas to Government: The Eritrean People's Liberation Front.* Oxford: James Currey.

Posen, Barry R. 1995. 'Nationalism, the Mass Army, and Military Power,' in *Perspectives on Nationalism and War*, edited by John L. Comaroff and Paul C.

# References

Stern. Amsterdam: Gordon and Breach Science Publishers.

Pottier, Johan. 2002. *Re-Imagining Rwanda. Conflict, Survival and Disinformation in the Late Twentieth Century.* Cambridge: Cambridge University Press.

Povrzanovic, Maja. 2000. 'The Imposed and the Imagined as Encountered by Croatian War Ethnographers.' *Current Anthropology* 41:151–62.

Prouty, Chris. 1986. *Empress Taytu and Menilek II. Ethiopia 1883–1910.* London: Ravens.

Prouty, Chris and Eugene Rosenfeld. 1994. *Historical Dictionary of Ethiopia and Eritrea.* Metuchen, NJ and London: Scarecrow Press.

Richards, Paul. 2005. 'New War: An Ethnographic Approach,' in *No Peace No War: An Anthropology of Contemporary Armed Conflicts*, edited by Paul Richards. Oxford: James Currey; Athens, OH: Ohio University Press.

Robben, Antonius C. G. M. 1995. 'The Politics of Truth and Emotion among Victims and Perpetrators of Violence,' in *Fieldwork Under Fire*, edited by Carolyn Nordstrom and Antonius C. G. M Robben. Berkeley, Los Angeles and London: University of California Press.

Robben, A.C.G.M. and C. Nordstrom. 1995. 'The Anthropology and Ethnography of Violence and Sociopolitical Conflict,' in *Fieldwork Under Fire: Contemporary Studies of Violence and Survival*, edited by C. Nordstrom and A.C.G.M. Robben. Berkeley, Los Angeles and London: University of California Press.

Robben, Antonius C. G. M, and Marcelo M. Suárez-Orozco (eds). 2000a. *Cultures under Siege. Collective Violence and Trauma.* Cambridge: Cambridge University Press.

—. 2000b. 'The management of collective trauma,' in *Cultures under Siege*, edited by Antonius C. G. M Robben and Marcelo M. Suárez-Orozco. Cambridge: Cambridge University Press.

Rodgers, Dennis. 2001. 'Making Danger A Calling: Anthropology, violence, and the dilemmas of participant observation.' London: Development Studies Institute, London School of Economics and Political Science.

Rosen, Charles B. 1975. *Warring with Words: Patterns of political activity in a Northern Ethiopian town.* Chicago: University of Chicago Press.

—. 1978. 'Tigrean Political Identity: An Explanation of Core Symbols,' in *Proceedings of the Fifth International Conference on Ethiopian Studies*, edited by R. H. Hess. Chicago: Chicago University Press.

Rubenson, Sven. 1976. *The Survival of Ethiopian Independence.* London: Heinemann.

Said, Edward. 1978. *Orientalism.* New York: Pantheon.

Salole, Gerry. 1978. 'Who are the Shoans?' *Horn of Africa* II:20-29.

Saltman, Michael. 2002. *Land and Territoriality.* Oxford: Berg.

Scheper-Hughes, Nancy. 1995. 'The Primacy of the Ethical: Propositions for a Militant Anthropology.' *Current Anthropology* 36:409-20.

Scott, James C. 1990. *Domination and the Arts of Resistance: Hidden Transcripts.* New Haven, CT and London: Yale University Press.

Shack, William A. 1974. *The Central Ethiopians – Amhara, Tigrina and Related Peoples.* London: International African Institute.

—. 1976. 'Occupational Prestige, Status and Social Change in Modern Ethiopia.' *Africa* 46.

Simmel, Georg. 1964. *Conflict and the Web of Group-Affiliations.* New York: The Free Press (Macmillan Publishing).

Simons, Anna. 1999. 'WAR: Back to the Future'. *Annual Review of Anthropology* 28: 73-108.

# References

Smith, Anthony D. 1981. 'War and ethnicity: the role of warfare in the formation, self-images and cohesion of ethnic communities.' *Ethnic and Racial Studies* 4: 375–97.

—. 1991. *National Identity.* London: Penguin Books.

Sorensen, John. 1992. 'History and Identity in the Horn of Africa.' *Dialectical Anthropology* 17:227–52.

—. 1993. *Imagining Ethiopia: Struggles for History and Identity in the Horn of Africa.* New Brunswick, NJ: Rutgers University Press.

—. 1998. 'Ethiopian Discourse and Oromo Nationalism.' in *Oromo Nationalism and the Ethiopian Discourse,* edited by Asafa Jalata. Lawrenceville, NJ: Red Sea Press.

Sorenson, John and Atsuko Matsukoa. 2001. 'Phantom Wars and Cyberwars: Abyssinian Fundamentalism and Catastrophe in Eritrea.' *Dialectical Anthropology* 26:37–63.

Taddia, Irma. 1994. 'In search of an identity: Amhara/Tegrean relations in the late 19th century.' in *Proceedings of the Eleventh International Conference of Ethiopian Studies,* edited by Bahru Zewde, Richard Pankhurst and Taddesse Beyene. Addis Ababa: Addis Ababa University Press.

Tadesse, Medhane and John Young. 2003. 'TPLF: Reform or Decline?' *Review of African Political Economy*: 389–403.

Tafla, Bairu. 1984. 'The *Awag*: An Institution of Political Culture in Traditional Ethiopia,' in *Proceedings of the Seventh International Conference of Ethiopian Studies, University of Lund, 26–29 April 1982,* edited by Sven Rubenson, Addis Ababa: Institute of Ethiopian Studies; Uppsala: Scandinavian Institute of African Studies; East Lansing, MI: African Studies Center, Michigan State University.

Tamrat, Taddesse. 1982. 'Feudalism in Heaven and on Earth: Ideology and Political Structure in Medival Ethiopia,' in *Proceedings of Seventh International Conference of Ethiopian Studies,* edited by Sven Rubenson, Addis Ababa: Institute of Ethiopian Studies; Uppsala: Scandinavian Institute of African Studies; East Lansing, MI: African Studies Center, Michigan State University.

Tareke, Gebru. 1983. 'Resistance in Tigray (Ethiopia). From Weyane to TPLF.' *Horn of Africa* VI: 15–29.

—. 1984. 'Peasant Resistance in Ethiopia: The Case of *Weyane.*' *Journal of Africa History* 25: 7–92.

—. 1996. *Ethiopia: Power and Protest. Peasant Revolts in the Twentieth Century.* Lawrenceville, NJ: Red Sea Press.

Tegenu, Tsegaye. 1996. *The Evolution of Ethiopian Absolutism. The Genesis and the Making of the Fiscal Military State, 1696-1913.* Uppsala: Uppsala University Press.

Tibebu, Teshale. 1995. *The Making of Modern Ethiopia 1896–1974.* Lawrenceville, NJ: Red Sea Press.

Tiruneh, Andargachew. 1993. *The Ethiopian Revolution 1974–1987. A transformation from an aristocratic to a totalitarian autocracy.* Cambridge: Cambridge University Press.

TPLF. 2000. *TPLF's Popular Struggle (1975–1991)* (in Tigrinya). Addis Ababa.

Triandafyllidou, Anna. 1998. 'National identity and the "other".' *Ethnic and Racial Studies* 21: 593–612.

Triulzi, Alessandro. 1994. 'Ethiopia: the Making of a Frontier Society.' in *Inventions and Boundaries: Historical Anthropoligical Approaches to the Study of Ethnicity and Nationalism,* edited by P. Kaarsholm and J. Hultin. Roskilde: Roskilde University.

—. 2002. 'Battling with the Past. New Frameworks for Ethiopian Historigraphy,' in *Remapping Ethiopia. Socialism and After*, edited by Wendy James, Donald L. Donham, Eisei Kurimoto and Alessandro Triulzi. Oxford: James Currey; Athens, OH: Ohio University Press; Addis Ababa: Addis Ababa University Press.

Tronvoll, Kjetil. 1995. 'Observation Report from the Elections to the Federal and Regional Assemblies in Region 1 Tigray, Ethiopia.' in *Diary Tigray: Politics and Elections 1995*. Oslo: Norwegian Centre for Human Rights, University of Oslo.

—. 1998. *Mai Weini A Highland Village in Eritrea. A study of the people, their livelihood, and land tenure during times of turbulence*. Lawrenceville, NJ: Red Sea Press.

—. 1999. 'Borders of violence - boundaries of identity: demarcating the Eritrean nation-state.' *Ethnic and Racial Studies* 22: 1037–60.

—. 2000. *Ethiopia: A New Start?* London: Minority Rights Group International.

—. 2001. 'Voting, violence and violations: peasant voices on the flawed elections in Hadiya, Southern Ethiopia.' *Journal of Modern African Studies* 39: 697–716.

—. 2008. 'Human Rights in Federal Ethiopia: When Ethnic Identity is a Political Stigma.' *International Journal on Minority and Group Rights* 15: 49–79.

Tronvoll, Kjetil and Øyvind Aadland. 1995. *The Process of Democratisation in Ethiopia: An Expression of Popular Participation or Political Resistance?* Oslo: Norwegian Centre for Human Rights, University of Oslo.

Turton, David. 1997. 'Introduction: War and Ethnicity,' in *War and Ethnicity*, edited by David Turton. Rochester, NY: University of Rochester Press.

— (ed.). 2006. *Ethnic Federalism: The Ethiopian Experience in Comparative Perspective*. Oxford: James Currey; Athens, OH: Ohio University Press.

Vaughan, Sarah and Kjetil Tronvoll. 2003. *The Culture of Power in Contemporary Ethiopian Political Life*. Stockholm: Sidastudies.

Waal, Alex de. 1991. *Evil Days. 30 Years of War and Famine in Ethiopia*. New York: Human Rights Watch.

WIC. 2000. *Dispatches from the Electronic Front: Internet Responses to the Ethio-Eritrean Conflict*. Addis Ababa: Walta Information Center.

—. 1999. *Ayder: An in-depth report on the massacre of school children in Tigray, Ethiopia*. Addis Ababa: Walta Information Center.

Williams, Brackette F. 1989. 'A Class Act: Anthropology and the Race to Nation Across Ethnic Terrain.' *Annual Review of Anthropology* 18: 401–44.

Wilmsen, Edwin N. and Patrick McAllister (eds). 1996. *The Politics of Difference. Ethnic Premises in a World of Power*. Chicago and London: University of Chicago Press.

Wilson, Thomas M. and Hastings Donnan (eds.). 1998. *Border Identities. Nation and state at international frontiers*. Cambridge: Cambridge University Press.

Young, John. 1996. 'The Tigray and Eritrean Peoples Liberation Fronts: a History of Tensions and Pragmatism.' *Journal of Modern African Studies* 34: 105–20.

—. 1997. *Peasant Revolution in Ethiopia. The Tigray People's Liberation Front, 1975-1991*. Cambridge: Cambridge University Press.

Zewde, Bahru. 1991. *A History of Modern Ethiopia 1855–1974*. London: James Currey.

—. 2002. *Pioneers of Change in Ethiopia: The Reformist Intellectuals of the Early Twentieth Century*. Oxford: James Currey; Athens, OH: Ohio University Press; Addis Ababa: Addis Ababa University.

# References

—. 2009. 'The History of Red Terror.' in *The Ethiopian Red Terror Trials: Transitional Justice Challenged*, edited by Kjetil Tronvoll, Charles Schaefer and Girmachew Alemu Aneme. Oxford: James Currey.

# Index

233

# Index

# EASTERN AFRICAN STUDIES

These titles published in the United States and Canada by Ohio University Press